ALSO BY ANN JONES

*Uncle Tom's Campus*

*Women Who Kill*

*Everyday Death: The Case of Bernadette Powell*

*When Love Goes Wrong:*
*What to Do When You Can't Do Anything Right*
(with Susan Schechter)

*Next Time She'll Be Dead: Battering and How to Stop It*

*Looking for Lovedu: Days and Nights in Africa*

*Kabul in Winter: Life Without Peace in Afghanistan*

# WAR IS NOT OVER WHEN IT'S OVER

# WAR IS
# NOT OVER
## WHEN IT'S OVER

WOMEN SPEAK OUT FROM
THE RUINS OF WAR

## ANN JONES

METROPOLITAN BOOKS   HENRY HOLT AND COMPANY   NEW YORK

Metropolitan Books
Henry Holt and Company, LLC
*Publishers since 1866*
175 Fifth Avenue
New York, New York 10010
www.henryholt.com

Metropolitan Books® and ® are registered trademarks of
Henry Holt and Company, LLC.

The contents of this book represent the views of the author and not those of
the International Rescue Committee.

Library of Congress Cataloging-in-Publication Data

Jones, Ann, 1937–
  War is not over when it's over : women speak out from the ruins
of war / Ann Jones. — 1st ed.
     p. cm.
  ISBN 978-0-8050-9111-3
  1. Women and war.   2. War victims.   3. Victims of violent
crimes.   4. Women—Violence against.   I. Title.
  JZ6405.W66J66 2010
  363.34'984082—dc22                                      2009050725

Henry Holt books are available for special promotions and
premiums. For details contact: Director, Special Markets.

First Edition 2010

*Designed by Kelly S. Too*

Printed in the United States of America
1  3  5  7  9  10  8  6  4  2

*To Frances Goldin*

To set aside the sympathy we extend to others beset by war and murderous politics for a reflection on how our privileges are located on the same map as their suffering, and may—in ways we might prefer not to imagine—be linked to their suffering, as the wealth of some might imply the destitution of others, is a task for which the painful stirring images supply only an initial spark.

Susan Sontag, *Regarding the Pain of Others*

# CONTENTS

# WAR IS NOT OVER WHEN IT'S OVER

# INTRODUCTION:
# WAR IS NOT HEALTHY

At the eleventh hour of the eleventh day of the eleventh month in the year 2008, as BBC TV presenters wearing crisp red paper poppy boutonnieres interview the last survivors of the Great War in Flanders fields, I sit in a sleazy hotel room off Hamra Street in Beirut, going over my notes of the day's interviews with refugees from the war in Iraq. After weeks of talking to refugees in Amman and Damascus, I met today in Beirut for the first time an Iraqi who actually was liberated by the American invasion of his country. His name is Ahmad.

As a young man, Ahmad worked as a mechanic in Baghdad and somehow managed to avoid being conscripted to serve in Saddam Hussein's war against Iran. By 1986, when he was twenty-six, the war had turned in Iran's favor. The Ayatollah Khomeini threatened to depose Saddam Hussein, and Saddam in turn cracked down on suspected enemies at home. He arrested Ahmad's sister and her husband, who were associated with a dissident party, and he arrested Ahmad as well. Charged as enemies of Saddam Hussein, Ahmad's sister and her husband were hanged, and Ahmad was sentenced to sixty years in prison.

Interrogators tortured him every day for two years, trying to elicit a confession worthy of his sentence. He had nothing to confess. Interrogators pulled out his toenails, burned and cut the skin from his lower legs, inserted a hose in his anus and pumped him full of water, administered electric shocks to parts of his body he cannot name, and beat his head and body with wooden clubs and steel batons. At last he told them to write down whatever they liked and he would sign it. After that false confession, his captors abandoned the most brutal "enhanced interrogation" techniques; they had what they wanted. But they continued to beat him routinely, less viciously and less often, for sixteen years. In 2003, two days after the American invasion, Ahmad and his fellow prisoners realized that the guards had abandoned the prison. They broke down the doors and set themselves free.

Ahmad returned to his parents' home and found work again as a mechanic. Two months after his escape, he winked at a woman working in a cosmetics shop across the road. She smiled and seven days later they married. Her name is Azhar. They moved into a house they bought together. Then in July 2005, as Iraq descended into chaos, Ahmad was kidnapped by men from the Mahdi Army who demanded $150,000 ransom. He says, "I had been so happy—loving life, laughing, spending money—they must have thought I was rich." The kidnappers also held two children, and when no ransom was paid, they cut their throats before Ahmad's eyes. Azhar borrowed $10,000 from her parents to arrange Ahmad's release after fifteen days in captivity. Soon Ahmad received a letter warning him to leave his house or be killed. He and his wife sold everything, repaid her parents, and fled to Syria where Azhar soon gave birth to a son. For a year they lived what Ahmad calls "a simple life."

In 2007, running out of money, Ahmad went to Lebanon. He had been told that he might find highly paid work in Beirut, but he didn't. Penniless and lonely, in November 2007 he sent for his wife and son. The family registered with the office of the United Nations High Commissioner for Refugees (UNHCR) and asked to be resettled in another country. Referred to the United States, they were interviewed by U.S. embassy officials. They wait for a decision in a windowless one-room apartment that reminds Ahmad of prison. Fear of being detained and deported by the authorities keeps him confined to that room. He suffers depression, anxiety, flashbacks. And he beats his wife as he was beaten. He was tortured. He tortures her. ("Domestic violence" is the euphemism we use to name torture that takes place in the home, but a comparison of standard techniques—from stripping and sleep deprivation to beating, burning, bondage, asphyxiation, and sexual assault—shows that torture by another name is still torture.) Slowly, with the help of psychotherapists at Restart, a UNHCR-funded program for survivors of torture, Ahmad is learning to stop abusing Azhar. "She is my life," he says. "I would die without her." (She says, "I choose to share this life of misery with him.") He suffers from diabetes, high blood pressure, and chronic back pain, the physical effects of his long imprisonment, and from the unrelenting depression of a man so poor he has only one set of clothes. The family of his youth is gone: three sisters in Sweden, one in Germany, one killed in the first American war, one executed, two brothers shot and killed during the second American war, one by an Iraqi militiaman in the street, the other by an American soldier in the living room. Ahmad fears for his child. Waiting for the American embassy to call, he says, "I need to know if my son has a future."

Today, in the bleak room he shares with Azhar and their young son in South Beirut, Ahmad removed his plastic shoes to show me his swollen feet, still purple and marked by sunken scars where toenails used to be. He says that when he has flashbacks he feels overcome by powerlessness and rage. What these feelings compel him to do threatens to destroy his life. He sometimes loses control and hits Azhar hard, and then he weeps and begs her pardon. His eyes seem to leak even as he says these things.

I am here to listen. I listen to what people like Ahmad and Azhar tell me about war and the violence that attends it because my own life—the only life I can know firsthand, and even that imperfectly—has been darkened by war. That war is now commemorated with paper poppies, the Great War, in which my father served with uncommon distinction and from which he returned a hero, irrevocably changed, subject to nightmares and sudden rages and drunken assaults upon innocent furniture and my mother and me, and tearful reconciliations we were not permitted to reject. I watch the BBC coverage of the distant ritual of Armistice Day and see many people, mostly women, advanced well beyond middle age, weeping with remembrance. Their memories, I imagine, might be like mine: the memories of people who never participated in the war and yet have never escaped it. My father, at sixteen, enlisted in the American Expeditionary Force to take part in the war to end all wars. But that's not how it worked out. In some ways, as the BBC presenter says, the Great War laid the foundation for more wars to come, and certainly for wars at home, like the one my father waged for twenty years and more against my mother and me in a dark-green-shuttered house in a small town in Wisconsin. The war my father carried home in his khaki canvas bag from the trenches of Flanders to the valley of the Chippewa is the shadow in which I've lived my solitary life. It is surely the reason that now in my seventieth year I sit in this seedy room in a fading hotel long favored by journalists and stare at cigarette burns in the worn carpet, and see only the purple toes of Ahmad and the fading yellow bruises on the face of his wife.

My father used to say that wars were made by men who had never been to war, men who didn't know that once started it never ends. The Great War ended with the Armistice in 1918, but my father lived another sixty years; and during all that time the war never left his memory or his nightmares. Nor is it ever far from mine, because the violence my father brought home fell on me and shattered whatever small childish trust I may once have had in the simplicity of love. The violence of war does not end when peace is declared. Often it merely recedes from public to private life. I am here in Beirut talking about war, writing about war, because my father fought bravely in a brutal one. And that changed everything for him, and consequently for me.

For many years I studied violence in the family and wrote about it in several books. I was part of a widespread movement of women in the United States and elsewhere who worked hard to change attitudes and laws about violence against women, inside and outside the home, and to provide services for women and child survivors. It was the home that I wanted to make safe for women and children because the home was what I knew, in all its fearful rage and sorrow.

Many of us who did this work argued that the violence of private life is not private at all. So often it spills into the world at large. An abusive husband shoots his estranged wife in her workplace and kills some of her colleagues as well. Another appears for a child custody hearing and shoots his wife, her lawyer, the judge, and other bystanders. We see such stories often in the media. Accounts of these routine rampages invariably accept the shooter's anger at his estranged wife or girlfriend as sufficient explanation for mass homicide. But where does such rage come from?

I still believe that violence in the home imperils us all. Just as it spills into the streets, it schools the next generation in violence. But now I wonder if that is truly where violence starts, at home. When my father attacked my mother or me, he was often angry about something altogether different. He laid into us—me especially—because I was there. But the response? The techniques? Those were things he had learned in the army. In fact it must have been his success in learning to act so swiftly, so effectively, so violently that made him a hero and earned him the highest honors of three allied countries. His medals hung on the wall at home, under glass. Friends of our family often said to me: "You must be so proud of your father." I was. I admired him and loved him, even though I knew what his heroism cost us, and him, at home.

One stronghold of the battered women's movement—in Maryland, if I remember rightly—distributed T-shirts bearing the words WORLD PEACE BEGINS AT HOME. I believed it. Raise up children in peaceful homes free of violence, I thought, and they will make peace. But now, having spent the last many years in and around wars, I think the motto is painfully idealistic. The relationship it describes is reciprocal, but not fair. World peace may begin at home, but violence just as surely begins in war; and war does not end.

Ahmad's cry—"I need to know if my son has a future"—is echoed by all survivors of the violence of war. What will become of the children? During the war in Vietnam, the peace movement had a slogan: "War is not healthy for children and other living things." In the violence of war, children are orphaned, maimed, mutilated, sexually assaulted, kidnapped, forced to be soldiers or servants or sex slaves, tortured, and murdered. The children who survive the violence of war may be deeply wounded, robbed of childhood, and poised to enter adult life already crippled beyond repair. Even children who know war only at secondhand, the children of soldiers returning from far-off lands, may be bent. Any of these damaged children may inflict the harm done to them upon others, even when it breaks their hearts.

Think of wars of recent memory and those still going on in the world today. Think of Iraq, Afghanistan, Gaza, Lebanon, Syria, Israel, Burma. Think of Darfur, South Sudan, Rwanda, Burundi, the Democratic Republic of Congo, Côte d'Ivoire, Liberia, Sierra Leone. Think of Sri Lanka, Kashmir, East Timor, Somalia, Ethiopia, Eritrea. Think of Kosovo, Croatia, Bosnia, Chechnya, Georgia, Salvador, Nicaragua, Colombia. Think especially of the United States, which has been at war, overtly or covertly, some place (or many places) in the world almost continuously since 1941.

Today children and their mothers are among the first victims of such wars. Despite the conventions of modern warfare that forbid armies to target civilians, it is civilians who die in far greater numbers than do soldiers. The more high-tech the army, the more sophisticated its weaponry, the safer the soldiers; but that shield does not extend to citizens. In fact, in many conflicts today, ruthless leaders use an effective strategy to destroy the civil society and culture of the enemy: a deliberate but unacknowledged war against women.

After 9/11, when America was seized by the Bush administration's ruinous enthusiasm for combat, I left the country to practice peace by working elsewhere with women. From 2002 to 2006, I volunteered with humanitarian organizations in Afghanistan. (I've written about what I learned there in an earlier book: *Kabul in Winter.*) Then, in the fall of 2007, I began to work as an unpaid volunteer with the International Rescue Committee, one of the oldest (more than 75 years) and most respected humanitarian nongovernmental organizations in the world. Its specialty is bringing immediate emergency relief to needful countries in the wake of war. That means mostly clean water, sanitation, basic health care, and basic education—all things I know only a little about. My experience lies in thinking about and working to stop violence against women. So the IRC assigned me to its technical unit that deals with GBV—that's Gender-Based Violence, a gender-neutral euphemism for violence against women. Among international humanitarian organizations, the IRC has taken the lead in working on GBV in direct response to the consequences of modern warfare, in which the principal casualties are not soldiers but civilians, and great numbers of those civilians are women, often targeted precisely because they are women.

Even when a conflict officially ends, violence against women continues and often grows worse. Murderous aggression is not turned off overnight; when men stop attacking one another, women continue to be convenient targets. Opposing factions of men sit down together to negotiate a peace settlement without ever letting up on rape, abduction, mutilation, and murder of women and girls. And whenever soldiers rape during war, rape becomes a habit taken up by civilian men and carried seamlessly from wartime into the troubled "post-conflict" time beyond that is labeled "peace." Wherever normal structures of law enforcement and justice have been disabled by war, soldiers and civilian men alike prey upon women and children with impunity.

So when the International Rescue Committee walks into any post-conflict zone, anywhere in the world, it walks straight into violence against women; and because its long-standing mission is to address human needs created by conflict, it must respond. The IRC recognizes violence against women as a fundamental issue of human rights, a central public health concern, and a major impediment to peacemaking, reconstruction, and development of war-torn countries.

The United Nations agrees and goes further. On October 31, 2000, the Security Council passed Resolution 1325, calling for women to participate fully at decision-making levels in every step of conflict resolution and peace building. Without the active participation of women, the UN argued, no just and lasting peace could be achieved. SCR 1325 was greeted around the world as a great achievement and a victory for women and peace, but later when men in post-conflict countries negotiated agreements, often with the guidance of the UN, they forgot all about it. The usual excuse was that they had to act fast, speed apparently being more important than justice or durability or women.

On June 19, 2008, the United Nations Security Council passed another landmark resolution. SCR 1820 demands "the immediate and complete cessation by all parties to armed conflict of all acts of sexual violence against civilians with immediate effect." It acknowledges the true state of millions of the world's women and girls: objectified, terrorized, brutalized, and violated in one conflict after another from the Balkans to Iraq and across the great sweep of Africa. More important, Resolution 1820 connects the dots: widespread rape of women in war effectively prevents the very participation in public life that Resolution 1325 identified as essential to devising durable peace. Resolution 1820 reframes the issue: widespread rape in wartime is no longer merely a woman's complaint, an instance of gender-based violence, or a public health concern—it is a matter of international security and peace. That makes it subject to sanctions, force, and the jurisdiction of international criminal tribunals and courts—if those with the power to act choose to do so. SCR 1820 sets forth the reasons why they should: Where women do not take part in peacemaking, there is no just and lasting peace. Where there is no lasting peace, no one is secure.

The principles set forth by the UN guide the work of NGOs like the IRC as well. We act as if the resolutions amount to natural law, but we act on a smaller scale, within the confines of specific conflicts, amid the rubble of particular wars. In my case, I sat down in New York with Heidi Lehmann, the head of the GBV technical unit, to see what I could do. Unlike many aid workers who have all-purpose answers, Heidi had questions. "We see all these statistics about the numbers of women raped and captured or displaced," she said, "but we don't know much about who they are." She wanted to know what ordinary women think about in the aftermath of war: what their problems are, and their hopes, and what international assistance might actually be of help to them. And she wanted to find a way to break the silence that seemed to surround them—to help them speak up for themselves. Women need more than the world's sympathy. They need the world's ear.

What we came up with was a simple project with a fancy title: "A Global Crescendo: Women's Voices from Conflict Zones." The title embodied Heidi's desire to hear a rising chorus; the tool we used was not musical, but visual. Here's how it worked. In different "post-conflict" regions, I loaned digital point-and-shoot cameras—good ones—to small groups of women volunteers and asked them to document their lives in photographs. I asked them to take pictures of whatever they wished, and to include a few shots that illustrated some blessings and some problems in their lives. The women shared cameras and worked together in teams. Few of them had seen a camera before, but many took hundreds of photos. For a month or more we met once a week—that was all the time they could spare—to look at their photos (in computer slide shows) and talk about the issues they raised. Then the women organized a "First-Ever All-Women's Photography Exhibition and Celebration" and invited all the local bigwigs. (The IRC brought refreshments.) On the appointed day, each of the women—few of whom had ever spoken in public before—presented two of her most important photos and made the case for action on the issues documented in the pictures.

By the time I collected the cameras to move on to another country, the women didn't need them anymore. They could look around, spot problems, and speak up—a process I called (off the record) "See, shoot, and shout." In *On Photography,* Susan Sontag observes: "To photograph is to appropriate the thing photographed. It means putting oneself into a certain relation to the world that feels like knowledge—and, therefore, like power."

"Knowledge" and "power" are the operative words here. One Global Crescendo participant put it this way: "Some people use cameras. Some people *become* cameras. Me, I'm a camera." The practice of photography had given her the skill and the confidence to be an advocate for herself and other women. The photographs were evidence of the truth of what she said. The impact on the community varied from place to place, but the changes in the way communities looked at women, and women looked at themselves, were real and often dramatic.

Because some readers might want to emulate this project, I want to say clearly that "A Global Crescendo" was not in the end about photography but about developing the particular skills (observation, analysis, articulation) and confidence that people need to advocate for themselves. There are now countless photo projects going on around the world in which artists or humanitarians give cameras to children or farmers or prostitutes and later present exhibitions as if the photographs are surprising documents of the lives of "others" or self-contained works of art: photographs that speak for themselves. "A Global Crescendo," on the other hand, is about photographers, women, who speak for themselves and go on speaking long after their cameras have left town.

Everyone I worked with on this project was a survivor of war, recently ended or still going on. Everyone had been affected by violence, displacement, loss, terror, and unimaginable brutality. I listened to hundreds of terrible personal stories. Sometimes when I got up to leave after listening for a long time, I found it hard to keep my balance and to walk away. A Congolese nurse in North Kivu province once told me about the way he and his medical colleagues reacted to the stories they heard from women who had been raped during a decade of war. He said, "We are obliged to weep. Sometimes we are obliged to hit our heads against the wall, and sometimes we just fall down."

I listened with a head full of memories of what I'd already learned about war in Afghanistan, and I saw that the practice and consequences of modern warfare are nothing like those planned and reported by American leaders. The architects of disastrous U.S. ventures seek unequivocal and terminal "victory," relying on bombing tonnage to erase enemies, both military and civilian, and enable marines to raise a final flag. U.S. leaders continue to measure success in terms of minimal American military casualties. They don't count civilian casualties among the "enemy" or even among the American civilian contractors who now do so much of the work and reap so many of the profits of waging the country's wars. They don't count the lost life of communities or social institutions. They don't record the moment in which a culture implodes. They don't acknowledge that when "peace" comes, the war against women continues. Given these limited terms of assessment, official American reports of the consequences of war serve only to misinform and mislead. They obscure the true nature and conduct of contemporary warfare, and what it does to people and societies.

The women who took part in "A Global Crescendo" help to set the record straight. Like most women and men around the world, they have no stake in America's wars or in their own. They care about their families, their children's education, their spouse's intermittent kindness, their income, their relationship to their gods, perhaps the acquisition of a new pair of sandals. My intention in volunteering with the IRC was to give the women who took part a chance to make their voices heard. I led the Global Crescendo Project in five countries—Côte d'Ivoire (Ivory Coast), Liberia, Sierra Leone, the Democratic Republic of Congo, and Thailand (where I worked with minority refugees from Burma)—and I came to feel an obligation to add my own voice by reporting what I learned about what these brave women want and what war has done to their dreams.

But you'll notice that the Global Crescendo isn't very global after all. Four of the five project countries are in Africa. We always hoped to carry the work to Iraq, but as my volunteer year neared an end, the IRC was feeling its way into Kurdistan while the rest of Iraq still lay off limits. And funders saw limited value in a project that sent groups of village women out to take pictures. (You can't quantify the results: so many wells dug, so many pumps installed, so many vaccinations given, so many school notebooks handed out.) So I went myself to talk to Iraqis, not in Iraq, but over the borders—in Jordan, Syria, Lebanon— where the country's most articulate citizens have sought refuge.

No project. No show. No refreshments. No cameras except my own—temporarily put at the service of UNHCR, the agency working overtime to register and assist refugees. But I'll tell you those stories as well. They *should* be part of a global crescendo. I keep hoping it might grow loud enough to drown out the drums of war.

# 1

## CÔTE D'IVOIRE:
## *"GRÂCE À L'APPAREIL"*

This is how it started. The IRC sent me first to West Africa, to Côte d'Ivoire, a country I'd visited a dozen years before on an overland journey that took me from one end of Africa to the other. What I remembered most about Côte d'Ivoire was the kindness of a man named Aka who ran a little campground on the outskirts of Abidjan where I parked my Land Rover and pitched my tent for many days. Sometimes we'd go out for yam chips and beer at one of the cheap open-air restaurants, and sitting up late under the stars, Aka would tell me about his family and his little coffee and cocoa farm up-country. He had lived there happily until something he didn't quite understand happened to the economy—something called "adjustment." After that, he couldn't make ends meet. He had to leave his small plantings in the care of his wife and children and come to the big city to enter the cash economy. He started Abidjan's first campground, a tiny well-swept space under palms rattled by winds off the wild unswimmable sea, and tried to make strangers like me feel at home. Yet he was a stranger himself in Abidjan, his family far away, separated by forces they could not comprehend. In Aka's late-night voice you could hear even then the sighs of a country coming apart. His story was one small sign of the decline that would bottom out in civil war.

From Aka's campground on the Gulf of Guinea, Côte d'Ivoire stretches north to Mali and Burkina Faso, sandwiched between Liberia and Guinea to the west and Ghana to the east. It is one of the largest countries in West Africa, just about the size of Germany, and for a long time it was part of the colonies known collectively as France Outre Mer, "France Beyond the Sea," or French Overseas Territories. Under French domination the nation of farmers began to cultivate crops for which the French had a taste, such as Aka's coffee and cocoa. The country had other treasures too: tropical timber, gold, and the tusks of the vanishing elephants that gave the country its name: Ivory Coast.

In 1960 Côte d'Ivoire gained its independence from France and quickly became Africa's rising star—one of the most prosperous countries on the continent. The father of the country, Félix Houphouët-Boigny, a doctor who led Côte d'Ivoire to independence and served as president until his death in 1993, had spent twelve years in France as the colony's representative to the French parliament and later as a member of the French cabinet. As president of Côte d'Ivoire, he welcomed French entrepreneurs who helped make modern Abidjan "the Paris of Africa." President Houphouët-Boigny, who had also been a successful planter and farm union organizer, concentrated on agricultural development to spread prosperity throughout the nation of small farmers. Then came worldwide recession in the early 1980s, accompanied in Côte d'Ivoire by drought. As the economy slumped, the World Bank offered loans and the International Monetary Fund (IMF) imposed ruthless "structural adjustment." Farm prices were cut in half, teachers and civil servants laid off, natural resources snatched away—almost half the virgin rain forest in a single decade thanks to an $80 million World Bank "environmental" loan, which in turn required more "adjustment" and more loans to pay the interest. By the time "the Old Man" Houphouët-Boigny died in 1993, Côte d'Ivoire was in debt for about $1.5 billion. The French had pocketed their money and gone home, the middle class was slipping into poverty, and Aka was taking leave of his family.

The story since then is all about political power plays—dodgy elections, coups and countercoups, successful and not, and ambitious politicians trying to succeed to the Old Man's power by stirring ethnic conflicts where none existed before. During decades of prosperity, Côte d'Ivoire was a magnet for migrant workers from poor neighboring countries; they brought their families and settled in. There was plenty of work and land to go around. But hard times and the politics of fear changed all that. Human Rights Watch reports that after Houphouët-Boigny's death, politicians scrambling for power "exploited ethnic divisions to oust political rivals in elections, using the state apparatus to repress opponents and incite hatred or fear among populations that had lived in relative harmony for decades." The ultranationalist definition of pure "Ivoirité" became the wheel upon which immigrants and minorities were broken. The breach widened between the Christian south, the seat of government, and the neglected, impoverished Muslim north.

In September 2002, northern rebels tried, and failed, to overthrow President Laurent Gbagbo, and the country fell into civil war. French, African, and later United Nations troops stepped in, and a peace treaty of sorts was signed in 2003. More than eleven thousand international peacekeepers monitored a buffer zone—*la Zone de Confiance*—running the width of the country east to west, separating the opposing forces. International intervention cut the war short, but the country had already been torn apart by animosity and violence such as peaceable, tolerant Côte d'Ivoirians had never known. When I returned to Côte d'Ivoire in 2007, the country was still trying to put itself back together—in the midst of continuing tension and rising poverty and a series of peace treaties, issued annually. It existed, as so many countries do these days, as a "post-conflict" zone. It was neither at war nor at peace.

I checked in with the IRC's main office in Abidjan and then headed up-country to Yamoussoukro, where I was to work. Although Abidjan is the country's largest, most fashionable city, Yamoussoukro is the administrative capital, a city purposely built for pomp and circumstance. Here in 1905, when the place was a tiny Baoule village, Felix Houphouët-Boigny was born. When the country prospered after independence, the president transformed his hometown into a modern city with a fancy hotel and a presidential palace set among gardens holding pools filled with crocodiles. Near the end of his life, as a gift to the people, he built the Basilique de Notre Dame de la Paix—an astonishing replica of Saint Peter's Basilica in Rome—with seating for seven thousand worshippers and standing room for forty-two thousand more. I was assigned living quarters on a nearby street, in a rented house with other IRC workers, and I used to walk out in the evening just before sunset to see the first stars appear above the darkening dome. It was the hour when brilliant streetlights came on—an oddity in Africa—and herdsmen appeared on the broad ceremonial boulevard, gently urging their bony cattle past the basilica to drink at a crocodile-free lagoon. I was there on September 19, 2007, the fifth anniversary of the beginning of the civil war. Some feared there might be trouble, but in Yamoussoukro it was a day like any other: hot, humid, overcast from time to time with clouds that gathered at dusk and rain that drenched citizens coming late from the markets. President Gbagbo was in New York, preparing to announce to the General Assembly of the United Nations on September 25, 2007, that the war in Côte d'Ivoire was well and truly over.

But when is war over? Long after treaties are signed, soldiers live with injuries, flashbacks, anguish, and remorse about things they saw and did during the war. Women live with the consequences of what was done to them.

Three years after the short war officially ended, Amnesty International reported:

> The scale of rape and sexual violence in Côte d'Ivoire in the course of the armed conflict has been largely underestimated. Many women have been gang-raped or have been abducted and reduced to sexual slavery by fighters. Rape has often been accompanied by the beating or torture (including torture of a sexual nature) of the victim. . . . All armed factions have perpetrated and continue to perpetrate sexual violence with impunity.

Human Rights Watch observed that "cases of sexual abuse are significantly underreported" because women fear "the possibility of reprisals of perpetrators, the negligence or retaliation of authorities, the ostracism of families and communities, and the unknown consequences that attend the violation of cultural taboos."

Amnesty International documented case after case of girls and women, aged "under twelve" to sixty-three assaulted by armed men. The more recent report of Human Rights Watch records the rape of children as young as three. It details how women and girls were seized in their village homes or at military roadblocks or discovered hiding in the bush. Many were too young or too old to run fast enough to escape. Some were raped in public. Some were raped in front of their husbands and their children. Some were forced to witness the murder of their husband or parents. Then they were taken away to soldiers' camps where they were held, along with many other women. They were forced to cook for the soldiers and repeatedly gang-raped. They were beaten and tortured. They saw women who resisted beaten and murdered.

Such violent rapes result in lasting injuries and pain. Amnesty International reports: "The brutality of rape frequently causes serious physical injuries that require long-term and complex treatment including uterine prolapses (the descent of the uterus into the vagina or beyond) . . . and other injuries to the reproductive system or rectum, often accompanied by internal and external bleeding or discharge." It notes that women can't "access the medical care they need." Some women—years after the official end of the war—find it hard to sit down or stand up or walk. Some miscarried. Many contracted sexually transmitted diseases and HIV. Nobody knows how many died, or are dying, as a result. And many are still missing, perhaps dragged across borders when rogue militias from Liberia and Sierra Leone were expelled from the country. Perhaps slaughtered along the way.

The Amnesty report traces this wholesale violence against women in Côte d'Ivoire back to December 2000 when a number of assaults targeted women of foreign origin, commonly referred to as Dioula. Amnesty documents the cases of Dioula women arrested, raped, and tortured at the government's Police Training School in Abidjan because their presumed ethnicity and political affiliation allied them with the opposition. Human Rights Watch notes that this well-documented Dioula affair is only one of many similar assaults incited at the time—before the war—by government-sponsored racist propaganda. No man responsible for any of these crimes has ever been "brought to justice." Amnesty International calls that "a disturbing signal to future perpetrators of sexual violence in Côte d'Ivoire." It later comes to be called "impunity"—because things set in motion by men grasping for power cannot be called back even when a war has been fought and ended, and a peace accord reached. Ignite misogyny and it will burn on its own.

The war in Côte d'Ivoire was a short one, over before most of the world noticed it had begun. If we did not have the reports of Amnesty International and Human Rights Watch, written by researchers who scoured the country after the war, we would have no idea what women had suffered. I certainly wouldn't know, for although I worked closely with village women and spoke with them of many intimate things, none ever alluded to the violence of wartime. It seems remarkable to me now, in retrospect, that they kept silent. Two of the villages where I worked were communities of foreign origin; some of the women had surely survived personal violence during the war, and their silence may well have been a measure of their fear of ostracism and "unknown consequences," as Human Rights Watch suggests. But there was more to it, I think. For village women who had to walk the roads still controlled by soldiers and police, the war was not over. They did their best to avoid the roads; some gave up going to market and packaged their produce in plastic to sell to motorists passing at the village edge, though even then the police harassed them. The women put a brave face on things, but they were plainly afraid of the gunmen. Their villages offered security, but at the price of the routine afflictions of daily life: forced labor, wife beating, marital rape. And now, more closely confined to home in the aftermath of war, these were the things they complained of. Women do almost all the work under penalty of punishment, while men reap the profits. With that imbalance come certain somewhat contradictory beliefs: Whatever goes wrong, a woman is to blame. Whatever is wrong, a woman is powerless to change. So it's no good voicing a grievance, or trying to cast blame on someone else, least of all a man. Better keep silent. What's past is past, and potential violence still lies all around.

In the aftermath of war, where do relief agencies begin? The IRC started working in Côte d'Ivoire in 2003 to help the masses of refugees flooding in from Liberia next door, fleeing from their own civil war. It stayed on to work on the fallout of Côte d'Ivoire's homegrown conflict. At first it focused on the basics: education and health care services. By 2007 it was running programs to deal with clean water and sanitation, primary health care and emergency obstetrical care, child protection and education, reintegration of displaced people and child soldiers, economic recovery, community building, and human rights. It operated out of three field sites in different parts of the country, hoping to encourage national reconciliation by serving three very different populations with different needs. Any well-planned humanitarian project to assist people damaged or displaced by war may be of some service to women. In the United States we usually think of women's rights as civil rights or legal rights, but the United Nations recognizes the full range of social, economic, environmental, political, and personal rights. Access to clean water and sanitation may be counted among the environmental rights of women, just as education and child protection may be considered among their social rights, and obstetrical care among their personal rights. All these rights are violated—violently—by war. And all of them are addressed in one way or another by humanitarian relief programs dealing with wells or schools or prenatal care. But all three IRC field sites also had strong programs in *"Violences Basées sur le Genre"*—Gender-Based Violence—because it is that added violence, that extraordinary personal violence women suffer in wartime, and after, just *because they are women*, that commands the full attention of GBV specialists.

In Yamoussoukro, the GBV manager was a big, beautiful Ivoirian woman whose name, written in the customary inverted order, was Tanou Virginie. Westerners intending to use her first name often mistakenly called her Tanou and she grew to like it. "It sounds more African," she said. Now that we were to work together on the photography project, "Tanou" she was to me. One morning we piled into a car with a couple of GBV field agents and set off for the village of Koupela-Tenkodoko. Not far out of town the grand ceremonial boulevard gave way to a skinny, potholed, asphalt and gravel strip, hemmed in by tall

When war is over, the military still controls the roads and all who travel on them. —Ann Jones

grass and punctuated along the way by military checkpoints where armed soldiers blocked the road with sharp-toothed chains. The checkpoints had been set up, as they are routinely in post-conflict countries, to keep the peace and provide security; but for women they prolonged the terrors of war. Only necessary errands to the clinic or the market could bring women out to run the gauntlet of policemen and soldiers. Yet all along the road women walked singly or in small groups with sick children slung on their hips or baskets of vegetables balanced on their heads. They would be harassed; some would be turned back; some would be robbed of their vegetables or their money; some would be beaten; some searched; some raped. We couldn't help them. We were a car full of women, all Africans except for me, and despite the IRC stickers on our vehicle, the soldiers pointed their guns at us and barked questions about our destination and our work just as they would lord it over the women who came on foot with their sick children and no defense.

An hour later, we turned off the highway and bounced the last few miles over a deeply rutted road. We drove past ranks of mud brick bungalows, through a ramshackle market, to the far end of the village where a meeting was in progress in front of the chief's house. A crowd of women lined the terrace and the steps, talking with the IRC health team. We paid our respects to the chief; and when our turn came, Tanou and I introduced ourselves and invited the women to take part in a special GBV photography project. We were about to describe it when a local man who had been translating for the health team started to translate for us as well, recycling our French in the local language. He had barely begun to speak when the women turned away, muttering among themselves. An old woman jumped up, put her hands on her hips, and shouted perhaps the only words she knew in French, "Men lie!" The men from the health team laughed. Even the stony-faced village chief cracked a smile. But the women weren't laughing. They supported the old woman's objection: their meeting, exclusively for women, should not be translated by a man. The man said that he, Malik, was the official translator for the IRC, as all the villagers knew. The women couldn't deny it, but they were skeptical nonetheless. The old woman glared.

I thought of all the women I'd met in Afghanistan who told me they wanted to learn to read so they could see if the Quran really said what mullahs and husbands told them it did. Here in Côte d'Ivoire, a world away from Afghanistan, women harbored the same suspicion that they were being conned. What could we do? Malik made a pretty speech, offering to hand over the translator's job to a woman. The women looked at their laps. That's when we learned what Malik must have known all along: that among the forty or fifty women crowded onto the steps, there was not a single one who spoke French. Among Côte d'Ivoire's population of more than sixty different tribes and tongues, French long ago became the common language of commerce and politics. Even in rural villages, many men speak French. The fact that women do not reflects their long exclusion from public life. And it means that all the information they get, including all they need to know to make sound decisions about such personal matters as their own health and reproduction and the well-being of their children, comes to them from the mouths of men.

Women have been bamboozled, and they know it. Take human rights, for example. In French that's *les droits de l'Homme*— the rights of Man. Spelled with a capital *H*, the word *Homme* is meant to include both genders; but when the phrase is spoken, the capital letter conveniently disappears. Men produce a literal translation. IRC field agents had astonished villagers with the news that *"Homme"* in that phrase about *droits* includes *"femme"* too. *Les droits de la femme? Impossible!* Even women think "the rights of woman" were invented by the IRC. But they like the idea. *Les droits humains.*

Still we were stuck with Malik to describe our project. Tanou and I explained that it would go on in the village for the next six weeks. We said it was meant to give women a chance to make a record of their daily lives, including their problems, their consolations, and their joys. We said it was meant to give them time to talk together and come up with a list of things they would like to change. And it was meant to give them a chance to make their lives known to people in other lands through photo exhibitions and publications. What Malik said, we couldn't be sure. The women declined to look at him, but they listened.

The first question came from a beautiful young woman in the front row. She asked, "How can we make this record?"

Malik translated the question for Tanou and me, and he added, smugly, "They don't know how to write."

Tanou replied that I would lend them digital cameras and show them how to take pictures. She asked how many of the women had used a camera before. She called for a show of hands. None.

Malik sneered, "They have never *seen* a camera before. They can't do this. This project should be for men."

I pulled out my camera—a little digital point-and-shoot. "This is a camera," I said, "just like the ones I will teach you to use." Malik said nothing, but the women were watching me intently. I held up the camera, pointed it at the women in the front row, and snapped some shots, then turned the camera around to show them the viewing screen—displaying images of themselves. Amazed, they gazed at the camera and at one another, eyes darting from the screen to the faces of the women represented there. They pointed. They grinned. They laughed.

I asked, "Who would like to volunteer?"

That needed no translation. They got it. A camera, pictures, no words. The hands went up, and began to wave. The old woman who had been so set against Malik pulled the volunteers to their feet and pushed them forward to give me their names. I wrote them down, as they spoke them, backward: Yougoubare Veronique, Baliman Safiatou, Zoumore Martine—sixteen women in all. The last was the elegant young woman who had asked how this record of their lives would be made. She had a baby on her hip: Samandougoulou Assetou.

A week later we were back in the village. Under the thatched roof of a small open-air assembly hut, we met the sixteen volunteers. Malik was there, standing beside me. The women seated themselves on benches around us. The younger women had brought their babies, bundled on their backs. I produced my shiny little point-and-shoot camera and held it aloft for all to see. *Voilà! l'appareil photo!* I anticipated smiles, but I saw only the blank-masked faces of women determined to keep their feelings under control. Still, I could see they were worried. A week later, they confessed that they had been scared to death. Intimidated by the tiny machine, the sort of technological gizmo men reserve for themselves, they feared they couldn't do what they would be asked to do. As I would come to understand, that is a terrible fear for village women.

Wives were told every day to do things they didn't have the time or strength to do, let alone the inclination. Failure brought punishment. When the women began to bring in their photos, I learned that men routinely beat their wives for their failures: to produce dinner on time, wash the clothes, sell tomatoes, stay at home, go to the field to work. The list was endless. Men also beat their wives for small acts of assertion: going to visit a neighbor, answering back, being tired or "lazy." Men referred to wife beating as "education." Men said that educating a wife in proper conduct was a great and tiring responsibility. Later one man tried to enlist the help of the GBV team, saying that women needed less talk about their rights and more about their bad behavior.

As I prepared to hand out the cameras, I was worried, too. The problem was the budget. We were doing this project on a shoestring, and the leading camera manufacturers we had asked for donations turned us down flat. So I had only five cameras for sixteen women, and there would be the same shortage in other villages. "I'm so sorry," I said. "You will have to share." I worried that our inability to give each woman a camera was a big mistake in our strategy, but it would turn out to be the best mistake we made.

I asked the women to arrange themselves in groups of three or four—each group an *équipe photo*, a photo team. Then I gave each team a kit consisting of a camera in a soft case, four rechargeable batteries, and a charger. (The village was not electrified, but the chief had a generator that powered a TV and lightbulbs in his home, and he'd given permission for the women to recharge batteries there.) When I asked the women to take out the cameras, one woman in each group gingerly did the job while the others clutched the rest of the gear. I held my breath as I watched the tiny, fragile cameras swallowed by big, callused hands. These women were farmers, used to swinging a heavy hoe. Then I saw Assetou pass a camera to her teammate as she swung the baby off her back and onto her breast. Her big work-worn hand offered a nipple to the child with the gentleness of a feather.

For the next hour I took the women step-by-step through

only the most basic operations of the camera, interrupted at first by Malik, who kept snatching cameras away from women and impatiently giving instructions himself. No woman could deny him his right as a man to take a camera out of her hands, until I asked him to leave the cameras alone. After that, when he snatched at a camera, he missed. We got down to business and learned to turn the cameras on and off. We learned to point and shoot. I finished by giving each woman her own personal memory card to use each time she had possession of a camera. We practiced the nerve-racking process of taking the itty-bitty cards in and out, and the women quickly developed a technique for catching dropped cards in their skirts before they could hit the dirt. I pronounced the camera training complete and sent the teams out to take photos. They huddled to consult with each other: Do I push this button, or that? How hard? Then, timidly, they walked off, and I followed.

The first team found a subject: two men sitting on stools in front of a house, smoking. One woman held the camera firmly, as I'd taught them, and pointed it. That was Veronique, wearing for the occasion a yellow IRC T-shirt. The heads of all the teammates converged at the viewing screen. What next? A teammate—that was young Safiatou—reached over Veronique's shoulder to depress the shutter button. An icon appeared on the screen to indicate that the subject was in focus. "It's green! It's green!" the teammates cried. "Push! Push!" Safiatou's finger came down. "Click!" The women screamed. They jumped up and down. They threw their arms around one another while Véronique held the tiny camera aloft for safekeeping. I joined the celebration, thinking that such teamwork—such solidarity— might be put to good use.

A week later, when we returned to Koupela-Tenkodoko, we

Yougoubare Veronique points the camera while her teammate Baliman Safiatou, with a hand on her shoulder, prepares to shoot the very first photograph of the Global Crescendo Project.

—Ann Jones

found Malik the translator out of a job. The women had told him not to come to the meeting. Tanou and I heard the news as we sat with a few of the women on Veronique's veranda. Most bungalows in the village opened onto bare, well-swept court-yards of red dirt that converged with the neighbor's. But Vero-nique's doorway opened onto a secluded patio enveloped in lush, cooling tropical greenery. No one knew where she got the idea for this extraordinary oasis, but we were all happy to gather there. Veronique was an enterprising woman, and the others seemed to look to her naturally for leadership. Out in the yard, beyond the cool veranda, Veronique ran a little beer business. She bought maize to soak and dry and soak again in a long process of fermentation that transformed golden grain into tiny bundles of gray muck, which when mixed with water and filtered through old grain bags became a sour and fairly potent brew. She employed her youngest sister and a niece in the business and turned a tidy profit for them all.

Assetou appeared in the doorway to tell us that the women from the other end of the village couldn't come to the meeting. She herself had come only to deliver the message. Tanou and I thought we understood. Ramadan had started, and hooch was *haram* (forbidden) in half the village, for Koupela-Tenkodoko was split into the Christian end of town (Koupela), where Veronique lives and brews beer, and the Muslim end (Tenkodoko), where the Islamic ban on alcohol is strictly observed, at least during Ramadan. A common marketplace lay in between. All the villagers were Burkinabe—originally from Burkina Faso—and most had lived here harmoniously for decades, but hateful propaganda had put everyone on edge. In these tense times, disharmony within the village would be intolerable.

The message from Tenkodoko sent the Koupela women into an uproar. That message hadn't come from the women, they said, even though Assetou had delivered it. It came from Malik. "He has to be in charge of everything," Veronique said. "If he can't come to our meeting, he won't let them come either."

"In that case," Tanou said, "we will go to them." It was agreed. We marched out of the cool veranda into the heat and dust of the village streets. We passed through the sweltering, slumbering market and made our way to Tenkodoko. We found the chief seated under the tree in his front yard, receiving visitors.

To explain our arrival in his end of town, I told him that I needed electricity to power the computer because we hoped to have a slide show of the women's first photographs. The old chief graciously suggested his reception hall and dispatched a boy to fire up the generator. An aide ushered us inside and produced an extension cord. The reception hall—the chief's living room—was furnished with overstuffed vinyl couches and chairs.

The Koupela women gingerly seated themselves beneath the oversized posters that decorated the walls—advertising shots of fancy resort hotels with inviting swimming pools. The women of Tenkodoko, with Assetou in the lead, soon joined us.

"How is your photography going?" Tanou asked in French. "How has the village responded to the cameras?"

Silence. Tanou looked around the room at each woman in turn, smiling. *It's all over,* I thought. *We have no translator.* Then Veronique said quietly, "I believe you asked how we are doing with the photography. And what the villagers think." I was amazed: Veronique was speaking French.

*"Exactement!"* Tanou said. Veronique turned to the group to voice Tanou's questions in the local language; thus a woman formerly intimidated became a translator.

Then the answers came quickly. The women said that "people" took them seriously now. Most of the men in the village were proud of them because using a camera is a very special thing. But they were jealous, too, because this honor had not been given to men, to whom it properly belonged, as anyone should know. The men were baffled by this and a little afraid of what the women might be up to. One woman reported that her husband, who had never before shared the proceeds from the family field, now proposed to give a little something to his photographer-wife. Another reported that her husband, who had never before provided money for a sick child's medicine, rode his bike all the way to the health center to make sure that his photographer-wife and the child, who had gone ahead on foot, were being served by the pharmacy. Another told of her neighbor, an habitual wife beater, never deterred by others who tried to intervene. When she threatened to fetch her camera, he stopped hitting his wife and ran away.

I was dumbfounded. In the space of a week, without anybody even getting a look at the women's photos, the village had tilted. It was the camera itself—the *appareil*—that seemed to have magical powers. It would expose bad behavior and petty tyranny. It would reveal the truth and command retribution. These were only the first reports of changes wrought in husbands and in photographers by the mere presence of the camera. The expression *"grâce à l'appareil"*—"thanks to the camera"—became a kind of mantra. Even Malik's mother, we learned from the Tenkodoko women, had turned against him. Malik was mean to his wife they said, but now his mother takes her side. Assetou said, "It is true."

As we talked, I downloaded the shots the women had taken during their first week as photographers. Then I unscrewed the electric bulb hanging from the ceiling, and there in the dark the images they had captured began to appear, one by one on my computer screen. The women were transfixed—silent except for an occasional gasp or cry. When all the images had marched past, they asked to see the parade again. This time they spoke up: "That's mine." "I took that one." "I helped." They laughed and slapped hands, dazzled by what they themselves had done. Then we were all up and dancing and singing songs that needed no more translation than the photos had. At last we threw open the doors of the chief's house and stepped into the blinding sunshine. When Tanou and I had first come to the village, we sat out there under the tree and proposed our project to the chief with the help of Malik the translator. Now, we had held our first slide show *inside* the chief's house, Malik had been fired, and the chief himself, I saw, was taking a nap, stretched out on the stones of his own front steps.

Koupela-Tenkodoko was only our first stop. We'd recruited groups of women in Zatta village, which lay on the way to

Koupela-Tenkodoko, and in Zokoguhe, a long drive beyond. The photo project was soon in full swing in all three sites, and the first assignment was this: take as many photos as you want to show what life is like for you and other women in your village; include three images of things that are problems, and three images of things that make you happy.

Finding problems was easy. In Zatta, that assignment had sent Zounan Sylvie running to the home of a woman she knew who had been badly beaten by her husband; when Sylvie reached her, the woman was slumped against the wall in despair because her husband had refused to give her the money she needed to have her injuries treated at the health center. Sylvie seemed to have a professional's sense of a story that must be told. "I am going to take your photo," she said, and she got the shot. Prudence in Zokoguhe photographed a man beating his wife with a broom. Martine in Zokoguhe photographed a woman landing in the dirt face-first and the man who had thrown her to the ground. Jeanette in Koupela-Tenkodoko photographed a man beating his wife with a stick.

Several women in Zokoguhe took photos of a penniless young woman abandoned by her husband living in the open under a thatched roof, with three tiny children. These images were most troubling to the women. The threat of abandonment was what made them suffer all other forms of abuse in silence. Anything was better, they said, than to be left homeless and alone. Most of the women actually fed and clothed themselves and their children by working their farms, selling produce in the market, making beer or other items for sale. But the house belonged to the man, together with everything in it and the land it stood upon. And money was needed for extras, like visits to the doctor and medicine—money the husband might give or not. Husbands were responsible for "important" things like

"The camera makes me strong to talk about this situation that happens all the time in my village. This is violence, and it is not acceptable. We cannot accept that men beat women. It is not the right way to treat any person."
—Goze Martine, Côte d'Ivoire

funerals. They paid the expenses. They invited the guests with whom they sat and drank beer. It was women who did the work. But a woman without a man to work for, without a man's house to live in, became an outcast. She could not survive.

What made women happy was easy too. Like the photo of a man who, when he saw that his wife was exhausted as she labored over dinner preparations, actually took the buckets and went to the well himself to fetch the water for his bath. There were other amazing photos of men in action: sweeping the courtyard, helping their wives pound rice, drawing water, carrying firewood home on their bicycles, and in a few cases actually holding babies. As we looked at a series of these shots, I could feel the women's hopes rise. Assetou asked: "Why *can't* a man bathe a child?"

And the other photos? In a week, some of the volunteers had taken hundreds. They showed women working in the fields with mattock and hoe, women chopping firewood with machetes, women building fires, women cooking over fires with cauldrons and grills, preparing rice, smoking fish, boiling fermented maize for beer, braising bananas and plantains, stirring sauces of egg-plants or peanuts or tomatoes with onions and chilies, women peeling manioc with machetes, grating manioc, boiling manioc, women washing dishes and clothes and children, women sweeping house and yard, women carrying burdens of all sorts on their heads—stalks of plantains, basins of tomatoes, bundles of firewood, baskets of laundry—walking to a distant field, or the market, or the river. One night I sat in my room in Yamoussoukro and reviewed on my computer the photos the women of three villages had made in the first week of their work as photographers. The number of photos of women at work was astounding. There were hundreds and hundreds. I realized that by the time this project came to an end in Côte d'Ivoire, in the space of a few weeks, I would have *thousands* of photos of village women doing chores. Most of them would show a woman alone, or surrounded by her young children, engaged in heavy labor.

I discussed the hard work of women with my French tutor, a forward-thinking Yamoussoukro schoolteacher, who had left his own home village and was usually eager to repudiate village traditions. Yet he saw the heavy workload of women as proof that the custom of polygamy must be maintained. The hard work necessary to support a man, he said, was too much for one woman to do alone. The idea that a man might share "her" work had not occurred to him. Yet what other solution was

there? Freeze-dried peeled and grated instant manioc would
not be available to village women anytime soon, and if it were,
they would still have to haul water and wood and build the fire
to cook it. In the villages, tasks were not allotted by physical
capacity but by gender alone.

What emerged from these massed photos was a bigger picture, a broader definition of gender-based violence. For village
women gender-based exploitation, enforced by violence, seemed
to be life itself—a life that demands relentless forced hard labor
*because they are women.* Here was the perfect political economy
of misogyny: gender-based servitude. Women labored. Men
profited. Women chafed under these rules, but one of the ironic
consequences of war was that they were caught in a state of
gratitude that they were still alive, still able to work, and proud
of it. But the aftermath of war had brought new demands.
Once it had been enough that they labored incessantly to
serve their husbands. Now they had to face the soldiers, the
police, the civil authorities who had become aggressive and
so intimidating that the women feared to photograph them.
War had made women vulnerable. War propaganda had made
minority women designated targets. Even health care workers
might shake them down for a little sex. Even peacekeepers. A
woman knew her husband's demands, but war had changed
her world.

As the weeks passed, and my collection of images grew into
the thousands, I realized that even though I talked with the
women every week and looked at their intimate photographs, I
still didn't know who among them had been raped during the
war, or assaulted at a checkpoint, or forced to watch a sister
dragged away. Somehow it didn't matter. I had been looking for
special categories of violence borne in on the edge of war, but
here were women—beautiful, spirited women—leading lives of

forced servitude. Their daily lives seemed like training grounds for ever more violent exploitation. If men in peacetime routinely view their wives as indentured laborers, in the field and in the bed, why shouldn't soldiers in wartime also view women as slaves to be impressed for labor or sexual servitude? Soldiers themselves referred to the women they abducted as "temporary wives"—short-term replacements, like interchangeable parts, for the wives they already had at home. For some women, it seemed, the difference between peace and war was not what was done to them, but which men did it.

The women gathered again to look at the work of their second week as photographers. They had documented their complaints: too much hard labor, too much violence, too much illness, too little attention and respect. At Koupela-Tenkodoko,

"This old woman peeling yams is a widow, left with nothing after the death of her husband. Her two sons live in the town, but they accuse her of being a witch and refuse to help her."
—Kouassi N'Guessan Françoise, Côte d'Ivoire

first one, and then another, of the older women said she didn't want younger women to suffer as she had. The younger women said they were hopeful that life could change because their work as photographers had already caused the men, especially their husbands, to look at them differently, with new respect.

"What would have to change," Tanou asked, "to free young women from suffering?"

As hard as they tried, the women could not pin down an answer. They offered concrete examples of suffering—the problems and complaints they had photographed. But they were used to thinking in specifics: one hard task after another. It was the generalizations that eluded them, the principles and rights. They said that there was too much heavy work for women. It would be fair—"just"—if men would help. But apart from the few men we had seen in photographs sweeping the yard or drawing water on occasion, men did not help at all. So the women couldn't produce examples of fairness or justice that might relieve women of their suffering. It was only injustice that came to mind. Even nature is unjust, they said, giving to women alone the pains of childbirth and the constant care of children. Nature made the rules. And men.

"It is true," Tanou said, "that nature gives women the task of bringing children into the world. But is it nature that says women alone must take care of them?"

The women pondered. Tanou threw back a question that Assetou had asked before: "Why can't a man bathe a child?"

Another woman said she knew of a man who once had done that very thing. Examples multiplied of other rare but real exceptions. Bit by bit distinctions emerged between the rules of nature that can't be changed and the rules of men that might perhaps be bent.

"What about the violence of husbands?" Safiatou asked.

"Can that be changed?" She directed her question to me. I said that in my country, women also had asked men to share the housework and the child care; and in addition, we had demanded punishment for men who harmed us, including husbands. "But you ask only for fair treatment," I said. "You want your husbands to be kind and helpful. Perhaps punishment is not the answer for you."

That prompted Damata to tell a story about a thief who lived in her mother's village. The chief ordered that he be stripped naked and paraded through the streets. After that ordeal, he never stole anything again. "Punishment makes people stop their bad behavior," she said.

"Ahh," Tanou said. "What if a chief thought that wife beating and rape were crimes as serious as theft?" The women began to chatter all at once. Tanou said, "Well, of course, the chief could order some other punishment. You probably don't want to see your husbands march around the village naked."

But the women slapped hands and playfully punched each other, and some of them doubled over in their chairs. The very thought made them laugh and laugh.

At Zokoguhe, we talked again—still—about the unrelenting work that filled the lives of these women. After all the unfairness they had photographed and described, after the long days of work in the house and the field, after the husband hopped on his bike and left his wife to hike home with the baby on her back and the firewood and a stalk of plantains on her head, after she hauled the bathwater and built the fire and cooked the dinner and did the dishes and made the bed, after all that, there was more. There was her duty. No use saying she was tired. Or ill. Duty called. If she refused to have sex with her husband, he might use force. He might beat her. He might rape her. Or, in Zokoguhe, he might eat a fat chicken.

He was entitled to it, by tradition, if she turned him down. Come morning he could go to the poultry seller and select the plumpest chicken in stock. He could arrange for someone to cook it. He could eat the whole thing. And he could send the bill to his wife. Some tribes from other villages required the wife to choose the chicken and cook it herself, but Zokoguhe rules prevented a wife from sticking her husband with some skinny bird. It wasn't a joke. When the poultry seller came around to collect, the wife had to find a way to pay. Which meant more work, more sacrifice, and probably greater submission to her duty.

We were nearing the end of the six-week project, and I had more than seven thousand photos in my computer, most of them showing a woman or women at work. Sometimes men could be seen in the background, riding their bicycles, or sitting together talking or drinking beer, or sauntering along in smart clothes freshly washed and pressed by some woman. In fairness, I have to say that we had photos of men at work as well, but not many. Somehow as we reviewed the week's work, the conversation had led us through the bedroom to the poultry market. Frankly, I was surprised because the women were extraordinarily reluctant to talk about any personal problem. It was as though they had sworn an oath of silence. To confide in another woman—other women—about marital difficulties or other personal problems was "shameful." It was a confession of guilt and inadequacy, since all women knew, as men so often reminded them, that every problem is caused by a woman. So the women blamed themselves, and to protect themselves, they shut up; while men, safe outside the wall of silence, went about their business and ate chicken.

I had told the women early on that in my country and many others the movement for women's rights caught fire when women started to talk to one another about their problems and to look for common solutions. Tanou had backed me up. Since then, a few women had spoken out from time to time. One wanted to tell about why she had left her husband in the city and come home to the village. Another wanted help figuring out how to get the man she had lived with for twelve years to marry her. (He wasn't "ready" yet, though they had six children.) Every time a woman spoke up, some other woman—often the imam's wife, or rather one of his wives—said that such problems should be discussed only with one's husband. Never mind that in most cases the problem was the husband. But lately I had noticed that when a woman spoke of personal matters, the admonition to keep silent came only after she had spoken, after she had been heard.

"What if you refused to pay for the chicken?" Tanou asked.

"You can't do that," Georgette said. She seemed horrified. "He's already eaten it."

"Did you eat any of it?" Tanou asked.

"No, no!" The women laughed at the impossibility of such a thing.

"No, you didn't," Tanou said. "So why should you pay for it? What would happen if you refused to pay?"

The women stirred nervously. Then Martine ventured, "Maybe next time the poultry man wouldn't be so quick to give my husband such a fat chicken."

"Ah-ha," said Tanou.

Julienne said, "Then he would beat me for sure." But she laughed anyway.

Georgette said, "What if we all refused to pay the poultry man?"

"Ah-ha," said the women.

That was something to think about.

Soon it was showtime at Zatta—the day the women were to exhibit their photos in the village. We had three big days ahead of us, one in each of the villages where we had worked on the project. To prepare for the shows, each woman selected two photos she considered to be the most important ones she had taken. Back at my room in Yamoussoukro I printed eight-by-ten color enlargements and spread them on every available flat surface to dry; my accommodating housemates went out to eat. Then I found a shop in town that could laminate the prints in plastic so they would be durable enough to pass from hand to hand.

A month earlier, during our first slide shows, I had made audiotapes on a little pocket recorder, asking each woman to explain why she had taken a particular photo and what it meant to her. I intended to use these responses as captions, but most of the women could scarcely speak into the machine. Their descriptions were short and painfully literal and specific. Speaking of the image of a young woman, chin in hand, looking utterly despondent, the photographer said, "This is a picture of a woman sitting in a chair." It took a lot of patient questioning to bring forth the explanation that the woman in the chair, pregnant, had been abandoned by her husband, and that this terrible threat of abandonment intimidates every woman. But during our discussions of the past month, as they searched their lives for answers to Tanou's questions, the photographers had somehow learned to generalize. They had begun to talk about "women," and not just that one individual in the photo. They had begun to talk in terms of fairness and justice. And knowing the exhibition was their chance to send a message to the village powers, they prepared.

At Zatta, the big chief, the subchiefs, and the *notables*

gathered in a semicircle under the trees that shaded the village meeting ground; for the first time, they invited women to join them. All along, we'd had one great advantage in dealing with the chiefs at Zatta, for the village spoke Baoule, which happened to be Tanou's first language as well. She knew the culture through and through, so she could speak to the chiefs with subtlety and tact. To open the show, she greeted the dignitaries, thanked them for receiving us, and explained the purpose of the Global Crescendo Project: to enable women to examine their problems and present suggestions to improve their lives and benefit the whole village. She asked the men to keep that purpose in mind, apologizing in advance for the discomfort they might feel on this unprecedented occasion. Women of the village would take the floor and address the chiefs, a practice never before permitted. They might show photographs of things the men did not care to see. They might speak some words, usually forbidden, related to matters usually not spoken about at all, such as sex. They might even express opinions that seemed to contradict the views of the assembled notables. But their aim, Tanou said, was benevolent and farsighted.

Then the women took over. They stood before the chiefs and said what they had to say about their photos while Tanou circled the crowd, displaying the images in question. It was the first time in their lives that any of the women had spoken in public, or addressed, or even looked at, a chief, something forbidden by tradition. Of their own accord, they stood up with their teammates so that every woman, as she spoke, had the visible support of others. They told the notables that women's tasks are too many and the work too hard. That men must help. That women must be allowed to rest. That men must bear some responsibility for the children. They spoke of the importance

of education for all girls and boys. They spoke of the enterprise and courage of women who sold their produce on the
dangerous highway, unsupported by husbands. The men listened attentively. With a gesture now and then, they silenced
the children playing nearby. They asked questions, and the
women responded as if they had engaged in public discussion
all their lives.

Then came Sylvie with a photo of a woman's leg. Sylvie's
first photo for the project was the picture of her friend whose
husband had beaten her badly. The battered woman had wanted
Sylvie to show the photo to the whole village, but the group
decided against it; they feared she would be recognized, and
they couldn't predict what her violent husband might do. So

"Why can a man beat a woman? This woman has just given birth,
and her husband has beaten her. Woman is like a pot; she is
breakable. A bad beating like this can lead to her death. We want
to say no to this situation, and we want it to change."

—Zounan Sylvie, Côte d'Ivoire

Sylvie stood up at the show and spoke about another photo she had taken on the same occasion, of the battered woman's bruised and bloody lower leg.

It caused the old chief to raise his arm and speak for the first time. "No," he said. "This is too much. I do not want violence of any kind in this village. Violence must stop."

The women applauded the chief. And when they stood together at the end of the exhibition, holding up their photos for all to see, the chief led the men in applauding them. I had arranged beforehand to take portraits of the chiefs after the show, and as I did so, the photographers ranged behind me with their cameras. Breaking with tradition, the women had looked the chiefs squarely in the face today; now they dared to photograph them. The photographers passed the cameras to their teammates so everyone could get a shot, and the chiefs sat still.

The next day the old chief sent word to the group: He had heard their message and he would honor it. I was skeptical. I didn't trust the leaders of my own country; why should I believe this chief? But Tanou said, "A chief is different. A chief must keep his word. The women of Zatta have won."

Two days after this triumph, Tanou and I set out for the exhibition at Koupela-Tenkodoko. The notables awaited us, seated on the stone steps of the chief's porch. Malik the tyrannical translator was in the front row. The photographers were offered chairs in the yard, facing the men; and the other women of the village gathered behind them. The chief of Tenkodoko himself was not present. He had gone to town, without explanation or apology, pointedly reclaiming his reception hall for his children—who were inside watching a loud shoot-'em-up movie on TV—and leaving this "woman's matter" to be dealt with in the yard by the village notables. The headman of the other end of the village, the chief of Koupela, was absent as well, though he sent word that I could come to take his picture. The balance of power in Koupela-Tenkodoko, once tilted briefly in the women's favor, had tilted back.

The notables had come to lock it down. When two women presented photos of an abandoned woman living with her children in a makeshift shack at the edge of the village, the men laughed. "Such a woman must still live," the photographer said. "The village cannot also abandon her."

Malik said, "If a man abandons a woman, she must have done something wrong." Case closed. One by one, the photographers presented photos of women doing heavy labor and suggested, again and again, that men could help. Again, the men laughed. Tanou asked how many of them ever helped their wives at home. Four men raised their hands. One of them was Malik. It was the women's turn to laugh. Tanou put a question to the village women: "Is there any man in this village who is known to help his wife?" A young mother pointed out a man seated in the top row. "He is a good man," she said. "Everyone knows it."

Tanou turned to the man and asked him to tell us, if he would, why he helped his wife. He replied quietly, "I loved my wife when I married her and I love her still. If I love her, I must care for her and help her. It is very simple. It gives me pleasure." Veronique stumbled over the translation; the man was her husband. He also said, "A woman is not a slave." It was something I had heard women say again and again. Why this word? It occurred to me that Veronique's husband meant it literally. He said that a woman is not a "slave" because in fact she is: a slave to work, a slave to sex, a slave to violence. That is the tradition, the custom, perhaps now even more rigorously upheld in the

"This is a picture of me, Assetou, doing a job my husband assigned. If the work is not finished when he comes home, he will beat me. He gives me so many jobs I have no time to sit down and rest and feed my child. This is not fair. Husbands must know that a woman is not a slave."
—Samandougoulou Assetou, Côte d'Ivoire

aftermath of war. Only the luck of marrying "a good man" might ease a woman's bondage. And there seemed to be only one "good man"—Veronique's husband—in the whole place.

Then it was the turn of Samandougoulou Assetou. She came forward to stand under the tree and present two photos. One showed a woman stirring her cooking cauldron over a fire while hungry children pressed her on all sides, holding out their empty bowls; the other showed a woman pounding rice with a wooden pestle in one hand while holding a child to her breast with the other. They were photos of herself and her children. She had set them up, she explained, and asked a teammate to press the button. She had taken them to make this point: "When a man assigns jobs to a woman, he should assign them one at a time. And he should do some work himself."

The men laughed, but she raised her voice and her fists to make herself heard. She was young and beautiful and utterly determined. Later she told us that her father had given her by force, as a young girl, to settle a debt with an older man who struck her every day, a man so mean that even her father now urged her to leave him. But she could not. She had five children. One of them was strapped to her back as she spoke, slicing the air with her arms, silencing the men. Her photos depicted a slave at work. One man in the front row looked away—the mean husband to whom Assetou had been given.

The high drama of this extraordinary confrontation left the women exuberant. Who knew they could fight so hard? They vowed to keep watch over Assetou and protect her from her husband; but she was euphoric with the giddiness of someone who had nothing left to lose but her life. When the women circled and began to dance, Assetou whirled and stomped at the center.

Tanou and I worried about her, though. At the thought that her husband might do serious harm, we chided ourselves for having let things go too far. On our way to our third show the following day, we stopped in Koupela-Tenkodoko, and there she was—composed, smiling, with her baby daughter on her hip. She told a story we could scarcely believe. Many of the notables had approached her husband after the exhibition and asked what he thought of the things she had said about him. He replied, "My wife has given good counsel." When she went home that day, he said nothing about the show or her part in it, but for the very first time, he gave her money to buy food for the children.

I asked Tanou to explain this miraculous conversion, but she couldn't fathom it. So off we went to our final destination,

At the First-Ever All-Women's Photo Show in Koupela-Tenkodoko, Saman-dougoulou Assetou denounces the demands of husbands. Yougoubare Vero-nique, smiling, is seated on the right.                          —Ann Jones

Zokoguhe, baffled but ecstatic; and there pandemonium awaited us. People of six different ethnicities speaking six different, mutually unintelligible languages live in Zokoguhe village. They get along by not listening to each other. One thing they do very well is dance—no language being involved. The whole village boogied out to greet us to the beat of marimbas, drums, and cymbals. They ushered us into the covered meeting hall, and danced some more. But once the show started, harmony went flat. There were translators—all men—for Bete and Gouro and More and Yacouba and Senufo and Baoule and a lot of shouting in Dioula, the somewhat mutually intelligible argot of the market. Each translator talked in turn, each translation longer than the one before, and while one language was shouted out, speakers of the other languages fell into noisy chatter with their neighbors. Meanwhile, all the village children—there were hundreds—played uproarious games around the perimeter of the open meeting hall. Tanou asked a drummer to call people to attention, but when he banged on his drum, everyone jumped up and started dancing again.

Somehow Tanou managed to introduce the show. The women came forward to present their photos and shout a few words into the din. And all the old men seated around the village chief—an aged and somnolent fellow in a battered fedora—stood up and shouted offensive things about women. "Whatever trouble women have, they earn it," yelled an old man wearing cool shades. "If they're abandoned, they deserve it," hollered another slick old dude. "If they're forced to do all the work, that's what they're here for," another one called out. "If they're beaten, they asked for it." They hooted. They slapped hands with the chief. Now I understood why women in Zokoguhe had taken so many photos of violence. It was routine here; there was nothing to deter it and certainly no tribal leadership to condemn it. A man could beat his wife in public without risking interference or even the bad opinion of his neighbors. Being caught by a photographer meant nothing. Yet the women chose not a single photo of violence for the exhibition. They already knew what the men would say. To show the photos of violent village men in action would have been only to ask for more.

It came to me then how much our work with women depended upon the goodwill of progressive leaders, and how different were the attitudes of leaders from one village to the next. In Zatta, only an hour away, one photograph of a battered wife had been enough to make the chief denounce all forms of violence. Since that show, he had summoned the photographers and invited them to join his council. But in Zokoguhe, where the violence was cheered on as if it were a sport, the women were silenced, condemned by a bunch of old men in power to more of the same.

Yet even here, in this hostile cacophony, the women managed to voice their concerns. One dared to show a photo of her family's cocoa crop. She said, "When it is time to work on the cocoa, the husband calls it 'ours.' But when it is time to sell, he calls it 'mine.'" Her photo showed her husband's harvested cocoa beans spread out like a gray carpet, with a tiny cluster set to one side for her, the wife who was the principal day laborer on the farm. For women it was a question of fairness. But the old man in the sunglasses shouted: "You will get in big, big trouble if you start talking profits." The warning was repeated at high volume in six or seven languages.

The women tried to talk about sharing household chores, as the women of Zatta and Koupela-Tenkodoko had done. Two showed photos of young husbands helping their wives pound rice, an onerous task performed with a wooden pestle as tall as a woman. I too had photographed young men in Zokoguhe helping their wives pound rice; but young men seemed to have no voice in the meeting. Arguments broke out in many languages, until the old chief rose to pronounce the last word upon the subject. "It might be permitted," he said, "for a husband to perform certain tasks from time to time, if he so wished, to assist his wife." Bringing a little firewood would be one such task, he said, but it was the only one he could think of. As for pounding rice or maize, that was woman's work, shameful for a man.

I might have wept about this deafening day except for two things. First, the women of Zokoguhe were just as proud of themselves for speaking up in public as the women of Zatta and Koupela-Tenkodoko had been. Never mind that no one seemed to hear. Nobody ever heard much of anything in noisy

Zokoguhe. The important thing was: They spoke. And when we held the final meeting of the photo group after the show, Assetou, who had accompanied us from Koupela-Tenkodoko, told her story to the women of Zokoguhe. "I spoke up to my husband," she said, "and my husband changed. It is a lesson. Do not be afraid."

With the project ending, we couldn't afford to give away the cameras; we needed them for use in other countries. But we couldn't bear to leave the women without a single magical *appareil*. In the end we presented one camera to each village group. I gave the photographers a few tips on keeping the camera in working order. I told them that if it broke, they should tell the IRC field agent—and no one else. She (or he) would take it to the city for repair and bring it back. If it couldn't be repaired, the agent would bring it back anyway, and they could go on taking pictures as if the camera actually worked. Tanou had told them weeks before that when it came to planning changes in their village, they didn't really need the camera. "Your eyes are the lens," she said. "The memory card is in your head. And the photo can come out of your mouth, for all of you can talk about the photos you have seen with your own eyes." Now they laughed at the thought of pretending to take photos with a broken *appareil*.

"Yes," said one. "It is a good plan."

All the groups saw that the project had yielded another benefit—the beginnings of solidarity. The Zatta women had decided early on to stick together. They elected officers and officially registered their organization with village authorities. They wrote a theme song. They adopted a Baoule cheer: *Anouanze!* (Unity!) They accepted the chief's invitation to join his council and help him devise effective laws to stop violence in the village. In the space of six weeks, the silent women of Zatta had become influential participants in local governance—a transformation that gave the lie to those naysayers who insist that social change takes a long time.

The Koupela-Tenkodoko group also decided to continue to meet together and intervene in families where women were abused, citing Assetou and her changed husband as role models of reform. The whole village knew that he now gave her breaks from her tasks and money for the children, and that he had taken up occasional child care and abandoned violence altogether. In January 2009, he escorted Assetou to the mosque and officially made her his legal wife. The whole group is waiting for him to give her permission to take their five children to the church at the other end of the village and have them baptized.

Even the women of Zokoguhe, that fractious village, planned to continue to meet and help women in need. At our meetings they had begun to collect food and clothing to carry to the abandoned woman and her children who lived in the shed at the edge of town. And later, after I had gone, Tanou wrote that the Zokoguhe women had become such strong campaigners for their rights that they had inspired others in neighboring villages with whom they talked on market days. On their own, the women of one village planned a march for "Fairness for Women" and invited the group from Zokoguhe to join them. The chief of the village in question refused to give his permission for the event, but the women marched anyway, and as they passed the chief's compound, all four of his wives came out to join the parade. None of them cooked his dinner.

Would it last? This spirit, this modest revolution? Who

knew? This is a country in which girls at the age of puberty massage their budding breasts with herbal ointments in hopes that they might not, after all, become women. But these women had taken a chance on our project. They had talked with other women, shared their ideas, become friends, and vowed to stick together. They did these things for themselves. They took the photos they wanted to take. They crafted the message they wanted to send. They delivered it with courage. And they saw some things actually change. Perhaps you wouldn't call that a crescendo—they never did speak up about what they suffered in the war—but it's not silence either.

One Sunday, just before I was to leave Côte d'Ivoire, Tanou invited me to attend mass with her and her daughter at the basilica. We sat together under the soaring dome and listened to a Polish priest give a sermon in French to a congregation of Africans about our obligations to our neighbors. I was carried away by the music of the choir, and for the first time, I saw Yamoussoukro's astonishing architectural wonder as a blessedly immense reminder that anything is possible. Not long after, Tanou sent me an announcement that an exhibition of forty-five photographs by women of the three villages—Côte d'Ivoire's First-Ever All-Women's National Photographic Exhibition—would open in the nation's capital at the Basilique de Notre Dame de la Paix and later travel down the road to the Grand Mosque. Tanou would be at the basilica with the photographers to open the show, but by that time, I had already traveled down the road myself to the ruins of another much longer war next door.

# 2

## LIBERIA: "LIFE CAN CHANGE . . ."

When I boarded my flight in Abidjan for the short hop to the Liberian capital, I was still high on the changes the women in Côte d'Ivoire had made in their lives. But the drive into central Monrovia brought me crashing back down to earth: wretched roads, paltry markets, ruined houses, blackened shells of government buildings occupied by long-term squatters, and the sprawling home of former big man Charles Taylor bearing a message inscribed in Christmas lights, now extinguished: "Season's Greetings." Liberian fighters had well and truly trashed their homeland.

I arrived at an IRC rental house in Monrovia on a Sunday morning in time to catch one of my new housemates leaving for the beach. I escaped with her. It was splendid and wild: the pale sand, the pale sky, and the sea the color of silver foil, crashing over a bar not far offshore. I stepped into the water just as a wave rolled back, sucking sand from beneath my feet. The rip caught me and hauled me far down the shore before I found my footing again. So much for swimming. I told my colleague I'd take a nice long walk down the beach. "Please, not," she said. She had warned me about the treacherous surf, and now the sand: "Some women have been raped. Men have guns. Friends can do nothing."

I met a young Brit at the water's edge. Like me, he was too wary to plunge. He was repairing sabotaged navigational equipment at the international airport. He said, "We haven't finished, but you'll soon be able to land."

I said, "I landed this morning."

"Oh, right." We stood there for a long while, watching the breakers roar ashore. "You should have been advised to come by sea," he said. And then, "It makes you think, doesn't it?"

That was the name of the beach: Thinker's Beach. What I thought was: If everything is so threatening to me, here on this beautiful shore, what must life be like for Liberians? I'd been in the country only about three hours, and already I felt lucky to have survived. Yet for a very long time Liberia had been awash in waves of war. Some Liberians speak of "*the* war," referring to fourteen years of intermittent conflict between 1989 and 2003. Others speak of the first world war, the second world war, and the third. (Any war must feel like a world war when you're caught in the middle of it.) They date the first war from 1980 and name it after Samuel Doe, whose bloody coup d'état in that year set the stage for more violence. The second war dates from 1989 and is named for Prince Johnson, who murdered President Doe. The third war, dating from 1999, is all Charles Taylor's. All three wars are named for Liberian leaders notorious for their appalling cruelty. Three wars, or one—it's more than enough.

By the time the fighting ended in 2003, 1.4 million Liberians had been displaced within the country. Almost a million others had fled. In a country of three million people, that's one in three citizens gone. At least 200,000 people were dead. Some sources say 300,000. That's 10 percent of the population. As always, women were targets. Lofa County, in the north, lay in the path of Charles Taylor's militia and the opposing forces of Liberians United for Reconciliation and Democracy (LURD). Both sides used rape and murder as weapons. A World Health Organization study in 2005 estimated that 90 percent of Liberian women suffered physical or sexual violence; three out of four women were raped.

A study by the IRC and Columbia University's School of Public Health in October 2007 reported: "While the war officially ended in 2003, the war on women continued." Well over half the women interviewed in two counties (including the capital city) had survived at least one violent physical attack during an eighteen-month period in 2006–2007, years after the end of conflict. Well over half the women reported at least one violent sexual assault in the same period; and 72 percent said their husbands had forced them to have sex against their will. We don't know whether marital rape was equally prevalent before the war; but war clearly demonstrated the efficacy of force and the disposability of women and girls. An earlier IRC study (2003) among Liberian refugees in Sierra Leone found that 75 percent of women had been sexually assaulted before they fled from Liberia, and after they crossed the border, 55 percent were sexually assaulted again.

After the war the Centers for Disease Control (CDC) and the United Nations Population Fund (UNFPA) surveyed surviving women in Lofa County. More than 98 percent said that during Charles Taylor's war they lost their homes. More than 90 percent lost their livelihoods. More than 72 percent lost at least one family member. Nearly 90 percent survived at least one violent physical assault. More than half survived at least one violent sexual assault. Such incredible statistics make you think, too.

Some people call Liberia America's stepchild, although some say "bastard child" is closer to the truth. It was founded by former slaves who were returned to Africa, bringing with them a few of America's worst features: elitism, discrimination, forced labor, religiosity, and a penchant for violence. They built small-scale plantations along the coast, established a nation, and lorded it over resident tribes. Leaders of America's only African "colony" set the model for autocratic African big men, until the "aborigines" rose up against them with greedy ambitions of their own.

The first African American settlers arrived on the west coast of Africa in 1822, shipped by the American Colonization Society. (Some members wanted to make amends for the slave trade by repatriating Africans; others just wanted to get rid of them.) The society bought a hundred-kilometer strip of coastal land from local tribes for $300 worth of dry goods and gunpowder. This wild coast was nowhere near the original homelands of the former slaves, but it was nearer than America. About five thousand freedmen and women soon followed the first settlers to the new colony. Nearly half of them died of disease, but in 1847, the survivors drew up a constitution, elected a president, and raised a simplified version of the American flag: the stripes with one lone star. They counted only themselves, the "civilized" Americo-Liberians, as citizens of the new Liberia.

For more than a century—until 1980—the Americo-Liberian elite ruled the land, while indigenous chiefs exploited their own system of forced labor. They hoarded women—many had a hundred wives or more—and put them to work. They made young men labor for years to earn a wife and sentenced poachers to servitude. Historians often cite this cruel system as the cause of the smoldering resentment and explosive violence of young Liberian men; but they don't say how women felt about it.

The country modestly prospered, especially during World War II, when the United States maintained military bases here, and afterward, when dozens of American corporations— led by Firestone rubber—invested in Liberia, conniving with the governing elite to cart off the country's natural resources. The long reign of the Americo-Liberians ended in 1980 when a group of young aboriginal soldiers, headed by Samuel Doe, murdered President William Tolbert and televised the execution of thirteen government ministers on a public beach. Doe continued what was by that time a tradition of governmental greed and corruption. International supporters vanished, leaving only the United States to contribute $500 million to the pockets of President Doe. He built a big stadium and named it after himself. Damaged by war, it was rebuilt by the Chinese and reopened in November 2006, still bearing Doe's name.

The rest is violence. In 1990, Prince Johnson—that's his name, not his title—murdered President Doe. Johnson had Doe's legs broken and his ears cut off; reports differ as to whether Johnson made Doe eat his ears or ate Doe's ears himself, though a video of the event shows Johnson merely sipping a Budweiser while his men do the carving. Reports generally agree that Johnson's men then dismembered Doe, and to impress the citizenry, displayed his body parts by hauling them around Monrovia in a car, or as some say, a wheelbarrow. Johnson tried to claim the presidency, but he still had to contend with Charles Taylor, a charming, American-educated sociopath, once a member of Doe's government and more recently allied with Johnson in the war against Doe. Taylor's forces were rolling through the country, terrorizing civilians, raping women, and murdering men, women, and children, even in refugee camps. Johnson's men held Monrovia and controlled the port.

An American warship lay offshore, sent by the first President Bush and filled with 2,500 American soldiers; they had the power to separate the contenders, as later the French would do quickly in Côte d'Ivoire to save their former colony from destruction. Liberians, who believed their country bore a special relationship to America, prayed for the troops to come ashore. But they didn't. Instead, they sailed away, and for the next five years, Johnson and Taylor and at least five other armed militias roamed up and down the country and laid it waste.

The strangest thing about this civil war is how little the militias actually battled against each other; they fought instead against civilians. When at last they signed peace accords in 1995, Taylor had the upper hand. Liberians elected him president by a landslide, perhaps reckoning (as battered women often do) that the best way to end the man's violence is to give him what he wants. It didn't work. By 1999 he was at war again with two opposition groups. Nevertheless, Liberians continued to return the most bloodthirsty men to high offices. Prince Johnson had fled to Nigeria, where he enjoyed a brief career as a born-again evangelist, but when he returned to Liberia, voters elected him to the senate.

President Taylor, having destroyed the country, finally abandoned it for luxurious exile in Nigeria, beyond the reach of his countrymen. International intervention and the election in 2005 of Ellen Johnson Sirleaf, Africa's first female president, offered hope of change. (Sirleaf was among the few in President Tolbert's government to escape Samuel Doe's 1980 massacre of ministers on the beach.) When I arrived in Monrovia late in 2007, things were much the same—tenuously balanced between hope and fear. Real fear arose from the mysterious absence of Senator Prince Johnson from public life—What was he up to?— and the public threats of his generals to assassinate Sirleaf. Hope, on the other hand, rested with her. For the first time, there was a woman in charge. One of her early achievements had been to press for the extradition of Taylor, setting in motion a process that eventually placed him in a courtroom in The Hague, on trial for war crimes.

Analysts trace the roots of Liberia's civil wars to "the emergence of a class of marginal young people." By "people," of course, they mean "men," oppressed by the system of the indigenous chiefs who monopolized the women and made the young "people" work to gain wives. But wives were not all the young men lacked. They had no land, no decent jobs, no money, no prospects. The generally accepted theory holds that "marginal young people" quite naturally worked themselves into homicidal rage, joined rebel militias, murdered and dismembered presidents, massacred political rivals, laid waste the country, and raped a lot of women and girls along the way.

What's odd about this as a theory is that for all the obfuscating talk of marginal "people," the women did not run amok with machetes and AK-47s or make lunch meat of somebody else's ears, although they surely had the greater cause. Enslaved in and out of the bedroom, their only possible deliverance lay in forced marriage to one of those resentful and violent young men, by then so fed up with labor that they would exert themselves only for revenge. Liberian women have always been exploited by men—rich and poor alike—yet they do not go berserk. Have they been so systematically enslaved by men that they've lost the capacity to act out anger? Have they been so traumatized by political and personal violence? Or do they just have better sense?

While I was in Liberia, road graders went to work on the streets of Monrovia and citizens were dumbstruck. Every president had promised to fix the roads; the woman everybody called "Ellen" had actually begun the job. It was a sign—superficial perhaps— that change for the better is possible. But when I first arrived in the capital city, driving the red dusty roads was an exercise in verticality as every pothole sank passengers and relaunched them toward the roof. I bounced along in an IRC van on my way to an outlying village called Bardnersville. The IRC GBV team had lined up a meeting for me there with ten women from eight distinct communities in urban Monrovia and the outlying suburbs of Montserrado County. In each community, IRC GBV teams had organized a Women's Action Group—WAG for short—to work on issues the members chose themselves. They had helped men too, in some communities, to organize groups known by an acronym that looked impressive on a T-shirt: MAPEVAW—Men as Partners in Ending Violence Against Women.

The GBV team wanted to involve all of the WAGs in the Global Crescendo Project. Before I arrived, they had asked every group to choose one aspiring photographer to take part. So instead of working in small supportive camera teams, as the women in Côte d'Ivoire had done, each photographer in Monrovia and Montserrado County would be on her own. These women were already better organized than the village women of Côte d'Ivoire. I hoped they would be as courageous.

Distant Bardnersville had been chosen as the meeting place because it had a brand new bright blue women's center, built with IRC support. The candidates stood waiting for us at a road junction where a dirt track trailed off into the trees. They were all dressed up in bright, bold African prints—snug blouses over skinny long skirts—but they packed themselves into the back of the vehicle like sardines volunteering for the can. One woman of especially generous size joined me in the front seat, and we strapped ourselves into a single seatbelt, instantly intimate friends. Together we jostled the last few miles.

To kick off the meeting I asked each woman to tell us what particular "action" her group was working on. What they said surprised me. Viola said the Central Monrovia group wanted to learn new job skills to increase their earning power. Patience said the women of Bushrod Island focused on "economic activi-

"This market woman was proud that Ann and I took her picture. She told us, 'No matter what men do to us, a woman can still sell fish.'"
—Patience Walker, Liberia

ties." Finda said the women from Chicken Soup Factory—a community named after a defunct Maggi bouillon cube plant—were learning hairdressing. Paynesville women were learning to sew, Vera said, but they had to do it by hand because they didn't have a sewing machine. Women from West Point and Slipway and Topoe Village wanted training in processes such as tie-dyeing and soap making, popular with NGOs. Some women confessed they had already learned these things in one NGO training program or another; but the course ended, the NGO went away, and they were left with forgettable skills and no materials to start up their new "livelihood." They wanted to try again.

When every woman had spoken, it struck me that not a single word had been said about violence. Yet Liberia was reeling from long, brutal wars characterized by unspeakable brutality and widespread rape. As in Côte d'Ivoire, when the fighting stopped, violence against women went on—especially rape; but the Liberian wars were more atrocious and much longer, long enough for violence against women and girls to have become the custom of the country. When the IRC surveyed Liberian women in 2006, 95 percent in Montserrado County named violence as their number-one problem. Up-country in rural Nimba County, 93 percent said the same. I wondered if things had improved so much that the violence had slipped their minds. So I asked, "Do you have any problem with violence in your communities?"

Heads nodded all around the room. "Yes," they said. "Of course." They began to talk of rape and wife beating and abandonment and the mental abuse of insult, public humiliation, and the like. They told me that every action group had an IRC social worker whose full-time job it was to offer psychosocial counseling and support to survivors. Some said their action group visited wife beaters at home to raise their "awareness."

Sometimes they imposed fines on wife beaters and tried to collect; sometimes they reported them to community leaders or
the police. The women said they found it very troubling to work
on rape cases when the victims were little girls, but they had to
face that all the time. The stories added up to an avalanche, and
an enormous, exhausting daily collective effort to hold it back.

As I handed out the cameras, I wondered why the women
hadn't mentioned violence in the first place. Their silence on
the subject suggested the depth of wounds suffered in the long
wars and after, and it seemed to me a kind of resignation to
what they were up against. They had seen and survived terrible
violence, and they still saw it every day; they worked to stop it,
yet it went on and on, always. What counted now was survival. Like the village women of Côte d'Ivoire, they seemed
determined to carry on with life, but for these urbanites the
terms were a little different.

After that first enlightening meeting in Bardnersville, I went
every day with an IRC social worker to the home community
of one of the photographers. We would sit in on a meeting of
the Women's Action Group to listen and learn. Then the designated camera woman would guide me through the community.
I would take photos as we walked along to model for her what
a photographer looks like, what a photographer does. Soon she
would be snapping too. Women from the WAG usually came
along as well to coach their photographer and make sure she
got the shots they wanted.

One of my first stops was West Point, the poorest, most
densely populated community in the capital: a garbage-strewn,
fly-infested warren of mud and zinc hovels squeezed between
beaches where a land spit slides into the sea. West Point's loca-

tion is so idyllic it might have been Malibu. But it's not. The Women's Action Group met in the town's justice hall, a rundown storefront badly in need of paint. Up front near the door a clerk took down the legal complaints of people who drifted in off the street, while I sat in the back of the room and jotted in my notebook the concerns of thirty women.

"Rape is rampant," said the first woman to speak. "It goes on every day. Young girls be raped. Children be raped."

"Then what happens?" I asked. I knew that one of the first acts of President Sirleaf's government was a strict new rape law. The legislature had excluded rape in marriage from the law— sexual service being considered a wife's duty—but a few men had received long sentences for raping women other than their wives.

"Nothing happens," women replied from all sides. "It is a shame for the family. The parents, the child, they don't talk about it."

"They make compromise," said the chairwoman. "For money. Maybe just small, small. Or maybe if the man is rich, the parents can get two or three thousand Liberian dollars." (That's $100 to $150 American.)

"So the parents know who the rapist is?" I asked.

"Yes, yes."

"But they don't report him? They don't go to the police?"

"No, no. It is a shame for the family."

At last I saw: the family is shamed because the rapist is part of the family. An uncle, a brother-in-law, a cousin's nephew. There are also other reasons for not reporting the rapist. Sometimes the family is afraid of him; often they feel sorry for him.

"Maybe he is a student," one woman said. "If he gets reported, his future is damaged."

"What about the future of the girl he raped?" I asked.

"Nobody thinks of that," said an old woman.

"Why not?"

The old woman looked at me with sad, patient eyes. "Because she be girl."

One woman wanted to blame the victims. "Look at the way young girls dress," she said. "Like they looking to be raped."

Another woman, displaced from the north, said, "Don't be blaming them. Even Muslim women who go with the whole body wrapped up, even they get raped."

The chairwoman said, "Even wives staying in the house can be raped by the husbands."

Another woman said, "My neighbor's daughter was raped. She is four years old."

We sat in silence for a while—just sitting with the presence of violence that for these women was as relentless as rain. Then they told me more, about all the men who impregnate girls, by rape or seduction, and then abandon them. About the Fulas who beat their multiple wives every day. About the man who, having paid the bride price, often beats his prospective wife with a canoe paddle in the public street. About men from Guinea who traffic young girls to Monrovia for prostitution.

"What can you do about these things?" I asked.

They said they reported some rape cases to the police. They brought survivors to talk with the IRC social workers, who were here in the community every day. They brought pregnant girls and women who had been abandoned, and they took their cases to the association of women lawyers to seek support from the fathers. They campaigned for government regulation of video clubs, private storefront businesses that show X-rated, violent, and pornographic films. The four-year-old rape victim had been attacked by a twelve-year-old boy on his way home from a video club, trying to practice what he had seen. In

2005–2006 a Médecins Sans Frontières study found that 85 percent of rape victims were younger than eighteen; 48 percent were between the ages of five and twelve. In 2008, more than 70 percent of the survivors of sexual violence treated by Médecins Sans Frontières in Liberia were children.

"Where you find poverty, you find hungry men," said the old woman. "Where you find hungry men, you find violence." She was talking about men hungry for riches, hungry for power. "Men who have a little something do violence to the vulnerable to get something more."

Later we walked through the back alleys of West Point. On the seaside at the far edge of the community, lean, hard-muscled men were making a fishing boat as their grandfathers had, digging out a massive log for the keel. Along the shore, women tended fires in sooty oil drums overlaid with wire screens. They spread the day's catch upon the screens and moved among the drums, through smoke and scorching heat, to flip silvery fish as they dried and blackened. These were old arts, but the fish were small now and sparse, the boats less tightly made. The broad beach beyond was buried in trash and reeking garbage.

As we walked back, women mentioned things we had not seen—government schools, a hospital, a clinic, a playground for children, a women's center. They did not exist. The women led me to a very small, unfinished building. This was all they had to show me of a "center" once promised by an international NGO that had abandoned the project after putting up the windowless ground floor and a stairway to a nonexistent second story. After many months, the action group had scraped together enough money to pay a carpenter to close the stairwell and put in a door so they could make use of the ground floor. Watching him work, the chairwoman said, "When we have our meeting place, we can make bread."

———

In Côte d'Ivoire, village women protested their relentless hard labor, at home and in the fields, day in, day out. In Liberia, women said just the opposite. Everywhere I went in Montserrado County they said, "We sit idle. We have nothing to do."

It turned out on closer questioning that "nothing to do" was not exactly nothing. They ran the home and looked after the children. They got the food and the firewood or charcoal to cook it. They washed dishes and clothes and children and floors, and they hauled the water to do these things. But being urban women, they didn't have to plant swamp rice or dig cassava tubers. Mainly they had to do what they called "housework."

But don't underestimate the labor involved in that. The Slipway community, not far from the center of Monrovia, had no safe water at all. Every day women walked long distances and waited in line to buy drinking water at 20 LD (Liberian dollars) a gallon. (That's nearly fifty cents, no small amount for a poor family.) Another long walk in another direction brought them to a polluted well where they bought water for bathing and laundering at 5 LD a gallon. Often the water was rationed, and they returned to a family of six or seven with only a gallon. There, near the heart of the capital city, women spent hours every day, morning and evening, hauling water on their heads. Slipway women said their husbands often beat them, but given a choice between ending domestic violence and gaining a source of clean water, they would choose water.

Still they said they had nothing to do. What they wanted, as the photographers told us at our first meeting, were "skills." They wanted someone to teach them to be taxi drivers or carpenters so they could make a decent living, but they would settle for less profitable occupations like tailoring or hairdressing—the skills

"This water, I say, we are suffering from it. The water is bad. When people drink from it they get sick. The children die. But if a woman does not carry the water home every day, the man will beat her."

—Hellen Mulbah, Liberia

that men deemed "gender appropriate." They wanted to learn to read and write and do sums and manage a business. They wanted jobs and money to feed their children and send them to school. Even a free government school cost money, for school uniforms and shoes and pens; and free schools were few and far between.

Women said, "When you are poor, you have nothing to do." What they meant was "When you are a poor woman doing housework, you have nothing to show for it."

I went to Bushrod Island to visit the Logantown Women's Development Association. They had a big sign on the storefront where they met. The group had been established in 2005 by Christina W. Cummings, who had worked for twenty-five years in the Ministry of Finance. She had made a career of thinking about money. Having given herself the title of Executive Director, she drove the membership to think about money too. Women in Bushrod Island suffered from familiar problems— no clean water, no sanitation, habitual wife beating, rape, and abandonment—but the Logantown Women's Development Association was focused on economic development. The members worked against violence too, raising awareness in the community and bringing survivors to the IRC social worker. But the bigger problem, Christina Cummings said, was that the women of Bushrod Island had nothing to do.

They introduced themselves. Patience, the group's photographer taking part in our project, said she was married with four children. Also, she said, she had a little business selling soap. The group secretary, Margaret, was married with three children. She sold fried and baked goods. Elizabeth, the community mobilizer, had six children and a husband out of work. She sold water and soft drinks. Martina, the peer educator, sold dry goods. Patricia, whose husband wasn't working, sold fried cookies. Blessing, whose husband was "away," sold dry goods. A widow said she took care of her grandchildren and sold peanuts to pay their school fees. Two other women, each with three children, had nothing to sell. As the introductions continued, I saw that these two were the only ones in the group who were not in business. Almost every woman at the meeting was the sole breadwinner in her family. They were thinking big. They wanted a vocational school where they could learn skilled trades and capital to upgrade their businesses and increase their income, which was never enough to go around or get ahead.

I was puzzled, as I had been at our first meeting with the Montserrado photographers. Why were the women in these action groups, supposedly devoted to ending violence, so eager to learn auto mechanics? But I was catching on to their reading of the political economy of money and sex. To acquire real skills was to acquire a trade that trumped the selling of fried cookies or cornrows in a market overrun with cookie sellers and hairdressers. You could send all your children to school; you wouldn't have to pick and choose among them. You could buy uniforms and shoes. You wouldn't have to ask your boyfriend or your husband for money, which he probably wouldn't give you anyway. He would see for himself that at last you were doing something. You were no longer "idle." He would respect you, and he wouldn't abandon you and the children for another woman in another part of town. Or, if he had already gone, he would come back. He would stay with you forever, and he wouldn't hit you anymore.

After three weeks of working with the photographers in and around Monrovia, I left them to work on their own and boarded a UN helicopter for the far north. The GBV coordinator for Liberia had made plans for me to do the photo project not only in the capital but also in rural villages of Lofa County, the scene of some of the worst violence during the wars. The long dirt road to Voinjama, the Lofa County seat, was always difficult, and heavy rains had made it temporarily impassable. Hence the helicopter. It was a spectacular flight, cruising at times over the canopy of intact rain forest. But often we looked down on forests decimated by logging—second growth, bush, and clearcut patches where forests may never grow again. Charles Taylor had financed his war and his presidency partly by selling off virgin timber to foreign loggers and diamond mining rights to secret entrepreneurs, including evangelist Pat Robertson. It was another kind of violation.

In Voinjama, at a tiny community center, I met ten Lofa County women: four from the town, four from a distant smaller town, and two from a little village along the way. They paired up in teams and plunged into lesson number one: how to point and shoot. Soon we were off on a walk through town, shooting as we went. The women took teamwork seriously: one asked permission of people they wanted to photograph, the other composed the shot. One snapped the photo, while the other explained to the photo subjects what a Women's Action Group does and what exactly is wrong with beating your wife. By mid-afternoon, they were heading home with their cameras carefully tucked in their bags.

For the next two weeks I traveled nearly every day with a GBV social worker named Hannah to visit the photographers in their home communities. As I had done in Montserrado County, I sat in on meetings of the local action group and walked through the community with our photographers, snapping. But Lofa County was different. Lofa County had endured the worst of Charles Taylor's war. Everyone lived in the midst of ruins. All around stood the broken shells of substantial and attractive houses of cast concrete that few could afford to build anymore. Domestic architecture had reverted to an earlier century, to huts made of mud and sticks and thatch. Here, sitting with women, I heard stories that made me weep.

One day I returned to the office in Voinjama to find a young American colleague visibly upset. She was reading a report on Liberia issued by a prominent international organization that repeated the popular historical theory about Liberian violence springing from the resentment of "marginal young people." Amid a hundred pages detailing the grievances of deprived young men, grievances so serious that they led the resentful young men—seemingly inevitably—to kill thousands of people and wreck their country, my colleague had come upon a single paragraph devoted to the subtopic "Gender." It included this sentence: "Women suffered greatly during the war."

"Suffered greatly? Suffered greatly?" Her voice slid up the scale. "Is that all they can say? This report goes on and on about what these poor men must have felt that turned them into such butchers. But they don't even say what *happened* to women, much less what they felt. Just this 'suffered greatly.' What does it *mean*?"

I could tell her something about what it meant because I had just come from Kolahun District, where a woman had shown me the scars on the left side of her neck: a series of parallel horizontal wounds starting just below the ear and slanting down toward the throat. Some guerrilla had locked that thin whisper of a woman against his chest and slowly, inch by inch, laid open the flesh of her neck in ribbons of blood. That wasn't all they did to her. Charles Taylor's men broke all the fingers of her left hand so they point backward, stuck at impossible angles. They slammed her in the back with rifle butts so that one leg is paralyzed, and one arm too, the one with the useless hand. She could still walk, leaning on a homemade wooden crutch. But that left her no good arm; and she couldn't carry anything on her head because she had lost the ability to balance. The soldiers had held her a long time. They had made her cook for them. How many raped her she couldn't say. She had five children, some of them fathered by rape. She told me that she had a problem: the room she now lived in leaked. Every day at this season it rained hard, and every day her children got wet. She wanted to be able to keep her children dry.

The day before, in the village of Dougoumai, one of the photographers had taken me to meet her sister, a woman people referred to only as "the sick lady," who lay on a bed in the one-room hut. She sat up to greet us, using twisted hands to move her swollen, useless legs. She had been captured by the LURD militia fighting against Charles Taylor and gang-raped repeatedly by ten men. Nobody could say how long they had kept her. They too had rammed rifle butts into her back—a common technique, it seems—so that her legs were paralyzed. They had smashed her hands. She couldn't hold anything or feed herself or comb her hair. Her face was oddly dislocated, too, from many blows. She spoke to me, but I couldn't make out the words. Her sister said she was asking if I could bring her a dish. Her mother and sisters cooked for her and fed her by hand. But she wanted to have her own dish, and her own spoon.

What do women think about the ravages of the marginal people? If violence is the heritage of Liberian men, the habitual response of women is to shoulder the blame. I heard women describe public humiliation, beatings, rape, gang-rape, and worse, and struggle to explain the violence as if it were their responsibility. ("I shouldn't have said that." "If only I had done something else.") Witness the entrepreneurial women of Logantown doing business—selling fried cookies or dry goods or peanuts—so their husbands won't beat them for being idle. But some were beginning to question the old excuses. Some Logantown members, including Patience, the photographer, reported that since they had gone into business their husbands had changed; they didn't beat them anymore, now that they were making money. But other women who worked just as hard, sold just as much stuff, and made just as much money said their husbands beat them just the same. One woman said, "Maybe us women being idle is not the true cause of wife beating at all."

Many women said men beat women because women are uneducated and need to learn to do what's right. This was another reason women wanted education: to relieve men of the duty of beating them. Annie from Voinjama said she enrolled in a literacy course for precisely that reason, but every day her husband ripped the latest exercise from her notebook and used it as toilet paper. Kebeh from Dougoumai, said that when she disobeyed her husband's order to give up her literacy class, he got out his gun—there are plenty left over from the wars—and tried to kill her. Annie and Kebeh reached the same conclusion and placed the blame where it belonged. Kebeh said, "He doesn't want me to be educated." Annie said, "He'd rather hit me."

But women like Kebeh and Annie who don't blame themselves come up against powerful forces that do. Liberia is layered with "culture" and traditions of different origins, different vintages, different potencies—all of them somehow arrayed against women. In the best of times, they're remarkably effective in keeping women in their subordinate place, but in wartime they become lethal, exposing those weak, second-rate, blameworthy creatures to a rush of violence so thrilling to the perpetrators that there seems to be no going back. That's another reason these women were working so hard right then, while war was in abeyance, to gain some education, some skills, some income, some respect, some standing as human beings before the soldiers come again.

A sharp old woman named Sarah blamed men for marital rape and coercion. "They say it's our duty to let them 'pleasure themselves' whenever they want," she said. "If you don't want to, they beat you until you give up. They think we are machines for their use." Both custom and law are against her. The only traditional recourse a woman has, besides giving up, is to ask a close male relative to convene a family meeting to settle her complaint. Most of these family adjudications—or home settlements, as they're called—find fault in the woman and advise her to change her behavior. Some require the husband to apologize—and the wife to accept the apology. By tradition, that's the worst thing that can happen to a man who beats his wife. He just might have to say, "Sorry." If he rapes her, he doesn't even have to say that.

Under new family laws a woman could report a battering husband to the police. But in Dougoumai police wouldn't take a wife beater to court unless the woman was badly injured or at least bleeding. Then the court might send the case back to the family for home settlement. Or the magistrate might offer to hear the case in exchange for the sexual services of the bleeding wife. The Dougoumai magistrate was notorious for it.

Then there is religion. Mention women's rights in Liberia and it's not long before some man marches out God. (Any god will do: about 40 percent of Liberians are Christians, 20 percent Muslims, and 40 percent followers of local faiths.) He'll say, "Men are in charge of women because that's the way God wants it. God set things up that way, so that's the way things got to be." That's what a Liberian man on the IRC staff said to me one morning, just as I was leaving the office to meet the photographers. I told them what he had said and asked what they would answer back. Kebeh, who is not literate and has never heard of Shakespeare, said, "Women and men are the same: born in the same way in the same place. If you cut us, we bleed."

Sangai said, "If God wanted woman to be under man, he could have made her from Adam's foot. But no, he took the man's rib—to show we supposed to be side by side."

"It's not God saying we supposed to be under men," Kormassa said. "It's culture."

Annie said, "Yeah, we used to have to walk on our knees because of culture." She was referring to a customary rule, still enforced in many places, that women must walk on their knees in the presence of men. "And we did it, too," she said, "because we always do anything to feed our children. But now we stand up." In fact, many of these women often bent over slightly to comply with the underlying principle that a woman's head should always be lower than a man's, but at least they were on their feet.

Kubor said, "It was only culture that made the boy child 'better' in the first place."

"Yeah," Oritha said. "And it was men that made culture."

"Women made culture, too," Kebeh said. "But men don't respect it. They use their power to keep it down."

"They use violence to keep it down," Hajah said. "That's what this gender-based violence is for." As these women analyzed life, it was men, not gods, who kept women down. But they were backed by the power of witchcraft or the spirit world, or what the women called "African signs."

"Women are not allowed to cut in the palms," Sangai said. She meant that women and girls were forbidden to climb palm trees and cut the fruit from which valuable palm oil is made. Some women had tried, and all of them had come to a bad end. First they were said to be not women but "monkeys." Then, if they persisted in climbing trees, they were killed. "They just die," Sangai said. "They are killed with spirits." This phenomenon has been well documented in Africa: a person violates a taboo, then quickly sickens and dies for no discernable physical reason. Western observers attribute such inexplicable deaths to the power of belief.

"But why would women be killed for climbing palms?" I asked.

"Ah," said Kebeh. "There's money there."

Musu told another story—about the firewood ceremony. Every so often women who had been genitally mutilated as initiates of the Sande bush were required to carry firewood to the head woman of that secret society. Wearing nothing but skimpy panties, and carrying the wood on their heads, they had to parade through the village and into the bush. All the village men stood by to ogle the procession of near-naked women. Musu said the ceremony was humiliating. She wanted to protest—to refuse to participate. But in recent years two women had done so, and both of them died—killed by African signs. Musu believed that if she refused, she too would be killed by the spirits. Even to speak of these taboos was to risk death.

Men had their own secret societies, including one that owned the largest building in the capital: an immense Masonic temple. Freemasonry was one more tradition, like Christianity, that the Americo-Liberians brought back with them from the New World. Until the reign of Americo-Liberians ended in 1980, every Liberian president was a master Mason. Some of their secrets spilled into the streets, and to this day the simple act of shaking hands is an intricate exercise in finger-snapping interdigitation that separates the elite from the excluded. Speaking of a rape case, a woman told me about the practical effect of the secret Masonic handshake: "A man walks into court, shakes hands with the judge, and the case is decided right there." Custom, law, religion, secret societies, and African signs merge and militate against women.

When talking about violence, the women always named—near the top of their list—denial: a man seduces a girl or woman with promises of love "now and forever," impregnates her, and then denies paternity. Women in Dougoumai said the local magistrate had done that recently to another young woman. The action group tried to help her during her pregnancy, but they said she often went without food for days on end. I met her when she came to a women's meeting without her new baby. She had taken it to the magistrate's office and left it on his desk.

"This girl lost her ma and her pa during the war. A man with plenty money fooled her. So now she is with these two babies. And where is the man? Abandonment. That is a problem we are suffering."

—Sangai Kamara, Liberia

Hearing the story later, the husband of one of the photographers remarked: "IRC is making the women frisky." His wife responded, "IRC just told me my rights. I can figure out the rest myself." But Liberian women did seem to be growing bolder.

On UNMIL radio, the popular station run by the UN mission in Liberia, cohosts Sharon and Fawzia broadcast a show called "Everyday Talk" each morning. Their show was nothing like the ponderous nighttime talk shows aimed at men who called in to voice their opinions about whether Samuel Doe or Charles Taylor was the better president. Sharon and Fawzia asked real questions, like "Is there any future in loving a married man or woman?" And when all the callers answered that they would never do it, Sharon and Fawzia said, "Hey, its goin' on out there right now, people! Get real!" Nearing graduation time, Fawzia sent out congratulations to her "little sister" about to "come out" from the University of Liberia: "Be all that you can be," she said. "Don't get married now. Go for the Master's first." Sharon and Fawzia were smart and funny. They gave good advice, and they didn't take any crap. A male caller addressed Sharon as "dear." She said, "My name is Sharon. You got that?"

And suddenly women showed up in jobs held only by men before. I was walking through Voinjama with the photographers when we came upon an incredible sight: a woman on a motorcycle. A big one. Wearing boots and jeans, she was straddling the machine, preparing to ride. She looked like one tough cookie. The photographers encircled her, snapping as fast as they could. She eased back on her bike and gave the women a big smile, the shot they wanted. Then she donned her helmet, revved her bike, and peeled off. The photographers burst into cheers, waving good-bye. They told me excitedly who she was. As superintendent of roads, she rode her motorcycle all over the county, checking on repairs. There weren't a lot of role models yet for these new frisky women. But despite all the forces ranged against them, what they wanted to be was Sharon or Fawzia. Or President Ellen Johnson Sirleaf, making the country new. What they wanted to be was County Superintendent of Roads.

Ambitious as they were, the photographers made the most of their new camera skills. During my last week in Lofa County, I was busy in the Voinjama office printing images photographers had already selected for the exhibition, and driving to the other sites to gather selections from the other teams. Hannah the social worker and I made one last run to Kolahun. Four photographers came running to greet us. Oritha threw her arms around me. She was a tiny woman, feisty and volatile, and terribly excited. All of the women were talking at once, eager to tell us that the day before they had visited every one of the little villages roundabout and photographed *everything.* "We have a thousand million photos for you," Oritha said, "and they're all good." But they wanted to take more.

So we set off through Kolahun about 11:00 a.m. just as the sun was approaching its blistering apex. Hannah followed Kpana and Hajah down the hill, while I joined Oritha and Sangai, who led me on a house-to-house hike through every hidden pocket and swamp rice paddy of rambling Kolahun District. We went from the doorstep of one suffering woman to the next. One woman had been abandoned. Another had raised her adolescent daughter all alone after the girl's father denied paternity. Another was a refugee from Sierra Leone who wanted to leave her abusive Liberian husband and go home. Another had been blinded during the war and her husband killed. She was raising her three young boys by herself. Another, who had been gang-raped, still seemed stunned and visibly depressed. An aging woman, whose children had been killed in the war, gathered and sold firewood to keep her grandchildren in school.

Nearly five hours later the sun was still hot and punishing overhead. We stopped at Sangai's little house long enough for me to run my head under the pump. "Now we can go back," Oritha said. We took to the dusty road again.

"We wanted to show you how big Kolahun is," Oritha said. "It's big, isn't it?"

"Yes, indeed. Kolahun is very big."

They had shown me every inch of it, and more. They had shown me how well organized a Liberian Women's Action Group could be, how in tune with the community, how ready and able to support women subjected to some permutation of the bottomless violence of this place. As we walked the streets, they were welcomed in every home, greeted with goodwill by every passerby, man and woman alike. They mattered to this community. They made a difference. They were speaking up and making change for women every day. That was the end goal of this project, and they were way ahead of it. They didn't need the cameras. They had their whole community in focus.

My time in Liberia was coming to an end. I returned to Monrovia to help the GBV coordinator, a formidable and funny Indian woman named Navanita, and her Liberian deputy Gertrude, plan a big two-day workshop—to culminate in the First-Ever All-Women's Photography Exhibition in Liberia. We invited all the photographers from Montserrado and Lofa counties, and for good measure we invited a delegation from Nimba County as well. Road conditions had kept us from traveling to Nimba County to conduct the project there, and we wanted them to be involved. On the first day, women from the three counties got together in small groups to talk about their photos—good practice for the upcoming show. Many of the photos depicted acts of violence committed in the plain light of day with complete impunity, intended to punish women for things they had done or force them to do things they did not want to do.

Navanita raised a question: "What problems do women and girls have as a result of this violence?" The women made a list, a long one that included many problems they said they hadn't had before. Whatever standing in the community may once have shielded them from such things had been shattered, like the community itself, by war; and they couldn't seem to get it back. The list read: HIV, AIDS, sexually transmitted diseases, excision (female genital mutilation), forced marriage, forced pregnancy, forced labor, rape, fistula, other internal injuries, broken bones, paralysis, miscarriage, stress, frustration, depression, fear, deprivation of education, exclusion from decision making, denial of choice, consignment to servitude, deprivation of health care, death." Patience, the photographer from Logantown, said, "If the violence continues, it will finish us. We must fight back."

The women illustrated their problems in drawings and dramatic sketches. We saw wives beaten, married women forced to submit to their sexual "duty," widows forced to yield their dead husband's property, women and girls forcibly impregnated, pregnant women and girls abandoned, young girls forcibly married, girls raped, girls kept from school, girl students seduced by their teachers, pregnant girl students expelled from school. Girls, girls, girls. Most of the women in the room were still very young. They had survived the violence of war, and the violence of the peace that followed, when everything was changed; but they worried about the young girls.

Navanita asked, "Can this situation be changed?"

The women shouted "Yes!" Confidently, they began to talk about great public concerns—health care, education, the law— and they went straight to the prejudice and violence against women that corrupted them all. Health care was insufficient and too expensive, they said, especially for women who had less money than men. It was violence that sent great numbers of women and girls in search of health care, yet few health care workers were trained to treat them. Education was thought to be the rightful province of boys. Girls were kept from school to labor at home, or to marry. Girls who managed to enroll in school were forced out by the sexual predation of their teachers. As for the law, it scarcely applied. There was no enforceable law against domestic violence or marital rape. Judges and magistrates were incompetent or venal. Many, like the magistrate at Kolahun, were sexual predators, exploiting women in need of legal aid. "Any man can put a flag in front of his house and

"We did not even know how to stand up and talk, but now we stand up to tell IRC thank you. They bring adult literacy into the community, and we go to learn how to write. We want to do more so we can learn more. We women want empowerment."
—Kebeh Jallah, Liberia

call himself a judge," said one woman. Police and magistrates regarded assaults on women as unimportant. They took bribes. They blamed the victim. They compromised rape cases at the expense of the victim. They exploited the victim, offering her a hearing in exchange for a little sex on the side. The law served only those with money—men.

Against such obstacles, Navanita launched the dreams of women. She asked, "What do you hope for?" One said, "We want to be safe in our homes, in our country, and that is our right." Another said, "We have a right to dream of a free, safe Liberia. It is possible."

Navanita asked, "What would you like to see in five years' time?" Vera dreamed that all the ruins would be rebuilt, and that all the girls and boys would go to school together. Anna hoped to walk freely in the streets, without fear of attack. Mantina hoped that women and girls would be safe in their homes. Annie hoped that women would be self-employed. Esther dreamed that girls would be educated and take up positions in government.

Navanita posed other questions: "What needs to be done to move in the direction of your hopes and dreams? Who will do it? How? And how will you know if it's working?" The women fell into heated discussion. They spread big sheets of paper on the floor, and using Magic Markers as bright as their dreams, they began to make plans.

By noon of the second day of the workshop, the women had produced finely detailed lists of answers to every one of Navanita's questions. Plus a timeline that outlined exactly what was to be done, and by whom, next year, next month, next week, and right then, that very day. Maybe some of the plans were a little unrealistic. Probably they wouldn't be able to jail all bribe-taking magistrates by the end of the week, but even to speak of it was an act of courage and self-affirmation—and a step in the right direction. The women were speaking of all kinds of brave, newfangled things. One said, "Your husband beats you, you take your case to court, your husband knows the judge, and the case is closed." But Annie said, "If we got together all the women this happened to, we'd have a big crowd. We could go back to court together." The women smiled at the prospect. Sangai said, "We could sit there. In the court. Together." Betty, from Nimba County, said: "We are like a bundle of sticks. If the bundle is loose, men can pluck us out, one at a time, and break us. But a tight bundle of sticks cannot be broken."

Then it was showtime. The First-Ever All-Women's Photography Exhibition and Celebration in the history of Liberia was about to get under way. The women had arranged their photographs on the walls in two groups. The first group showed the problems they had found in their communities: environmental pollution, lack of clean water, poverty, hunger, child labor, absence of affordable schools, inadequate health care, unemployment, and raging violence against women and children. The second group showed their hopes and dreams. There were photos of women attending literacy classes, selling fish and fabrics in the market, cleaning their own communities with brooms and wheelbarrows, doing hairdressing and tie-dyeing and tailoring, and—most important—little girls in uniform laughing and striding to school. There were men in the photos too, though not many. Some could be seen working side by side with women harvesting rice. Three others were laughing together by the fire in an outdoor kitchen as one of them prepared dinner for his wife and children. That was Oritha's photo; she proudly titled it "Gender Equality." Finally there was Annie's photo of the Lofa County Superintendent of Roads mounted on her motorcycle, about to don her shimmering red helmet striped with green and gold. The woman of the future.

But Kulah, the photographer from West Point, was missing. At last she rushed in and explained in an unsteady voice. She had been busy all morning with police and community leaders and the family of a girl found early that morning raped and mutilated and drowned in a pool of wastewater where only a short time ago another girl, a teenager, had been discovered raped and murdered. The girl found that morning was still wearing the pretty ruffled dress she had put on to go to church with her mother. It was the mother's duty to tally the collection, and when she looked up, her daughter was gone. The child was two years old.

Thus was the future eclipsed by the violent present even as

"This woman supervises the road construction in Voinjama. See, woman riding motorcycle. Anything man can do, woman can do!"
—Annie Koiwu, Liberia

the guests invited to the photo show began to take their seats in the hall. Early in my stay, a market woman had told me that even after all the years of warfare, rape, violence, desperation, and death, "Women can still sell fish." I could only wonder where she found that fortitude. Now, one by one, the women rose. Each one stood alone before her photographs and spoke of things she hoped to change. It was their custom to introduce themselves by saying, "I stand here before you." I found the practice deeply moving, emphasizing as it did the solitariness and vulnerability of the speaker—her evident and undeniable courage. Some were beyond courageous. They pounded their photos for emphasis and knocked them right off the wall. Unfazed, they slapped them back in place and carried on. Anna spoke of the waste that buried Slipway and polluted the water supply. Kebeh, thinking of her crippled sister, spoke of justice for women sexually enslaved during the war. Hellen spoke of justice for women and girls raped and abandoned. And Kulah, fresh from a murder scene in West Point, spoke of the need to educate girls, not rape and mutilate and murder them.

Then Hajah stood up to talk about what the photo project had meant to her. "My parents never sent me to school," she said. "But now I stand here before you. IRC came and gave us cameras to take photos. I was afraid because I have not touched a camera before, but I begged my husband to let me go to Voinjama to take photos. Yes, I begged him because he still has power. And he allowed me to go. I got the camera and carried it home and sat down. My husband said, 'What is this?' I said, 'We women, we coming together.' He said, 'I see that camera. What can you do with it?' I said, 'Sit down. Let me take your picture.' I took it and showed it to him. I said, 'You see this? You must know that women, we are able to take pictures too.'"

The audience was on its feet, clapping and cheering, when Sangai rose and filled the room with the call-and-response song that had become the anthem of our project in Liberia. She had a big, bold, edgy voice that couldn't be denied. When she sang, and the women responded, even a skeptic like me had to believe.

She called out, "People, life can change. We never knew."

All the women joined her, as they had done so often during the past weeks, swaying and clapping, harmonizing the repeated response: "My life can change. I never knew."

"I used to beat my wife," Sangai sang. "I will never beat my wife. We never knew. A bad man can become a good man. A good man can become a better man. We never knew."

The women responded, "Our life can change. We never knew."

"A woman can become a president," Sangai sang. "Oh, a

woman can be a minister. We never knew. People, oh, life can change. Oh, go tell the people that life can change. We never knew."

"Our life can change. We never knew."

The audience joined in the chorus, stepping to the rhythm of the music. There were colleagues and friends from many local and international NGOs, including a big delegation from the IRC, looking smart in bright new T-shirts. But the hall we had rented for the grand occasion had not filled to capacity. We had waited as long as we could for invited guests conspicuous for their collective absence: prominent lawyers, judges, politicians, officials of government ministries, including the Ministry for Women. The audience, now enthusiastically shaking hands with the photographers, consisted of local and international humanitarian workers dedicated to helping Liberian women make the case for nonviolence and peace; but the Liberian bigwigs, both men and women, with actual power to make change, seemed to have more important things to do than attend the grand opening of the first-ever in Liberia all-women's photo show and celebration. The frisky women of Liberia were speaking up and singing out, but who was listening?

# 3

## SIERRA LEONE: GIRLS

The West African wars that began in Liberia moved northward into Sierra Leone. On the map of West Africa, little Sierra Leone looks like a left-handed mitten, grasping the edge of the continent, reaching inward, trying to hold on, and poking a thumb into Liberia. Sprawling Guinea wraps itself around Sierra Leone and most of Liberia as well. Just there, at the thumb, the three countries interpenetrate, making it possible to set foot in all three on a short hike. A place like that, at a crossroads where cultures meet and mix, is a perfect location for a market; and that's what the town of Koindu has been for as long as anyone can remember. It's right there on the inner edge of the thumb, no more than a mile from Guinea and about four miles from Liberia. People on both sides of all these borders were farmers with fresh produce to sell; and the produce market naturally attracted tradesmen peddling dry goods, fabrics, knives, locks, cooking pots, and plastic housewares in a riot of bright colors. In Koindu market you could get your shoes stitched, your hair cut, or new trousers tailor made in minutes. You could buy eggs, chickens, goats, blackened smoke-dried monkeys, and if you were lucky a nice fat porcupine freshly killed and stripped for the pot.

But not now. Not anymore. Because that border where three countries meet is also a perfect place for a guerrilla invasion. Just step across the shallow stream and carry war from one country to the next. That's what happened in 1991 when Foday Sankoh, a fat fifty-three-year-old rebel commander with a band of men behind him, walked across the border from Liberia. The war he brought to Sierra Leone lasted nine years.

In Koindu market long ago, in peacetime, you could find just about anything an African villager might want. The merchants prospered, as did the town. People built spacious houses of concrete blocks cast with decorative curves. The houses were embraced by terraces and embellished by colonnades. Within lay courtyards screened by perforated walls or iron filigree. The market stalls, too, were arrayed in pillared ranks, spacious and graceful, reminiscent of ancient agoras.

Then, during the war, Koindu was destroyed. Every house, every market stall, every public building was strafed or burned. This was guerrilla warfare with lethal but fairly modest weapons—machetes and Kalashnikovs—at least in the beginning. No B-52s, no high-altitude heavy bombing, no bunker busters. So parts of the houses and market stalls still stand, in outline at least, though the roofs are gone and the rooms stripped. Koindu lies only seventeen miles from Kailahun, the district capital where I came to live while I worked on the Global Crescendo Project in Sierra Leone; and the work sometimes took me there. It was a long, jolting drive, close to two hours over derelict and sometimes impassable dirt tracks. But I liked to walk the quiet streets of Koindu. I liked to photograph the ruins—where some people still lived, huddled in the corner of a room under a bit of zinc or a scrap of blue tent. They cooked outside on open fires. I was always on edge there, fighting the urge to sit down in the dust and weep, but what I cherished in Koindu was the peculiar quality of its ruination: everything was gutted, but you could still glimpse what once was. You could see what had been lost in war.

As a young man, Foday Sankoh joined the British colonial army of Sierra Leone and was cashiered. After independence, in the 1970s, he worked against the governing party and spent some time in jail as a result. Sometime around 1987 he went to Libya where, in the midst of the Cold War, Colonel (and President) Muammar Gaddafi ran a kind of boot camp for rebel guerrillas. Gaddafi, who had come to power in Libya in 1969 as the leader of a military coup that deposed the king, called the political system he imposed "Islamic socialism"; but unlike Osama bin Laden, whose camps would later train men for the Islamist jihad against the West, Gaddafi supported all sorts of national liberation movements. To maintain order in his own country he imprisoned, exiled, or assassinated Libyan dissidents, but he took an uncommon interest in fomenting disorder and instability elsewhere.

Gaddafi's camp was a kind of finishing school for paramilitary groups and potential dictators. I imagine it as a small-scale version of America's own Cold War academy, the U.S. Army School of the Americas (SOA)—known in Latin America as the School of Assassins. Like the SOA, Gaddafi's school taught such skills as kidnapping, torture, execution, assassination, and the multiple uses of fear. And it made use of U.S. Army equipment: huts, trucks, uniforms, and other gear abandoned at a base in Libya where once American soldiers trained for the war in Vietnam. There Gaddafi schooled recruits from dozens of countries, including several that became scenes of long-term suffering: Sri Lanka, Sudan, Zaire (later the Democratic Republic of Congo), Colombia, and Haiti.

It was at Gaddafi's training camp, probably in 1987, that Foday Sankoh met Charles Taylor from Liberia and perhaps Prince Johnson as well. Four years later, when Sankoh walked into Sierra Leone to start a war, he led a small band of men armed and trained in Liberia and financed by his friend Taylor. Sankoh had studied the Liberian way of war, murdering men, raping women and girls, and stealing anything of value. When he stepped across the border into Sierra Leone, he used those tactics from the start.

Sankoh's band of guerrillas—the Revolutionary United Front (RUF) of Sierra Leone—reportedly numbered at first no more than one hundred and fifty men. So, as Taylor had done in Liberia, Sankoh began by intimidating civilians and recruiting more troops. Women in the village of Pendembu took me to see a bombed-out house he had once occupied, now thoroughly overtaken by the bush; and standing amid the ruins in the yellow grass, they told me a story. An old woman was huddled over her cook fire, frying some nice tasty frogs, when RUF rebels entered the village. They surrounded her, peering into the pot to see what she was cooking, and one of them said: "We are freedom fighters of the Revolutionary United Front. We have come to save you from the government." The old woman said: "Then you must go to the capital. The government is not in my pot." The women of Pendembu repeated this story many times and laughed. They were proud of the courage and common sense of that lone, bold old woman, though they must have known that the rebels probably shot her and ate her frogs.

That's how Foday Sankoh worked. His men invaded a village and terrorized the people. They tortured and killed those who seemed worthless to them and those who resisted. They forced villagers to watch. Or they forced villagers to do the dirty work, to torture and kill their neighbors and their own families. They shot those who refused. They forced boys to commit atrocities that were literally unthinkable: torture, rape, murder of their own parents or grandparents—acts that cut them off at once from their families and from themselves. Such boys made the best soldiers. The rebels took them away, along with other villagers forced to serve as porters, laborers, temporary wives, and sex slaves. Many of those killed in every village and most of those abducted were women and children. Human Rights Watch reports:

> The RUF committed crimes of sexual violence—often of extreme brutality—from the very beginning of the war . . . during which thousands of women and girls were abducted and forced to "marry" rebel "husbands." These abducted women and girls were repeatedly raped and subjected to other forms of sexual violence throughout the duration of their captivity, which in many cases lasted years. . . . An unknown number of abducted girls and women still remain under the control of their rebel "husbands."

When RUF fighters were ready to leave a village, they set it on fire. People in villages nearby, seeing the smoke, ran to hide in the bush. RUF boys picked those deserted villages clean. When two of Sankoh's top commanders who also had trained at Gaddafi's camp objected to his brutal tactics, Sankoh had them shot.

Official reports document appalling crimes: fathers forced to rape their own daughters; brothers forced to rape their sisters; boy soldiers who gang-rape old women, then chop off their arms; pregnant women eviscerated alive and the fetus snatched from the womb to satisfy the soldiers' bet on its sex. A brother is hacked to death and eviscerated; his heart and liver are placed in the hands of his eighteen-year-old sister, who is commanded to eat them. She refuses. She is told that her two children and her sister have been abducted. She is taken to the place where her sister and two other women are held. She sees them murdered. Their heads are placed in her lap. Such crimes deliberately violate primal taboos; they aim to crush not only the individual victims but also those who physically survive the violence. They are meant to destroy a way of life and the values that inform it. Yet the individual victims are important in their own right, and in most cases they are women and children.

The RUF was the worst, but all parties to the spreading conflict committed atrocities. (I am leaving out the worst stories; they are too hard to take in.) Soldiers targeted young girls, especially, for "virgination." Cases of girls as young as eight or nine brutally gang-raped, have been documented. Human Rights Watch interviewed one ten-year-old girl who, while living in a refugee camp, saw the bodies of eight young girls about her own age lying on the ground, their dresses pulled up, their legs spread, bloodied, their mouths stuffed with cloth. They had been raped to death, and because they had already lost their parents, they lay there for a long time before others came to bury them.

Many commanders, like Sankoh, forcibly conscripted children—mostly boys, but many girls as well—and turned them into armed guerrillas as bad as themselves. In *A Long Way Gone*, Ishmael Beah describes his career as a boy soldier fighting on the other side, in the national army of Sierra Leone. Fleeing from his village during a rebel attack, he was separated from his family; he roamed the countryside, falling in with other lost boys, until he was captured by the army, trained to fight, kept high on drugs (as all soldiers were), and forced to kill. At the instigation of men, boy soldiers began to take the initiative, willingly, to torture, rape, mutilate, and murder girls and women of all ages. Sometimes, just for fun, they buried them alive.

Within a matter of months, Sankoh and his traumatized recruits, permanently high on palm wine, marijuana, and heroin, gained control of Eastern Province and its diamond mines. Sankoh's tactics cleared communities out of the diamond fields and secured a labor force of men and boys, and girls to supply sex, all enslaved by terror. The mines had been Sankoh's goal, and Taylor's, all along; diamonds would finance two wars, and then some. When the RUF advanced on Freetown, officers in the national army staged a coup and outsourced the war to a private South African contractor—Executive Outcomes—who for $35 million fought the RUF for nearly two years (1995 to 1997) and pushed them back to the edges of the country. They lost the job when Western countries persuaded a new president that putting down rebellion with a private contractor was "politically incorrect." They left, and once again the RUF rampaged through the countryside in an onslaught of looting, rape, atrocity, and murder universally described in the press as an "orgy."

Early in 1998, Nigerian forces led an African peacekeeping intervention. They seized Freetown, restored the rightful president to power, and arrested Sankoh. He was sentenced to death for war crimes. But within a year, the RUF recaptured Freetown and set him free. The Western powers called for an end to the war, and President Clinton dispatched Jesse Jackson to persuade Sankoh to sign a peace agreement. He had already signed one at Abidjan in 1996, and then ignored it. But the new peace accord he signed at Lome (Togo) in 1999 was the first one to give him everything he asked for. It elevated him from death row to the vice president's office and gave him command of four government ministries, including the one that controlled the country's natural resources—diamonds and all. It granted amnesty to him and all his RUF fighters. Already, in Liberia, Charles Taylor had signed a similar peace agreement, and the people had elected him president by a landslide. From that office, he had continued to support his friend Sankoh in Sierra Leone. Now Sankoh too was rewarded with high office and with full control of the mines that had made both men rich and both wars profitable.

Western governments responsible for arranging the Lome Accord called it a landmark "power-sharing agreement," and indeed for ambitious sociopaths yearning for profits and power, it taught a powerful lesson: get a gang of thugs, get your hands on drugs and natural resources, assault civilians, commit a lot of headline-grabbing atrocities, and you'll be invited to the power-sharing table in no time. It also made clear that these wars were never about ideology, or even politics. They were about greed, about the power to grab and sell the region's natural wealth—Liberia's primal rain forests and Sierra Leone's blood diamonds. West Africans will tell you that these wars took place simply because a few "bad, bad men" craved power and riches. In colonial days, Western powers stole the wealth of Africa. With independence, African "big men"—Mobutu, Mugabe, Amin—enriched themselves by selling their country's resources to Western contractors and pocketing foreign aid as well; they established beyond doubt that government is the road to riches. This new generation of rebels took a shortcut: kill the government, terrorize the people, grab the stuff and sell it.

In 2000, when additional UN peacekeeping forces entered Sierra Leone to disarm combatants, the RUF seized five hundred of them as hostages and moved to take the capital again. That last outrage brought in the British air force to crush the RUF and turn Sankoh over to a Special Court for Sierra Leone, established jointly by Sierra Leone and the United Nations to try cases of those charged with war crimes and crimes against humanity. To her credit, Mary Robinson, UN Commissioner for Human Rights, refused to honor the amnesty provision of the Lome Accord. Sankoh's crimes could not be written off by any gentlemen's agreement. But before his trial could begin, he died of natural causes, leaving Charles Taylor, flushed from posh exile in Nigeria, to stand before the court in The Hague and face eleven charges for war crimes—related to matters including terrorizing civilians, murder, rape, sexual slavery, amputations, and enslavement—committed not against the citizens of his own country but against his neighbors, the people of Sierra Leone.

During the war about fifty thousand people were killed and one hundred thousand men, women, and children mutilated. About four hundred thousand people fled the country, while another million were displaced; that's one person in three forced from their homes, including most of the residents of Kailahun District there on the border where the war began. About forty-eight thousand children fought in the war; many grew accustomed to the rush of rape, murder, and mutilation. When it was all over, Sierra Leone replaced Afghanistan as the poorest country on the planet. It also surpassed Afghanistan as the country with the highest rates of maternal and infant deaths. Tens of thousands of the war dead were men who left wives and children behind. Thousands of widows had no livelihood. The war in Sierra Leone had become notorious for its trademark atrocity: amputation—chopping off arms, legs, hands. But atrocities committed against women—rape, enslavement, torture, disfigurement—although less publicized, were far more widespread. Many women suffered permanent disabilities. Many gave birth to children of rape. Women were learning to live with the consequences of all that. They found their lives much harder than they had been before.

In the immediate aftermath of the war, the IRC responded with a range of projects designed to meet the emergency with quick relief. When I got there, nearly six years after the end of hostilities, the IRC had narrowed its focus to Sierra Leone's most conspicuous long-term needs and the IRC's core strengths: health, education, and gender-based violence. One IRC health project focused on obstetrical care, promoting survival of mother and child. Another worked with the government to combat childhood illnesses, such as malaria and pneumonia, that kill one child in four before the age of four. An education project pried child laborers from the muck of the diamond mines and got them into school. Another education project helped local governments manage schools and train teachers, to keep those kids in school. Many NGOs worked to replace 1,270 primary schools destroyed in the war.

The GBV program planned for the future too, but it still had to respond to wartime violence against women and girls that continued after the fighting stopped. Human rights organizations placed the number of women and girls sexually assaulted during the war at more than a quarter-million. GBV's first program was aimed at those survivors. In 2002, it established Rainbo Centres in three cities—Freetown, Kenema, and Kono—to provide free medical care and psychosocial support to survivors of sexual violence. Five years on, the program had served thousands of women and girls and been cited for international awards as one of the best GBV practices in the world, but its future was uncertain. The IRC wanted the Ministry of Health to take it over and keep it going, but many officials in government and donor agencies thought the time for such emergency services had passed. The war was over, the emergency finished. Planners had already moved on to issues of development. Why couldn't women move on too?

But women and girls were still being raped every day. The Rainbo Centres received at least eighty new cases every month, almost all of them referred by the police. Studies done by Physicians for Human Rights and Human Rights Watch noted that sexual assault of women and girls had exploded during the war. It continued at a high level after the war and found new victims. Sixty percent were between the ages of eleven and fifteen. Twenty-three percent were between the ages of six and ten. The youngest was three years old. Only 17 percent of rape victims were adult women.

"Only 17 percent" is still too many. But the prime targets of rape—the preferred victims—were little girls. We know that when rape is used as a tactic of war it becomes a habit hard to break, popularized by soldiers and taken up by civilians as well. But after war, when militias split up and a UN disarmament team takes away the automatic weapons, a man finds it harder without his buddies and his gun to attack grown women. Girls are easier—smaller, weaker, more easily overpowered and intimidated, more easily persuaded not even to tell. In Liberia too, after the war, girls became the preferred targets of rape; but in Sierra Leone, the rapists' preference for young girls was even more pronounced, perhaps because the use of so many young girls as wives during the war had made the convenience of the arrangement so evident.

Of all the victims recorded at the Rainbo Centres, 84 percent knew the man, or men, who had assaulted them. Half of the victims had to return to the same residence where they had been raped before; and of those who returned, nearly half were assaulted again by the same man. Here, as in Liberia, the rapist is often a member or friend of the extended family, and usually he can persuade the impoverished parents of the rape victim to compromise—that is, to let the matter drop in exchange for cash. In Buedu village, I met a widow who had settled with the man who raped her ten-year-old daughter for the equivalent of $13.35. That small sum was a measure of her poverty. Later, when she regretted the compromise and wanted to cancel it, she couldn't raise enough money to pay the rapist back.

The war in Sierra Leone left many, many widows like this with young children to raise and no means of support. Widows worried themselves sick because they couldn't afford to send their children to school. Often they couldn't feed them. War also left many orphans; many girls and young single women were on their own. Such girls growing up in poverty, without education, were easy prey for men on the prowl. Sexual exploitation was commonplace. In this part of the country, men drifted over the borders all the time, from Guinea or Liberia, to get a girl. When the girl "got a belly," the man got out, leaving her with an unwelcome baby, an additional burden on her own or her family's scant resources. Schoolgirls too were sexually exploited by their classmates and their teachers. They left school in droves not long after puberty, an exodus that education experts usually attributed to girls' "natural" loss of interest at that age in anything but getting married. The official story concealed the real, unmentionable reason for their flight: the unnatural interest of their teachers in sexually harassing, seducing, and raping them. A girl who tried to stay in school and became pregnant was expelled, disqualified from further education, though the man or boy who impregnated her suffered no consequences.

Girls who dreamed of becoming nurses or teachers to contribute to their communities became shameful liabilities instead, leaving a hole in the future of a small town.

In Kailahun District, the region hardest hit by the war, the IRC helped four communities build substantial women's centers. The communities donated the land, the labor, and the materials they could fabricate themselves—mud bricks and lumber. The IRC provided "store-bought" materials, such as zinc roofs. GBV helped the communities organize Women's Action Groups, like those I worked with in Liberia; and once the groups had their centers, they came up with plans. When women had a place to meet and talk and work together, it made a world of difference.

When I brought the Global Crescendo Project to Sierra Leone, the GBV team in Freetown, the capital, decided that I should work up-country in devastated Kailahun District, among people who had survived the worst of the war. The obvious place to start was with the groups in the district's Women's Centers. One of them was right there in Kailahun town, less than a mile up the road from the IRC office and the staff house across the street where I was given a room. At our first meeting, I passed out cameras there to six teams of photographers, twelve women in all. Two days later, I traveled over the rough road to Pendembu village, about an hour and a half away, to dispense cameras to twelve women there. Then I drove down the road to another part of Pendembu village, forded the stream where women wash clothes, and climbed the hill to the Roman Catholic Girls' Primary School. It is girls who are at special risk in Sierra Leone, and girls we wanted to talk to about their lives.

In Kailahun District, GBV supported Gender Clubs in a number of primary and secondary schools. They were meant to fill a need created when the public schools, for lack of funds, dropped Family Life Education courses that used to give students basic information about sexuality and gender roles. With the courses gone, most students got few facts. They learned about sexuality and "love" from pop songs and music videos. It was a suicidal initiation in a country where HIV/AIDS is epidemic, and doubly dangerous for young girls, leaving them starry-eyed candidates for sexual exploitation. IRC-sponsored Gender Clubs were meant to arm both girls and boys with information they needed to stay safe and healthy. When we presented our project to the Gender Club at the Girls' Primary School in Pendembu, twelve girls jumped at the chance to become photographers. The oldest was fourteen, the youngest ten.

I'm not a parent, so that first day I didn't know quite what to expect. But neither, I think, did my two codirectors on the project, both mothers—Christiana Massaquoi and Christiana Gbondo. (I call them Auntie Chris and Chris G.) Auntie Chris was a tall, slim, happily married forty-year-old mother of three. A former high school science teacher, she had worked with the IRC for years, managing a refugee camp during the war and lately assigned to the Rainbo Centre in Kenema. Chris G., from Kailahun, was a vibrant thirty-year-old single mother of two little boys and a mainstay of the local GBV office. I counted on them to help me understand these girls, but from the start we all underestimated how smart they were, and how quick. The girls got the jump on us in no time.

That first day I asked them to group themselves in teams of three—each trio to share a camera. They teamed up with their age mates, but Mr. Shariff, the volunteer schoolteacher who was their Gender Club adviser, quickly shuffled them to put one older girl on every team. Mr. Shariff was young and very good-looking, but the girls' devotion to him was based on something else: trust built up through long experience of his good teaching and advice. Quickly they rearranged themselves and sat looking at me expectantly, ready to begin. In Côte d'Ivoire and Liberia, camera instruction with adult women nervous about merely holding a camera had taken time and patient repetition. In the past few days I'd had the same experience with the women's groups in Kailahun and Pendembu; but the girls caught on right away. Their small, dexterous fingers easily manipulated tiny controls that sometimes confounded grown women. Nevertheless, I made them practice sitting down together to extract one girl's memory card from the camera and replace it with the next. I warned them not to run with a camera, for fear of stumbling. I mentioned over and over the danger of falling with a camera or dropping it. All the girls were learning English in school, and some of them understood; but Auntie Chris and Chris G. went over the warnings again in Mende and Krio. The girls wiggled and fidgeted and yawned and stretched their arms and put their heads in their hands, overcome with boredom.

Soon we set off walking through the village to take their first photographs. I had intended to have an adult accompany each team, but my colleagues had wandered off ahead, deep in conversation. The girls seized the moment to scatter in all directions, like cats let out of a box. I watched them run screaming over the rough ground, the fragile cameras dangling from waving arms. I spotted the slowest runners and ran after them. When I caught up, they were strolling along the road, casually swapping memory cards as they walked along, chattering happily. Chris G. came running and chastised them loudly in Mende for not following instructions. The scene drew a crowd of curious villagers. I nudged Chris G. "Please don't yell at them. Just explain." She did, while the girls squirmed and fidgeted, looking bored again. One of the older girls, Lilian, took the lead, saying in English, "We are sorry, Auntie. We will do good." The others

In Pendembu village, the IRC's Christiana "Chris G" Gbondo (in jeans) herds the girls' photo group out to practice shooting.          —Ann Jones

pulled long, straight faces and nodded somberly, but they were itching to get going.

We set off again, this time at a brisk walk. I accompanied Lilian and her younger partners, Ruth and Jenifer. We walked miles and miles, through every neighborhood of the sprawling village, crossing vacant lots and fields, clambering over the rubble of fallen buildings. The girls seemed drawn to the skeletons of smashed and abandoned houses, as I was haunted by the ruins of Koindu. They snapped away. Then, to humor me, they sat down together in a shady porch to change memory cards. I knew they felt sorry for me—a poor old auntie who didn't even know how easy it is to change a memory card one-handed, standing up, strolling along. And running with a camera?—there's nothing to it. Three hours later they'd worn out the batteries meant to last a week.

I climbed into the vehicle for the hard road back to Kailahun. Auntie Chris and Chris G., who had been dragged about
by other groups of girls, sprawled exhausted in the backseat,
already dozing. Our driver, Sowa, looked at me and started to
laugh. "I know," I said, wiping the sweat and dust from my
face. "Let's just go home, please."

Home was the second floor of a rundown house near the end
of the main street in Kailahun, a space I shared with Auntie
Chris and Natsnet Gebrebrhan, a young workaholic from Eritrea
who managed the GBV program. Natsnet was happy to have
us; she'd been alone there for months, depending on the Al
Jazeera English channel on TV for company that spoke a language she knew, although like most aid workers in impoverished places like Kailahun, lacking diversion, she worked nearly
all the time. Most evenings, before supper, Natsnet and I would
make time for a good, brisk walk—usually out the main road,
through the fields, and up over the hill to the camp of the UN
peacekeepers and back. Occasionally, when we had some small
victory to celebrate, I'd walk the half mile to a store in the
center of town and buy a can of beer for each of us. Once a
British woman, a supervisor with a large international NGO,
came to town for a few days and invited Natsnet and me out
for a drink. Natsnet was thrilled. She said, "All this time I've
been here, I never knew there was a social club you could go to
and have a drink!" We got dressed up in our best shirts, and
Natsnet put on lipstick. The British woman picked us up in
her Land Rover and drove us the half mile up the road to the
beer store. Natsnet shot me a look. We followed our hostess in
to the store, ordered beer, and carried the cans outside. "Isn't
this lovely?" Natsnet said as we sat on the steps, sipping. Later

she said, "It was my first social event in Kailahun. Wasn't it fun?"

Natsnet, Auntie Chris, and I shared a local cook named Agnes who shopped for food in the local market, and if she found any, cooked it and left it on the table, under a cloth. At six o'clock in the evening, one of the guards turned off the generator at the office across the street, and the staff went home to eat supper. At our house there was always a hush akin to prayer as we lifted the edge of the cloth to discover the results of Agnes's efforts. Usually a pot of rice. Boiled greens occasionally, or fried plantains. Once, a wiry chicken. The meagerness of our dinner was a measure of the state of the district where derelict farms and half-abandoned markets had yet to recover from the war. We ate. We did the dishes. Then I holed up in my room at my computer while Natsnet and Auntie Chris returned to the office. Chris G. would have gone home to feed her boys, tucked them under their mosquito nets, and returned to the office already. I would hear Natsnet and Auntie Chris come home at ten, just before the house generator went off for the night. Sometimes we'd sit together on the porch in the dark, talking quietly, drinking a cup of tea. Then I would stretch out under my bug net, listening to the sound of the latest shoot-'em-up blasting from the video club on the hill behind the house and think about the girls of Sierra Leone.

One day the two Chrises and I drove to Buedu, a village about an hour and a half away, where the IRC had also helped build a women's center. We sat in the yard, in an open-air work area where the women had gathered. One woman was weaving, and a man—the tailoring instructor—was working at a sewing machine. We explained that we weren't able to invite Buedu women to join the photo project because the road from Kailahun was so often impassable at this season, but we wanted to know what was on their minds. The chairwoman said the biggest problem in Buedu was teen pregnancy. Then everyone was talking at once. Some sounded angry and bitter. They said they struggled to get money for their daughters' education, and look what happens. "It's not just girls," said another woman. "I paid for my son's education all the way to college, and then the war came, and now he is out of his mind and I am still taking care of him." The others knew her story and sympathized, but they turned the talk back to girls.

One said, "These traders come from Liberia, grown men with wives at home, full of sweet talk, and next thing the girl gets a belly."

Another said, "We need sex education, family life education, to make these girls smart."

Another said, "That don't help. A girl gets smart, she says no, she gets raped. You get sweet-talked, or you get raped. Those are the choices."

I asked why these things happened, and the women had a single clear idea. Poverty has a lot to do with it, they said. "Parents can't afford to keep their girls in school," the chairwoman said, "so the girl's only future depends upon getting a man. Parents can't afford to buy pretty things the girls want to have. Then a man comes along who can, and he looks like the future. Then he's gone. And she has another mouth to feed when she can't even feed herself."

A young, pregnant girl said that when she was in school she had a romance with a boy in her class. They planned to get married. Then she got a belly, and he denied everything. She wants to go back to school after she has her baby, she said, but her father won't support her anymore and the school won't allow it. A widow said she had no money to send her four chil-

"The girl in this photograph is washing her child. She is not even fifteen and doesn't know how to take care of a child because she is only a small girl herself and has dropped out of school."
—Musu Koroma, age eleven, Sierra Leone

dren to school. Another widow who has the care of three grandchildren said she had the same problem.

Every woman at the meeting wanted to earn money. They had all taken IRC-sponsored courses in income-generating skills such as tailoring, tie-dyeing, or making *garri*, a quick-cooking form of shredded cassava. But they had no materials to carry on. The chairwoman said, "If we had materials, you'd see a lot more women working here today. You'd see a lot more women coming to the meetings." It was a familiar story: they had learned a skill, made a product, and then to meet immediate needs they had sold it for less than cost, leaving no money to buy more materials. It's not that they don't understand the principles of profit and loss; they are market women. But they are poor and without access to credit that might enable them to hold their goods for a better price. Even the best NGOs with the best intentions get tired of this common complaint and refuse to buy more materials for women who seem to throw them away. They could teach women something truly useful and profitable—like how to make mud bricks (mud is free) and build houses—but they don't. And perhaps men would not let the women learn. Women who had learned to make *garri* said they could turn a profit if they didn't have to buy the cassava, but they can't grow it themselves because they're not allowed to clear land and turn the soil; that work is reserved for men, and no man will help them.

But if they could turn a profit, would that protect their daughters? In Liberia, women thought that if they made money, their husbands wouldn't beat them. In Buedu, women thought that if they made money, their girls would not get pregnant. They knew instinctively that economic self-sufficiency was a step toward respect, equality, and the power to protect themselves and their daughters. But a pot of dye, or of *garri*, is not a diamond mine; and at the center of these mass delusions, always, stood a solitary woman, responsible for everything.

One evening, over dinner, as we talked about women who'd come to the office that week seeking help, Natsnet said: "Sometimes I feel like such a negative person. I live with so many sad stories." By nature she was just the opposite: fun-loving, optimistic, kind—but I knew what she meant. Women came day after day with stories of domestic violence—beatings, rape, emotional abuse, torture, death threats. The stories seemed to grow worse and worse. One day Natsnet called me to photograph the wounds of a twenty-five-year-old woman whose husband—a forty-year-old former combatant still in the army—broke into her house, tore off her clothes, beat her, bit her, and slashed her face with a knife, all in front of their children. The man had abandoned her and the children to live with a new wife, but he said he heard that she was seeing another man. While he was at it, he stole all her money—the profits of her own business that had supported the whole family for years—and all her trade goods. She felt lucky to have escaped with her life. A week earlier, in a neighboring district, a man had cut off his wife's head.

Natsnet had been working for a long time on one disturbing case. About three months earlier in Koindu town, a seven-year-old girl was raped. The girl's mother went to the Family Support Unit (FSU) of the local police to report the crime. (Sierra Leone has a law against rape, except in marriage.) The plainclothes police officers—women and men—of the FSU are specially trained, and they take their job seriously. In this case, they investigated the complaint, questioned the alleged perpetrator—a twenty-five-year-old man, a relative of the child's father—and took down his confession. They reported their findings to the prosecutor.

Members of the FSU often complain of frustration. There are two systems of law in Sierra Leone—formal law and customary law—and in regard to marriage and the family, Muslims may apply Islamic law as well. All of these systems were devised by men. Prosecution of rape fell under formal law, but in fact few complaints ever reached the magistrate's court. In most cases, as in this one, the rapist was a family member or friend. The family and the perpetrator usually arranged a compromise for the sake of friendship or family honor. The victim was not consulted about her feelings, thoughts, or wishes. Especially if she was only a little girl. Even cases that did reach the court were often dismissed or simply delayed until the complainant gave up. During a six-month period in 2007, the three Rainbo Centres handled 528 cases of sexual assault. Bravely, 396 of the victims filed legal complaints. Of all those cases, only thirteen were successfully prosecuted in Kenema and Kono and none in Freetown.

But in this particular case the mother also went to see the GBV social worker at the Koindu Women's Center. The name of the center is painted in big letters over the entrance: DIOM PI LOOR—that's "Unity" in the Kissi language. The social worker gave the mother comfort, advice, and some small financial assistance—enough for her to travel to Kailahun to be present in the court when her daughter's case was first brought before the magistrate. With the evidence gathered by the police, and the perpetrator's confession, it seemed open and shut. Nevertheless, the magistrate postponed the hearing. The mother traveled back to Koindu. Again the case was called, and again the social worker paid the mother's fare to Kailahun. This time the perpetrator did not appear, and the magistrate postponed the proceeding again. This time he spoke of the "alleged" perpetrator and suggested that the man might not have confessed at all. Natsnet visited the magistrate in his chambers—a courtesy call, she said—to let him know that the IRC was concerned. At the same time, rumors came to the IRC that the perpetrator's mother was spreading money around. She was said to be well connected to the magistrate. Natsnet and other GBV staffers made another courtesy call.

So the dance went on—and off—for months. Any mother trying to bring a complaint before the court would have been forced to quit long before by the sheer cost of hiring a ride on a motorbike to get from Koindu to the court in Kailahun. The round trip cost more dollars than this mother saw in weeks. But the IRC kept coming up with the fare. And Natsnet and others from the Kailahun GBV team kept going to visit the magistrate, who seemed to suggest, more and more strongly, that there was little evidence against the confessed perpetrator.

Then the case was called again. The mother came from Koindu, again at the IRC's expense, and this time she brought her seven-year-old daughter, the rape victim. This time the GBV team also asked women from the local Women's Action Group to come to court. Men sympathetic to the issue came too. They sat there—ordinary women and men—filling the benches of the courtroom, and among them sat a seven-year-old girl. Some said the magistrate seemed terrified. All these women were watching.

Within minutes the magistrate found ample cause, as he should have done months before, to refer the case to the High Court in Kenema where the judge is a woman who follows the law. It was likely the confessed perpetrator would serve some time in jail and everyone in Koindu would hear about it. The case would be a precedent—and a warning. It had already made big news in Koindu.

This result was brought about mainly by one brave, persistent mother and the intimidating presence of women in the courtroom, watching. And Natsnet, of course. It wouldn't have happened without her. But now the local women knew how to do it for themselves. The Krio language has a term for occasions like that, when a feeling of triumphant exultation comes from deep within. They say it makes you, "plenty, plenty gladdy." I thought about all the people involved, all the time spent, all the work done to gain merely the possibility of eventually winning this one single case. I walked into town and bought Natsnet a beer.

Every day in the streets I saw photographers from the Kailahun women's group snapping away, but when we went to meet them again, they reported a problem: men were giving them a hard time. They said the white woman was using them to show bad things about Africa. They said the white woman was going to make a lot of money; she was going to use their photos in a pornographic movie. They said the women weren't really taking photographs, that the IRC would not be crazy enough to give real cameras to stupid women—opinions confirmed by the town's one professional photographer who said he knew for a fact that these cameras were fakes. Men wouldn't allow the women to take photos of the mosque, the ruined houses, the video club, the motorcycle gang, the lane beside the peacekeepers' camp where girl prostitutes waited, or the police station, especially on a day when one team found the cops out behind the building, dead drunk.

The women were angry, but also afraid. Forbidden to snap men, they snapped women instead. Theresa took a photo of a pregnant teenager; her parents had sold her to a temporary husband because they needed the money. Satta photographed another pregnant teenager; a man had raped her, made a deal with her parents to marry her, and then passed her off to his family, who used her to labor on their farm. Mariama snapped another pregnant girl, forced to drop out of school while the child's father continued his studies and pretended not to know her. Messie took a shot of a beautiful young woman with two children, abandoned and looking for work. Sattu photographed a widow, half-naked, sitting on a mat beside the burial mound of her husband; Sattu said every widow was forced to sit on a mat for forty days, while the men of the family divided up the dead husband's property among them. Amie got a close-up of a stillborn child, born of a mother forced to work the upland rice harvest; because she had complained of being in pain, her husband had forced her to work harder, without rest or food.

Aminata shot a tiny girl at a well, struggling with a blue bucket almost as big as she was; she was made to do all the work at home because her widowed mother wasn't well. Aminata had also taken a photo of a man lying drunk in the street. She said, "If a woman passed out like that, men would rape her and say it was her own fault." Natsnet's words came to my mind: "I feel like such a negative person; I live with so many sad stories." But Gbessay showed us a photo of two young women working at sewing machines in a shop where paper dress patterns were tacked up on the walls. "These girls are my daughters," she said. "They learned in the wartime, in the refugee camp in Guinea, to do this tailoring, and now they make a living and contribute to our family." Mamie Sampha offered a photo of a girl in a school uniform reading a notebook. "This girl is my niece," she said. "Her parents support her in school, and they don't allow her to do housework, but only study; now she is sitting her final secondary school exam." Maybe the women of Buedu were right after all; a little money, a skill, a trade, and somebody to watch your back—these were the keys to a better life.

We sent them off for another week of shooting, and we went the next day to see how the women were doing in Pendembu. There the situation was completely different, for on our first visit, the progressive chief had invited us to meet with the elders to tell them about our project and get them behind it. After that, the elders had paid a formal visit to the Women's Center and requested that the photographers shoot the half-ruined mosque, the war-ravaged houses, the inadequate clinic, the struggling widows with too many mouths to feed—all problems the elders were already trying to address. The women showed us their photos—and they too had taken some pictures of pregnant teenagers—but the spirit was different. They were not afraid. Watta said, "I was proud to take photographs for the

"Our problem here is resettlement, especially for some of us who dropped out of school and now are widows with children to care for. An example is myself. This is our house that was broken by soldiers, and I have four children. We are now staying in a hut that leaks. When am I going to get another husband to help me rebuild this house?"

—Sao Kallon, Sierra Leone

whole village." I turned to the IRC community organizer, who knew Pendembu well, and asked, "What makes this chief so progressive?" She laughed and said, "He is married to the chairlady of the Women's Action Group."

When we met the Pendembu girls' group, they were buzzing. They were angry with a teacher who had found them dancing in a classroom and said, "You'll all be pregnant before you get to secondary school." They told the teacher he was wrong to think that just because they had high spirits they would get pregnant. "It's the quiet girls you should watch," they told him. They cited as evidence the unfortunate case of an introverted classmate impregnated by a man who denied all responsibility. She had been taken away to another village to have the baby.

This problem of teen pregnancy, which effectively ended a girl's education and her marriage prospects all at once, turned out to be the single biggest problem in every community we visited. The girl was stigmatized. Her family was shamed. Her parents were deprived of the expected return on their investment in the girl's education: that she would be in a good position to care for them in their old age. Everyone lost, except the man who impregnated the girl. Many girls had been denied the sex education that might have armed them against seduction when local counseling agencies lost their American funding under the Republican "gag rule" that forbids any mention of abortion, no matter what other essential services such agencies provide. (Repealing the Bush gag rule was one of President Obama's first acts in office; but in my view, the health and safety of women and girls around the world should not be subject to the toss of an ideological coin in Washington.) In any event, abortion was illegal. It was also forbidden by Islam and most, if not all, Christian denominations. Illegal, or "criminal," abortions were performed, but they cost more than any village girl could imagine, and they were not safe. A pregnant teenager must have felt doors slamming on every option.

Auntie Chris asked the girls provocatively, "What's wrong with getting pregnant?" The girls gave her an "Are you crazy?" look and bombarded her with answers.

"You cannot continue your education."

"Even if you could, your attention would be divided between your baby and your schoolwork. You couldn't do well."

"Your body is not developed. You may have to have surgery."

"You could even die."

These medical warnings were no exaggeration for girls who have been subjected to female genital mutilation. Excision greatly increases the incidence of life-threatening complications during pregnancy and childbirth, just as it increases the chance of contracting HIV/AIDS when, during rape or intercourse, old scars tear open with bloody violence.

"Your parents will put you out of the home," said Mattu.

"You will face stigmatization," said Comfort. "You will have no support for yourself or your child." I waited for the next nail in the coffin—that though you have been taught to depend on a husband for support, no man will marry you—but I didn't hear it. That might be just too hard to think about.

"And if you do *not* get pregnant as a teenager, what will you do?" That was my question, and the girls fired answers at me even before they got a translation.

"We will enjoy our education," said Lilian.

"We will enjoy encouragement from our parents," said Lucinda.

"Our parents may even allow us to travel outside of Pendembu," said adventurous Katumu.

"If we are educated before we have children, we will be able to support them and help our parents too," said Bintu.

"We will ensure that our children also have a good education," said Lucy.

"We will not hurry to marry," said ten-year-old Jenifer, "and we will plan our families."

I was floored. Who knew these girls had so much information and such strong opinions? Did I know about family planning at age ten? Was this what a Gender Club could do? Mr. Shariff, the faculty adviser, sat quietly in the back of the room, smiling.

"Can you imagine your future life?" I asked. "Say, in ten

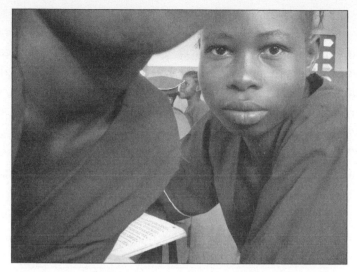

"I took this photo of my classmates at the Girls' Primary School. We think it is important for every girl to finish her education so she can contribute to her family and to our village. I am hoping to be a Catholic sister and a teacher."

—Lucinda Jamiru, age fourteen, Sierra Leone

years' time. What would you like to be doing?" They were shy about answering this question, maybe reluctant to expose a dream to daylight. But Lucy, who had been eyeing my computer, said she wanted to be a computer specialist. Musu said she wanted to be a nurse to help the people of Pendembu. Comfort said, "I do too." Mary, Lilian, and Katumu wanted to be nurses as well. (Becoming a doctor seemed beyond imagining.) Isata wanted to be a teacher. (There were no female teachers in the school.) Musu's sister Mattu wanted to be a lawyer because Pendembu needed one. (There was only one lawyer, a man, in the whole district.) Jenifer wanted to be a government minister. Both Lucinda and Ruth said they wanted to be Catholic sisters. (Ruth's brother was already a priest.) I asked Ruth if she wanted to be a teaching sister. "No," she said firmly. "I will be a praying sister. Pendembu needs prayers."

I asked the girls to bring their memory cards and come one by one to sit with me at the computer. Musu was first. I put her memory card in the card reader, and soon her photos were flashing fast on the screen as the computer took them on board. Later we would watch a slide show of all the girls' photos, but as they were loaded in the computer they were visible only to Musu and me. Auntie Chris and Chris G. had been carrying on the discussion with the other girls, but suddenly the room fell silent. I looked up to find all the girls gazing intently at Musu, who was staring at the screen. She had shot 330 photos; she and I saw every one of them. There were a lot of shots of her pals— girls in blue uniforms at school, making faces at the camera or peeing in the bush—and some of people and places in the village. Musu watched the screen, her face a perfect mask. What was she thinking, this pert little girl, seeing pictures of her own making? I couldn't tell.

To me that was strange and disappointing. I had already shown the women photographers in Kailahun and Pendembu their first photos, and their reactions had been completely different. At the Pendembu meeting, Habibatu had raised her fist and shouted "Yes!" at every photo. Fatmata had sung out "Fine!" and slapped my thigh for emphasis 310 times. At the Kailahun meeting, Mamie Sampha had put her arm around me as I downloaded her photos, and as each one of her 248 images flashed by, she squeezed me tighter and tighter and tighter. Now this enigmatic girl stood up, put her memory card in her pocket, and sauntered back to her seat. Her sister Mattu came next with 176 photos, then Bintu with 431, and later Comfort with 542. It seemed to me you had to enjoy snapping to do it 542 times in a single week, but Comfort was just as self-contained as the rest.

These little girls appeared to be as calm and disinterested as fish. I had to ask Auntie Chris, "Can you tell how they feel?"

"They are very happy," she said. "Can't you see?"

"No," I said. "I can't see." What was it about their lives, I wondered, that made them hide happiness? But the older girls had a harder time containing themselves, and fourteen-year-old Lilian, the last to come forward, finally broke into a big grin. "I think my photos are very fine," she said. I slapped her hand. "Yes, Lilian," I said, "your photos are very fine. Your photos are super." Then the girls erupted—a sudden explosion of grinning, shrieking, hand whacking. Musu whooped and ran around the room. Big girl Lilian had made it okay to cut loose. The excitement passed, like a sudden storm, and the girls settled down to watch the full slide show. Each girl jumped up again to identify her photos when they came on the screen, and the others studied the images with great seriousness—not half-scared little girls anymore, but photographers at work.

One evening I sat in my darkened room, listening to the rain dance on the zinc roof, and scrolled through the photos these promising little girls had produced. The girls were bright, eager, sassy, bold, full of life and hopes for the future, but I had only to raise my eyes to the window and the skeleton of the house across the way to glimpse the unforgiving dangers that lay all around them. Here was a photo that ten-year-old Jenifer had taken of Ruth and Lilian standing with their backs to the camera looking at the shattered concrete shell of what once had been a spacious and graceful home. The image held me: small girls in their pretty dresses facing the ruin of war. Lately I'd been looking at things in that polarized way. On the one hand there was humanitarian relief, on the other destruction. Food, clean water, and schools on one side; rape, murder, and ruination on the other.

The world and its activities, seen from the vantage of Kaila-hun, seemed split in this binary way. There were the women and children and their concerns, which happened to be also the concerns of civil society and progressive elders and the humanitarian community: health care, education, agriculture, good governance, prosperity, and durable peace. And then there were the sexual predators and armed men in gangs. The division was not simply a matter of gender, for the armed men had wrecked the lives of other men, the great majority of them, and of boys as well. Often in the ruined market of Koindu town I saw a few men sitting together, empty-handed, talking—people who once were peaceable merchants back in the days when Liberians who walked over the border were tradesmen like themselves.

The weeks passed quickly, and soon it was nearly showtime again, time for the women and girls to review their photos and pick two—just two apiece—to present to their community. Choosing was never easy—these women were rarely, if ever, asked to make a choice or a decision about anything. And they had a lot of images to choose from. Altogether 17,792 images to be exact. I knew they would need a lot of patient support.

The trouble was, I couldn't make my limbs move to get my body out of bed. One by one my African colleagues crossed the road from the office, climbed the stairs, stuck their heads around my bedroom door, lifted the mosquito net to peer at me, and said: "Malaria. That's malaria all right." They were used to it—this scourge that kills more Africans each year than does that other plague, HIV/AIDS. I had seen my colleagues break into a drenching sweat, pop a couple of pills, and carry on working. Not me. I was flattened. If malaria attacked Americans at home, the government would launch a war against it.

Chris G. perched on the bed, notebook in hand, for some quick computer instruction. Then she and Auntie Chris set off for Pendembu to help the photographers make plans for the show. The IRC dispatched Dr. Jeff Kambale Mathe, a Congolese physician with the health program in Kenema, to drive for four hours over rough roads, carrying a plastic bag full of pills, to save me. He brought Gatorade too. "Don't worry," he said, grinning, as I washed down the pills. "In forty-eight hours you'll either be up again or dead. I'll stay to see how it turns out." Thanks to him, I did get up again, just in time to print the photos that Auntie Chris and Chris G. had helped the women and girls choose. Right on time, we hung the shows.

Then, as we might have predicted, the two First-Ever All-Women's Photography Exhibitions held in Kailahun town and Pendembu village turned out very differently. The women of both groups had worked hard to produce good photos, and they would speak clearly about the community problems their cameras had captured. But what happened after that depended—just as it had in Côte d'Ivoire—on the chief. In Pendembu, the large crowd gathered in the Court Barrie included the village elders and high-ranking officials from the district government and police. With the entire village in attendance, Chief Cyril Foray Gondor II seized the moment and the microphone to explain recently passed national gender laws that raised the legal status of women by registering customary marriages and criminalizing rape outside of marriage. He went further to admonish the men of his chiefdom: "Do not force yourselves upon your wives. That is rape, even if the law does not yet say so." He closed with a stirring reminder to men to respect women as their equal partners in life. Then, as if to offer an example of the behavior he had just recommended, he handed the microphone to his own formidable partner, Auntie

Lucy Foray Gondor, the chairwoman of the Women's Action Group. She wore a gold dress for the occasion and a fabulous hat of gold and black satin, puffed and shirred like a turban bursting into bloom. The chief and his wife were the ultimate power couple, bravely hauling their ruined village into a new century.

Auntie Lucy summoned the women photographers one by one to present their photographs, and then she held forth herself to make sure that no one missed the point of gender equality. Here were the photos the elders had requested: the damaged mosque in need of repair, the inadequate clinic short of supplies and equipment, the ruined houses that spoke of widespread homelessness and insecurity, the poor widows who couldn't support their children. But here too were images of pregnant teens, exploited and abandoned women, little girls forced to do the work of adults, women doing the hard labor of mules— transporting lumber on their heads—and by contrast, beauti- ful portraits of proud girls in the bright blue uniforms of school. The photographers spoke forcefully about each one. The elders applauded. The audience gave the women a stand- ing ovation. A disc jockey put some music on the rented public address system, everyone danced, and the photographers took more pictures.

Two days later at a meeting hall in Kailahun the district chief rose to greet the audience of townspeople. He began with an angry warning: "Do not speak of FGM (female genital mutila- tion). It is our tradition. We do not want foreign traditions." The audience applauded. Even the women photographers of the Women's Action Group, dressed for the grand occasion in matching light blue dresses and head wraps, applauded the local tradition of cutting away with razor blades the genitalia of little girls. I was taken by surprise, for the chief had welcomed us warmly when we first paid him a formal visit to request permission to carry out our project; and in the whole course of the work nobody had ever spoken about FGM. We discuss only issues women themselves raise with their photographs. FGM is an atrocity, but it is also a potent taboo.

Since the chief had brought it up in this public forum, the IRC countrywide GBV leader, who had driven up from Freetown for the show, tried gently to reply. A native of Sierra Leone, Amie spoke in Mende, the language of the chief, but he didn't want to listen. He stomped out of the meeting, followed by his cronies. After the show, when Amie and other national staff members went to the chief's house to make peace, he said that he knew FGM was a bad practice and should be stopped, but gradually. Although he held the power to end FGM throughout the district overnight, he clung to the notion that "change takes a long time." African "tradition," here as in Côte d'Ivoire, rests on the courage or conservatism of such chiefs.

A week later, after I'd left Sierra Leone, five hundred women marched through the town of Kailahun in a display of support for FGM, a display of loyalty to the chief, that made headlines around the world. They carried signs that said in Mende and English, "We don't talk about it." To me, this was our greatest defeat. Then I got an e-mail from Chris G., who in recent years had saved three young cousins from the knife. "This is really a very good thing," she said. "Before, nobody could even mention FGM. Now, thanks to the chief, people are talking about how they can't talk about it. That's progress." Maybe so.

The girls' show came last, before a packed house in the big assembly hall of the Girls' Primary School. All the students attended and many parents and teachers from other schools. Chief Foray Gondor sent a representative, as did the District Office of Education. The Family Services Unit of the police sent a uniformed policewoman, who delivered a rousing diatribe against rape and sexual exploitation. Then it was the girls' turn. They had mounted their photos on the blackboard at the front of the hall, and one by one they rose to speak about them. Mr. Shariff accompanied each of the girls, lugging a big battery-powered megaphone that carried their reedy voices to the far corners of the auditorium. They spoke of the importance of girls' education. Their photographs were a catalog of things that prevented girls' education and things that furthered it. There was Musu's image of a torn antiviolence poster that showed a man beating his wife with a whip, and Bintu's image, on the other hand, of a good father—a smiling young man minding a toddler and scrubbing the family laundry. "Our mothers have too much work to do," Bintu said. "Our fathers must be kind to them and help them and help the children. We need the support of our families." They asked their parents to free them from housework so they could concentrate on their studies as boys were allowed to do. The photographers had taken many pictures of little girls doing dishes or laundry or toting water buckets on their heads or selling things in the road—all girls kept from school to labor at home. Pointing to her photo of four little girls with buckets, Katumu revealed something else: "The water well is far from the town," she said, "and very often girls are sexually abused along the way. If you cared about us, you would make another well."

It wasn't that girls weren't willing to work; several of them presented photos of girls in the classrooms, taking notes, reading books, responding to teachers. Other photos showed squads of blue-uniformed classmates armed with mops and brooms, cleaning the school and the grounds as they did every Wednesday. But Katumu said, "I'm asking parents and relatives to wait until girls grow up before assigning us domestic work. Please let us girls go to school, and let us finish."

Some girls spoke of the dead-end danger of sexual exploitation and early pregnancy. Two girls presented photos of men bathing in the stream that crossed the road just below the school. Comfort said, "It is not right that young girls must walk past naked men every day to go to school." Musu showed a photo of a fifteen-year-old mother with a toddler. "She cannot take care of this child," Musu said, "because she is only a small girl herself and has dropped out of school."

Then it was the turn of twelve-year-old Isata. She had chosen a photo of Mr. Shariff leading a class and told us she would

At the One-and-Only All-Girls' Photo Show at the Girls' Primary School in Pendembu, twelve-year-old Isata Amadu points to her photograph of Mr. Shariff, the teacher and gender club adviser, who holds the megaphone as she speaks. Isata is about to bring down the house.                    —Ann Jones

speak about the importance of good teachers. We didn't know that she was about to connect the dots between girls' education and sexual exploitation. There she stood, a tiny girl in a too-big hand-me-down faded blue school uniform. Tight braids rose from her head like antennae. She pointed to her photograph of Mr. Shariff, who stood behind her at the time, looking a bit embarrassed as he held up the megaphone. "Good teachers are very important," Isata said, "and Mr. Shariff is a good teacher. He gives us information to help us in our lives. I took his picture because all teachers should follow the example of Mr. Shariff." She paused for a moment to catch her breath, and then in a louder voice, she said, "And they should stop impregnating schoolgirls."

Parents gasped. A woman shrieked. The room buzzed. The headmistress put her head in her hands. Isata walked back to her seat while the other girl photographers whooped and threw her high fives. Their schoolmates cheered and clapped and stomped their feet. Shy little Isata had voiced the unspeakable truth that everybody knew. She spoke for every girl in the room. She spoke for every girl who wants to get an education, every girl who wants to contribute to her community, every girl who wants to be all that she can be. Isata herself wants to be a teacher. All the schoolgirls clapped and clapped.

Later, when everyone had calmed down and we had handed out certificates to the girls and congratulated their parents, everyone adjourned to the schoolyard. All the schoolgirls sat under the trees sipping pink Kool-Aid, provided especially for the grand occasion. In Sierra Leone, for once, for girls, it was a Kool-Aid kind of day.

# 4

# THE DEMOCRATIC REPUBLIC
# OF CONGO: RAPE

The history of nations is complicated, but not the modern history of the Congo. It's a simple tale of unremitting greed and
exploitation—omitting the interests of the Congolese people
altogether—that begins with a Welshman working as a journalist
for the *New York Herald*. In 1871 Henry Morton Stanley went to
Africa on assignment and made himself famous by finding the
renowned Scottish missionary Dr. David Livingstone, who—
from Dr. Livingstone's point of view—actually was not lost. An
ambitious adventurer in an age of robber barons, Stanley saw
there was money to be made in Africa. He returned to explore
the Congo as private emissary for Leopold II, king of the Belgians,
carrying a pack full of contracts to be signed by tribal chiefs
who agreed, or were persuaded, to hand over natural resources.

Leopold laid claim to the Congo, a land many times the size
of Belgium, not for his country but for himself. He called it
the Congo Free State—that's "free" in the neoconservative sense:
free for the taking. The Congo Free State was not a colony but
a private enterprise; and there, for almost a century, under the
guise of bringing civilization and Christianity to black men,

white men seeking profits carried out an African holocaust. Their aim was not to exterminate Africans, however, but to make them work. Free state, free labor.

Leopold first seized ivory and then moved on, after the invention of the pneumatic tire, to rubber. At that time there were no tidy rubber plantations such as those Firestone later exploited in Liberia; rubber trees grew wild. In tropical forests, trees of a single species are widely dispersed, so gathering rubber in quantities sufficient for European demand was a big job. Leopold's Belgian-led Congolese mercenaries—the Force Publique—provided incentives. They imprisoned workers' wives and children without food to encourage men to work hard and fast. (What else they did to imprisoned women they did not report, and Victorians did not inquire.) They wiped out rebellious tribes—though many fought for years—with the Maxim machine gun. They chopped off the hands of the dead and carried them back to their commanders; the hand tally could be checked against the number of bullets spent, thus discouraging waste of ammunition and keeping overhead down. Amputations in the Congo were the mean, thrifty idea of greed run amok.

Toward the end of the nineteenth century, Leopold was shipping out millions of tons of rubber every year and drawing a profit of $1.1 billion from his personal empire. No such careful accounting was made of Africans, but ethnographers estimate that between 1880 and 1920 at least half the population of the Congo died of starvation, exhaustion, exposure, disease, and murder. That's ten million people. Congolese remember it to this day as "the overwhelming."

When word of Leopold's atrocities finally reached Europe, he was forced to sell out (at a profit) to Belgium, which then administered the Congo as a colony and continued to exploit

its resources until 1960, a triumphant year of African national-
ism when colonial powers pocketed their profits and went
home. Patrice Lumumba became the first democratically elected
prime minister of the newly independent nation, and his call
for the economic independence of Africa resounded throughout the continent. Political independence would mean little,
Lumumba insisted, if the former colonial powers continued to
exploit the natural resources that rightfully belonged to the
African people. Lumumba's message was heard in Washington,
too, where the National Security Council subcommittee on
covert operations ordered his assassination. Before he had been
two months in office, he was shot with the connivance of the
CIA and then dismembered and disappeared in a vat of acid.

After that, Joseph Desiré Mobutu, who had facilitated
Lumumba's murder, was our man in Africa. Mobutu, the son of
a cook, had become an officer in the Force Publique and an
informer for Belgian intelligence, assigned to shadow the rising
Patrice Lumumba. That put Mobutu in an excellent position to
make himself useful to the CIA, and then in 1965 to seize the
presidency himself—gratefully backed by Belgium, France, and
the United States. He renamed the country Zaire, forbade the
use of Western names and Western neckties, and started selling
out his country's natural riches once again to the West.

Over the years, Mobutu pocketed more than a billion dollars
in U.S. aid, and more from France, to secure his place as Africa's
most enterprising and enduring neocolonial puppet, and for
another generation of would-be bosses—men like Samuel Doe,
Prince Johnson, Charles Taylor, and Foday Sankoh—the very
model of the clever kleptocrat. He took over the Congo's mines
as his own, and he stashed away a fortune much larger than
King Leopold's. He visited President Kennedy, who gave him an
airplane and a U.S. Air Force crew to fly it. He visited President

Reagan and President George H. W. Bush, who hailed him as "one of our most valued friends."

In 1994, when Mobutu had ruled Zaire for more than thirty years, the civil wars next door in Rwanda and Burundi climaxed in genocide. After the slaughter the defeated Rwandan Hutu *génocidaires*—the Interahamwe—fled through the mountains to Zaire. They brought with them their intensive experience in butchery, and something else: an attitude cultivated by Hutu Power propaganda that as a matter of ethnic pride and political policy, Tutsi women must be raped. But once Hutu men got the hang of rape, they branched out to other ethnicities. They would rape any female: young, old, babies, grandmothers, tiny girls. The Interahamwe continued for a long time to be the worst, the most brutal, offenders; but soon all the guerrilla factions in Zaire took up rape, and Mobutu's national army adopted the practice as well. The Congo was on its way to becoming the rape capital of the world.

And the Interahamwe continued their war on Tutsis inside Zaire. They took control of refugee camps that had been established by international agencies to aid Tutsi survivors of genocide. They attacked Zaire's Tutsis, the Banyamulenge, who had lived in Zaire for half a century. Zaire's President Mobutu, for reasons of his own, backed the Interahamwe and sent them arms to kill his own Tutsi citizens. The Banyamulenge fought back, and Tutsi forces from Rwanda entered Zaire ostensibly to support them, though some say they were drawn by the magnetic pull of minerals in the earth. In 1996 they teamed up with Laurent Kabila, a longtime Congolese rebel who aimed to overthrow the ailing Mobutu in what became officially the First Congo War.

Kabila bragged that anyone could make war in the Congo with $10,000 and a cell phone. The money would buy an army, and the cell phone would be used to make deals: to sell off gold, diamonds, and coltan to international "investors" who would pay a premium to remain anonymous. Neighboring countries intervened, on both sides, with an eye on the same resources. A single helicopter could lift out a load worth millions. Kabila reportedly made sales worth $500 million even before his cut-rate army took control of the capital. Old and overmatched, Mobutu fled to Morocco where he died within a few months of cancer.

Soon the new self-appointed President Kabila turned on the Tutsis who had helped him to power, and their allies, triggering a Second Congo War that became the largest war in modern African history and the deadliest on the planet since World War II. Observers of world conflicts use the term "privatization of violence" to describe a new and increasingly popular form of war—that is, war waged by individual men who in their drive for personal wealth and power use private armies and paramilitary groups, or rouse ethnic militias to wreak private vengeance. Laurent Kabila's Congo Wars involved elements of both. The privatization of violence also delivers the destruction of the public good; the privatized war, driven by crazed personal greed and ambition, has nothing whatsoever to do with the welfare of the people who happen to live in its path. When peace accords were signed in 2003, eight African countries and twenty-five armed groups were involved in the war. Many of them continued to fight, especially in eastern Congo, long after the official end of conflict. Most of them went on grappling for the DRC's riches. All of them went on raping women and girls.

But more than that, throughout the wars and after, the militias counted on women for subsistence. They were not paid or provisioned but launched upon the land to enjoy the traditional spoils of war—that is, whatever they could seize. They counted on women for food. They raped women harvesting crops. They raped women carrying produce to market. They stole their goods. They dragged women off to their camps to cook their food, do their laundry, fetch their water and firewood, mend their clothes. The wars in the Congo could not have continued without the services of women—their produce, their skills, and their labor—seized by force. And their enslavement included sexual servitude that amounted to prolonged torture and often ended in death. The national army of the Congo might have achieved a military advantage by freeing captive women and protecting them from militias, but instead it raped them too.

Joseph Kabila succeeded his assassinated father as president in 2001, and the international community, desperate to stop the fighting and stabilize the Congo, put up $500 million for a special election in 2006 to affirm his presidency. That placed Joseph Kabila at the head of a government fabricated to appease and include all factions (except women) among its four vice presidents and thirty-six cabinet ministers. It's one of those unwieldy creations, by now familiar in failing states, in which officials find the means to enrich themselves, but nothing to support institutions or pay salaries to civil servants, teachers, doctors, soldiers of the national army, or police. People in eastern Congo complained that $500 million might have been better spent on something else because for them, far from the government in Kinshasa, the war went on. And so did rape.

When I traveled to the Congo for the IRC in 2008, it was to eastern Congo, to Bukavu, the capital of South Kivu Province. The town occupies hills that rise steeply from the shores of the southern end of Lake Kivu. The lake, which covers more than a thousand square miles, is one of the chain of great inland seas cradled in the volcanic eastern rift valley: Lake Tanganyika to the south, then Kivu stretching more than fifty miles north-ward to North Kivu Province, and beyond that, Lake Edward. This Great Lakes region, in its natural state, is a stunningly beautiful piece of the planet, though Lake Kivu is one of those rare, strange lakes—full of submerged methane gas and lethal carbon dioxide—that could, at any moment, turn over. A good friend, an African with whom I'd worked in Liberia, refused to go swimming with me. "And set off the gas?" he said. I went swimming anyway, as many expats did, in the cool, sweet water of the lake. Still weakened by my bout with malaria, I often had to roll onto my back to rest. And there, floating atop an antici-pated eruption that could kill within minutes two million people living near the lake, I gazed at the blue sky and tried to make a metaphor of imminent disaster. But it seemed meager in a land where history itself is catastrophic.

Although almost everyone in the DRC is desperately poor, some people have lived very well in Bukavu. I know because I lived very well in a house that someone else had built many years before on the crest of a hill just above the lake. The house and another next door had been rented by the IRC for staff members; it opened onto a lawn that sloped away toward the tranquil explosive lake and the blue mountains beyond. I used to sit there at sundown to watch the mountains fade into the dark, the view interrupted only by the coiled razor wire atop the wall at the foot of the garden and the gatehouse tower where the guards stood. Then from the neighboring compound just below would come the sound of drums and bugles: the Pakistani peacekeeping troops, beating some military tattoo.

Just down the road lay the border of Rwanda, and just up the road—a short walk, past the banana sellers—stood the IRC office; there with the GBV staff I went over plans for the photography project. They had scheduled me to work in three different villages, as I had done in other countries. But despite the official peace that existed in the DRC, the war in eastern Congo had never really stopped, and now hostilities were heating up again. Armed men stalked across the land, attacking each other, attacking villagers, pillaging, raping; the "security situation" was murky. The international aid agencies and MONUC, the UN mission, monitored events and issued warnings when armed men were on the move. That was the situation near one of the villages in my work plan; security had put it off-limits. "You'll go to the other two villages only," the GBV manager said. I could see the change meant nothing to her. She must have been used to plans gone awry.

"You might not want to go to Walungu either," she said. "There's been a lot of fighting around there lately. Last week when CNN was here, we had to bring people from Walungu for the reporter to interview because he didn't want to risk the trip."

"I need to go to the village," I said.

"Okay," she said. "And then on Wednesday you can go down to the Ruzizi Plains, to Kamanyola." It was a start.


The red clay road climbed straight up the mountain and traced the ridges until it dropped, nearly two hours later, into the green valley of Walungu. All along the way, spectacular vistas of lush forests and fields opened to one side or the other. But the narrow space between the roadway and the precipice was crowded with crooked houses, cobbled together from rough planks of dark wood. In the road women porters trudged, bent double under the weight of the burdens they carried suspended from straps worn around their foreheads. It was as if the life they led bore no connection to the landscape spread before us with the promise of rich profusion. Their life was not out there on the horizon. It was right here, close at hand, behind the doors of dark houses. It was here in the rutted road, and it was wretched.

We slid the last few miles over a muddy lowland road to Mubumbano. It was a fair-sized village with a main street lined with the same low wooden shacks. They were shells, really: thin, rough planks nailed horizontally to four corner posts that had been pounded into the ground, a dirt floor, a makeshift roof, a door with a big padlock. One of these small shacks was a community women's center, home of a women's group called MED (Mamas pour l'Education et le Développement), supported by the IRC. The women were waiting to greet us. Marlene, the Congolese assistant GBV manager, had come with me to make the introductions, along with Francine Nsinda, a recent graduate of the English literature program at a Bukavu college, who had been hired especially to translate for the project. We plunged into the darkness of the shack. The women squeezed themselves together on skinny plank benches and rolled out their beautiful Francophone names: Inviolate, Patientie, Immacule, Nathalie, Evelyne, Jacqueline, Muleha, Kusinza, two Charlottes, and Joelle. I took out my camera and began the project all over again.

Later we walked through the streets of the village, cameras in hand. But the people of Mubumbano were different from the villagers I'd grown used to in West Africa, who seemed always ready to pose. Here men ducked their heads, turned their backs, or confronted the camerawomen, demanding payment. I'd told the group about the pitch West African women had used to sell their photo project to potential subjects: that documenting life would prove helpful to the whole community. That carried no weight here. Men wanted to know how they would benefit as individuals. What was in it for them? How much was the white woman prepared to pay?

We walked far down the road and out into the fields before we met a woman sitting on the ground in a plot of cassava, peeling tubers with a big knife. When the women told her what they were doing, she said, "Please take my picture. It is important that people see how to peel cassava in the correct way." She offered to show me how to cook it correctly too. The women happily passed the cameras to their teammates so everyone could take a lot of photos suitable for publication in a cassava cookbook. And they promised to take many more photos on Sunday, when they would all be well dressed for church.

Two days later we drove south to the plains of the Ruzizi River and the village of Kamanyola, very close to the Rwandan border. In fact, to reach Kamanyola by road we had to exit through the DRC immigration checkpoint, enter Rwanda, passing through the checkpoint, and then, after a short drive, pass back out of Rwanda and into the DRC again, getting our papers stamped at every crossing. Driving to Kamanyola became a complicated exercise in the courtesies of border control and made clear how simple it would have been—how simple it was for drifting gunmen—to just walk through the forest.

The women's group at Kamanyola had a little office on the main road, right next to the base of the DRC national army, with a big sign out front: COLLECTIF DES FEMMES DE KAMANYOLA. We had just pulled up, and the women were hurrying out to welcome us, when my phone rang. Security again. "You can have a short meeting," the GBV manager said, "but you can't give out the cameras. It's too dangerous for the women."

We crowded into the little office, and I told the women what had happened.

At our first meeting, the leaders of the Collectif des Femmes de Kamanyola posed in front of their office. Founder Fatuma Kayangele (wearing a
dark head scarf) is directly in front of the sign.          —Ann Jones

"Security is wrong," one said. "Things are not as they say."

Another said, "If there is danger it will fall on us. We are
prepared to take a chance."

"The decision is not mine to make," I said. That was a situation any African woman could understand, but they were disappointed and angry.

"Why do you bring us this false information?" asked one.
"Do you want to make us afraid?"

"I'm very disappointed, too," I said. "But perhaps security
will let us use the cameras next week." We talked about the
purpose of the project and decided that we would use our time
together to practice the "crescendo" part—raising voices. Some
of them would speak about their concerns; Francine and I would
listen.

The leader of the group, a slim, sharp-faced woman, said, "I am Fatuma, and I can speak about how I learned about rape and started this group."

From a dark corner came another voice: "I am Charlotte, and I can speak about how this group saved me when I was raped."

A tall woman standing at the back said, "I am Kipendo. I say let them speak, and you will understand."

Fatuma took up her story from a day seven years earlier, in 2001, in the late afternoon, when her husband sent their daughter and her cousin to the market to buy oil for the lamps. When the two fifteen-year-old girls turned to go back home, they found the way blocked by soldiers who took them away down the road. As darkness fell, Fatuma and her husband went in search of the girls and learned of screams and crying coming from the school. There they found the girls as the rapists had left them. They went to the police station for help, but the police said there was nothing they could do about soldiers. Fatuma's husband grew angry and shouted at the police until they threatened to arrest him. Fatuma was thankful the girls were still alive. She walked out of the station and took them home.

I already knew what a brave act that was. In the DRC, a rape survivor is an outcast, blamed and shamed by local tradition and religion. The rape is all her fault. She becomes dirty, and worse, her sexual contact with another man shrinks the stature of her husband or her father, the man to whom she belongs. To regain respect he must cast her out.

Fatuma said she was thankful that her husband behaved differently: he stood by the girls. But as Fatuma watched her daughter's suffering, she felt powerless. The girl was her firstborn child, the eldest of nine. "At that time," she said, "I didn't even know enough to take my daughter to the hospital." She decided then to try to learn how to help her daughter and other survivors of sexual assault; but because rape is a crime that women and girls suffer in shamed silence, she had no idea how many there were. She didn't know that in the DRC, even then, there were thousands upon thousands.

When a French aid organization announced a women's meeting in a town not far away, Fatuma attended. There she learned for the first time that women could help rape survivors and fight back against the terror. She and a few others called a meeting in Kamanyola and more than a thousand women showed up. In a short time, Muslim women had to drop out, grounded by their husbands, and Protestants chose to go back to their church groups and rely on prayer. That left about two hundred Catholic women to form the Collectif des Femmes de Kamanyola (CFK), with Fatuma in the lead.

GTZ, the international development arm of the German government, worked with CFK and taught them the importance of getting rape survivors to the hospital within seventy-two hours; they needed medical treatment and a package of three drugs (called a pepkit) to prevent sexually transmitted diseases, HIV, and pregnancy. Under the administration of George W. Bush, American aid went mainly to faith-based facilities that omitted the emergency contraceptive from the pepkit, leaving many rape victims pregnant. Fatuma and her group learned from the Europeans to double-check the contents of the kit. Fatuma hoped to help dozens of rape survivors. During the first year, while GTZ provided transport to the hospital, CFK helped hundreds.

Then, after peace accords were signed in 2003, came another wave of warfare and another wave of rape. Fatuma and the women of CFK saw that medical treatment was not enough. Women were torn apart by rape, but so were families and communities. Everything was falling apart. The CFK women decided to break the cultural silence and begin to talk to survivors and their families. Fatuma also began to travel to outlying communities to talk to women about how they could help survivors and hold their communities together. When the IRC started to work in the area, CFK applied for help. The IRC GBV specialists taught them to give supportive counseling to rape victims and told them about women's rights.

To help Fatuma's group become self-sustaining, the IRC bought them a field. The CFK women are experienced cultivators, but the IRC taught them some advanced farming techniques to increase the crop yield. In their first season the women produced three tons of maize. The IRC bought them two more fields and taught them how to organize their activities and keep useful records. The women set up an office on the main road next door to the army base and began to talk to the commander about what his soldiers were doing. (At that time, the Congolese national army was thought to commit 70 percent of the rapes in eastern Congo.) They visited the homes of outcast women to persuade husbands and mothers-in-law to take rape survivors back.

Then they began to visit the fathers of raped girls to ask them not to compromise with rapists—not to accept a payoff— but to prosecute. They publicly denounced known perpetrators and helped take cases to court, calling both rapists and jurists to account. In a province where the justice system is a shambles, Fatuma said that CFK had seen a few cases through to convictions. José, the group's advocacy leader, added that she takes a CFK delegation to the prison periodically to see if the few men convicted are there. Most of them, she said, bribe their way to "escape." "It's true in everything we do," Fatuma said. "We win something, and then we lose." They faced both old attitudes and new appetites for rape.

Charlotte told us that she had been tending her small field alone, three years earlier, when she heard a rustling in the bush. Her heart leaped at the thought that her husband might have come to help her, but she looked up to see two armed militiamen emerging from the forest. They threw her down and raped her. Afterward she managed to get home, but she was afraid to tell her husband. She had heard of the work Fatuma was doing, and she sent a child to fetch her. Fatuma took Charlotte to the hospital and counseled her to stay in her rightful place at home; when Charlotte's husband guessed the truth, Fatuma and others from CFK talked with him as well. Charlotte was now the "soldiers' wife," he said, and useless to him. He refused to give her money for food for herself and their two children. He refused to pay the children's fees, and they had to leave school. He denied Charlotte clothing and shoes. He ordered her to leave the house.

"After the rape," Charlotte said, "I could not greet anyone or pass before other people. I felt they could see my evil. Slowly I got over that because of what I learned from CFK. I learned that I was not the first woman raped. Not the only one." She paused, and then she said something that struck me like a blow. "To be raped by gangs of men," she said, "it is very normal for women."

Charlotte had begun to feel better about herself when Fatuma and others told her that most of the women for miles around had also been gang-raped. Later I found confirmation in a 2005 report of research conducted by two local women's organizations in South Kivu, Réseau des Femmes pour un Développement Associatif and Réseau des Femmes pour la Défense des Droits et la Paix: "79% of the women interviewed had been raped by at least two attackers, either one after the other or (in 30% of the cases) simultaneously." The number of attackers ranged from two to twenty. In South Kivu, being gang-raped was still a shameful crime; yet it had become routine.

"But still," Charlotte said, "my husband chased me from the house and made me suffer. And the children too." At last Fatuma led a delegation from CFK and Charlotte's family to tell her husband that he must go to court, divorce her properly, and allow her to take her children home to her parents' house. Charlotte said, "The power of CFK made him very afraid. He looked again and he could see me in a different way." After that, they reached an understanding. They had another child. And with her husband's approval, Charlotte went to work with CFK. She said she believes that God worked through CFK to bring her back to life and restore her family happiness.

It was astonishing that Charlotte, so well trained in the tradition of shame and silence, could speak so openly. It was powerful evidence that the women of CFK could change the lives of survivors and their families, and perhaps even the community. Charlotte had become a leader in CFK, working on the cases of young girls who had recently been raped, not by militiamen but by civilians right there in Kamanyola. A twelve-year-old girl was raped by her teacher. A nine-year-old was raped by a young boy. A seven-year-old was raped by a middle-aged man. An eleven-year-old was raped by her father. A seven-year-old was raped by her pastor. Charlotte was one of the women who visited the parents, persuaded them not to compromise, and helped them take their child's case to court. But the rape of these young girls by civilians—by teachers, pastors, fathers—this was something new in the community, since the war, and the women of CFK were struggling to understand it. Later I told Charlotte and others about the way the habits of war carry over into peacetime, the way the habits of soldiers are taken up by civilians. I told them about the civilian rapes of little girls in Liberia, snatched even from church, and in Sierra

Leone. Unknown before the war, civilian rapists and child rape in Kamanyola—like gang rape—were becoming normal.


The next week, Francine and I returned to Mubumbano to see the photos the women had taken. It seemed there wasn't much to photograph in Mubumbano. Men intimidated the photographers, demanding money. But that was not the whole story. One woman had taken a photo of her wooden house. "My house is a fire hazard," she said, which was certainly true. "IRC should buy me a better one." Another had taken a photo of her tiny mud hut. "My house is full of insects," she said. "IRC should build me a new house." Another had taken a photo of two children. "These are my children," she said. "IRC should send them to school." I began with the obvious questions. Are there any other houses like this in the village? Are there any other people who lack the money to send their children to school? And slowly, slowly we began to explore the difference between a personal complaint and a social problem. We had only just begun to raise the next question—If the IRC were not here, what could you do for yourselves?—when the driver came to fetch us. It was going to rain heavily; we couldn't risk getting stuck in the mud, not even if the fate of Mubumbano rode on the answer to this question.

Driving back, watching the clouds mount over the valley, it struck me that I had not met women like those in Mubumbano since I'd worked in Afghanistan. "Traumatized" is the word that came to mind. Whatever they had been through, they did not speak of it, but lived in survival mode. The sense of community, of common humanity, had disappeared, if indeed it had ever existed. In West Africa, women had photographed problems they knew to be problems for many, many women: lack of money, lack of water, lack of housing, sexual violence. Here in Mubumbano, women photographed my house, my children, my problem. Was this lonely individualism—each woman marooned in her personal distress—something new? Or was this simply life as it had always been? Only one Mubumbano woman, Charlotte M'Rubangiza, had taken a photo of another woman, close up, standing in the market area on the main street, clutching at her face with one hand, her forehead and her eyes a map of anxiety. "I took this picture of a woman to show how hard women in our community are working," Charlotte said. "As you can see, she looks very tired and worried. We don't have any electricity or any clean stream. We all have to go out and look for firewood, water, food, and such things every day. We are all tired and worried."

"I took this picture to show how hard women in our community are working. . . . We are all tired and worried."
—Charlotte M'Rubangiza, DRC

Back at the office, the GBV manager said, "You can't work in Kamanyola. The office in Kinshasa says so." Kinshasa? The capital was twelve hundred miles away. What did they know about the Ruzizi Plains? A gang of armed men had hijacked a vehicle belonging to another Bukavu-based NGO on the road not far from Kamanyola and stolen a payroll. All the NGOs in Bukavu had already signed a letter to the government saying they wouldn't drive that road again unless the government guaranteed their security. They seemed to believe that the government, such as it was, would care. "Don't question it," the manager said. "It won't do any good."

With the project slipping away, Francine and I set out to learn more about rape and the part it played in this unrelenting war. Whenever we had time and a vehicle, we drove out to Panzi Hospital to visit patients and talk with nurses, doctors, and psychologists on the staff. We walked through the wards, stopping to visit, and sat outdoors under the trees with patients who were weaving tote bags—something to sell—from bright plastic cord. Many were stuck in silence, but here in the hospital, in the presence of countless other survivors, and with the support of counselors, some opened up and told us their stories, several on videotape, wanting the world to know. But the stories were so awful, I wondered if the world could bear to hear them.

Francine and I took a boat up the lake to Goma, the capital of North Kivu Province. We visited a hospital there, damaged both by war and by the eruption in 2002 of the local volcano; the streets of Goma were buried in lava that quickly shredded the national flip-flop footwear. It was one more daily trial for ordinary people who had no proper shoes. We drove north to a Catholic hospital at Ntamungenga and a rundown Baptist mission hospital at Rwanguba that was trying to cope with an

inexplicable epidemic of pregnant adolescents—all impregnated by older men, civilians, who denied responsibility. Nurses
and midwives said they hadn't seen this in the past, and they
didn't know what to do about it. Like the women in Kamanyola, they were struggling to understand. We talked with doctors and nurses and survivors. We went to women's community
meetings in the villages with aid workers from the local IRC
office. We gathered stories, statistics, and case studies, and then
one day, back in Bukavu, late in the afternoon, I sat down in
the garden with my notebook and stared at the darkening
mountains and the beautiful threatening lake and tried to
make sense of things.

It seemed clear that in the Kivus alone at least forty thousand women survived wartime rape, but most of them—the
report of the two Réseaux said 95.1 percent—suffer at least one
enduring symptom of psychological trauma (such as depression, anxiety, sleeplessness, or despair) and debilitating physical
problems: crippled or missing limbs, blindness, damaged or
destroyed internal organs and/or genitalia, and sexually transmitted diseases, including HIV. Thousands have been left with
fistula, a complaint often mentioned but misrepresented by
male war reporters with only vague notions of female anat-
omy. Broadly, "fistula" refers to any perforation in the tissues
separating the vaginal canal from the urinary tract and/or the
rectum. There are several different types of fistulae, depending
upon where the holes occur, but the typical result is uncontrollable leakage through the vagina of urine or feces or both. In
less violent times, fistula most commonly results from prolonged labor in childbirth when the fetus presses upon maternal tissues, cuts off blood supply, and effectively creates dead
spots that give way. The younger, and therefore smaller, the

mother, the greater the likelihood of prolonged labor and fistula. When women have access to adequate maternal care, fistula is easily prevented.

In the last several years, Dr. Denis Mukwege has become the world's most famous fistula surgeon, widely praised in the international press for his work as the head of Panzi Hospital. We saw him there often on the lawn, wearing an immaculate white smock, speaking to international TV crews; but he was frequently away, carrying the story of the Congo rapes abroad—a doctor who had become an international advocate for his patients. When we spoke, his eyes gave away his profound weariness. "It's the way they do the rapes," he said. "It's monstrous. The damage is terrible. We treat them, as best we can, and then they go back home and are raped again. They come again, or they come too late. Then there is nothing more I can do." He was a healer at war with armies, and despite all his victories, he was losing.

An obstetrician/gynecologist, Dr. Mukwege trained in fistula surgery before the war to treat the complications of childbirth; but between 2004 and 2008 at Panzi he treated more than ten thousand rape victims, surgically repairing thousands of fistulae, most of them caused by traumatic injury—by brutal multiple rapes and other "foreign objects." The oldest patient was eighty-three, the youngest nine months. In 2008 the hospital regularly received about two hundred rape survivors a month—that is, six or seven women and girls a day. Most of them came to the hospital about a year after the rape, only when the consequences—STDs, HIV, fistula—became harder to bear than the shame. But Dr. Mukwege told me in April 2008 that he was feeling heartened because the number of cases of traumatic fistula had been going down for about a year, along with a decline in militia activity in South Kivu. (During that year, 2007, Panzi Hospital recorded 2,583 rape cases, 299 fistula surgeries, and 16 cases of pregnancy as a result of rape.) But even then among the surgeries he was performing for obstetric fistula, one in three patients was a teenage girl, a former captive "wife" of soldiers, who had given birth years before and lived ever since as an outcast in the forest, reeking of urine and feces, unaware that she might find help. Panzi's patients came from the vicinity of Bukavu; but now the hospital was adding a mobile unit to venture farther afield. Dr. Mukwege said, "We will find many more."

The GBV manager had an idea: we could invite some of the CFK women to come to Bukavu for a meeting. If CNN could do interviews "from the field" in an office in Bukavu, why couldn't I? A few days later, five CFK women arrived on a local bus, accompanied by several children and two adolescent girls to look after them. Marlene settled them into the guesthouse at a mission school near the IRC office, and we gathered in a conference room there to continue the conversation begun at our first meeting in Kamanyola. Fatuma, the leader, was there, and Charlotte, who had told us her story of rape. José, the head of advocacy, was there, and willowy Kipendo and cheerful young Isabelle.

Kipendo, a nonliterate farmer, was in charge of CFK's fields. Isabelle, in possession of a diploma, was the best educated, and she had chosen to be Kipendo's assistant. Isabelle was good at keeping the records and accounts, and Kipendo said she was becoming a good farmer too. The women worked their communal fields in groups, for companionship and efficiency, and more important, safety. There were groups that took the produce to market too—some of the sharpest members, who wouldn't be fooled by the slick city market women who weighed the maize with a finger on the scale. They were doing well, making enough money so that every woman made a small profit, enough to convince her husband that her work with CFK should continue. But what they needed now, Kipendo said, was a mill so they could process the maize themselves and carry the meal to market. Isabelle had the projected figures, showing a substantial increase in the profits. Short of that, Kipendo said, they needed a warehouse so they could hold some of the crop off the market and wait for a better price. They had worked out the figures on that, too.

But the whole point of the farming, José reminded us, was to make money for CFK to continue its work with rape survivors and their communities. That's where the women's hearts were. Yet they'd argued at our first meeting that there was more to it than taking raped women to the hospital. I wanted to know what was involved in "more to it." I wanted them to show me.

So I presented a slide show of images from the photo exhibitions we had held in West Africa, and Francine translated into Kiswahili the statements each woman had made about her photographs. The CFK women were full of questions, and we could answer many of them in the West African women's own words, filtered through multiple translations. It was an odd sort of teleconference with the West Africans' photos standing in for them, but the connection was palpable. I asked the CFK women to ponder overnight the photos they might have taken in Kamanyola, if only Security had let them take a chance with the cameras.

In the morning they drew pictures, with inspired artistry, and each woman presented her drawings to the others, as if we were having a real photo show. Then they put their heads together and arranged their sixteen drawings in order of importance. Number one was Charlotte's picture of a big angry man throwing

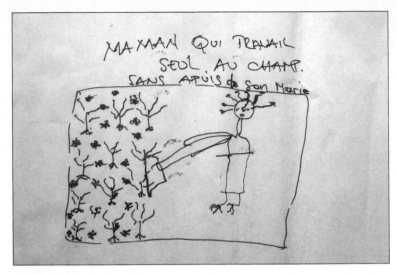

"I drew this picture to show that every woman works very, very hard on her farm, but working alone, she is in danger from roving men." The caption written on the drawing reads, "Mama working alone in the field without any help from her husband."

—Josephine Mugoto, DRC

his raped daughter out of the house. (The father was an enormous bloated figure, the daughter tiny.) Number two was Kipendo's drawing of a woman alone and pregnant after rape. Three and four were Kipendo's as well: the parents of a rape victim going to the police, and a rapist being arrested. José drew number five: the local pastor who raped a little girl. Isabelle drew number six: economic discrimination hiding behind a "tradition" that only men can grow banana trees. ("Banana trees grow by themselves," Kipendo said. "Men only sit under them in the shade, and take the profits." Isabelle added, "They take bananas too.") By contrast, both Charlotte and José drew pictures—numbers seven and eight—of lone women cultivating their separate plots. They were meant to show the isolation and the dangers—like Charlotte's rape—of women working alone. (José said, "We were all so busy working alone on our *shambas*, we had no time to be friends. Now look at us.") Next came two pictures by two different artists of women cast out and abandoned, living in small huts. There were pictures of little boys begging by the road, and children malnourished, and other children sitting on the floor in a school without chairs or desks or books. Finally there were two pictures by Fatuma: one of a community meeting led by a woman with men in the audience, listening, the other of women and men marching together, as they had done not long before in Kamanyola, to demand an end to silence about rape. These, the evidence of progress, came last, I thought, only because the troubles were so immense. You could see why the women looked to Fatuma as their leader; they searched out the problems, while she optimistically kept her eye on the goal. But what they wanted was clear: an end to violence against women and children; an end to traditions and customs that masked male violence and economic oppression; education, health care, and opportunity for children; and cooperation between men and women in reaching these objectives.

I broke the security rules then and handed each woman a camera—to be used only in the next few hours on the mission grounds. Thrilled, they took photos of each other and of the children and of the beautiful lake, and then they handed back the cameras and raced for the bus back home. I photographed their drawings, printed enlargements, and had them laminated, just as for any other Global Crescendo first-ever all-women's photo show; and I printed up all their snapshots of themselves and their kids. I bundled everything together and arranged for the package to be delivered to CFK by a person not yet paranoid who still drove daily down the forbidden road to Kamanyola.

Then I printed the photos the Mubumbano women had selected for their show and set off once again for the Walungu valley. This time most of the members of the GBV staff came along to see what we had been up to. More than a hundred people gathered in a big, timeworn meeting hall in the compound of a large mission church. All the village elders and officers were there. Kusinza, the head of the women's group, presided jointly with the principal chief, who happened to be the husband of Patientie, one of our best photographers. Somehow the women, who had seemed so wrapped up in themselves, had worked together to make all the arrangements for the hall, the invitations, and the program. And the community bigwigs had turned out to support them. I guessed that Patientie's husband had something to do with that—another example of the difference a progressive chief can make.

After the protocol of prayers and welcoming speeches, Marlene and I explained the purpose of the project, and then it was the women's turn. Jacqueline showed the photo of her little mud hut, the one she had wanted the IRC to replace, but this time she said she wanted people around the world to know that a woman who lived in this "small, unsatisfactory hut" had successfully brought up four children in it. "We women suffer in such places," she said. "Yet we succeed." Charlotte M'Rubangiza showed the photo of her hazardous wooden house, and Charlotte Nabintu followed with a photo of a man cleaning up after a house fire; but this time they called for a village meeting to figure out better safety measures, and maybe even better house plans. Jacqueline showed her neighbor's children, as well as her own, coming from school and said, "I wish all our children could be sent to school so that they could avoid becoming street children." Some way must be found, she said, for poor children and orphans to be sent to school. Nathalie followed up with a photo of five

"These orphans in our community have no one to care for them. They live in poverty. They are not studying because they have no one to pay their school fees."

—Nathalie Mirindi, DRC

orphan boys mugging for the camera. "They are street children," she said, "and most of them are joining the army because there is nothing else for them to do. The community must think of the problem of these boys and what can be done for them." Then she put an arm around Francine, who had been translating, and said, "Look at this young woman standing here speaking four or five languages, helping to bring people together. We need more educated young women like this. We do not want more soldiers." That brought the chiefs and elders to their feet to applaud.

The women kept coming with their photos, almost all of them depicting problems. There were more orphans and many widows without support. There were abandoned women, one of them living with her children in a derelict poultry cage made of twigs and straw. There were women and children doing heavy labor, pounding cassava, carrying enormous loads; some of the women were pregnant. There were people toiling over broken bridges and washed out roads. There were children fetching water from a polluted well, women hauling firewood, and Charlotte M'Rubangiza's portrait of the worried woman, the face of the village. Then came Kusinza and Evelyne with a ghostly photo of a recumbent figure, swathed in a white sheet. She was a rape victim, Kusinza said, just one of many the women's group tried to help and counsel. She explained, "My teammate took her photo with her face covered because we wanted to protect her privacy. We also wanted to suggest that she is not the only one. It is a great shame that there are thousands of women like her."

When the women had finished, and Marlene and I had presented their certificates, dignitaries rose one by one to congratulate them and thank them for photographing problems they somehow had failed to notice. When the chief closed the meeting, the audience lingered. They lined up to congratulate the photographers and fell into spirited conversations about things they had seen, things that needed to be done. Francine said, "The women surprised us, didn't they? They have done very well." And so they had.

But I was going over the photos and the Kamanyola drawings in my mind: widows, orphans, abandoned women, lone women, malnourished paper-thin women and big-bellied children, all the broken things—houses, roads, bridges, schools, families—and all the women raped. Rape was not just one item on a list of miseries. Looked at in the way the women of Kamanyola and Mubumbano had been trying to show me, rape lay behind everything, and everything was about rape.

As direct targets of men at war, women and girls suffered terribly. This armed group or that might be singled out as the

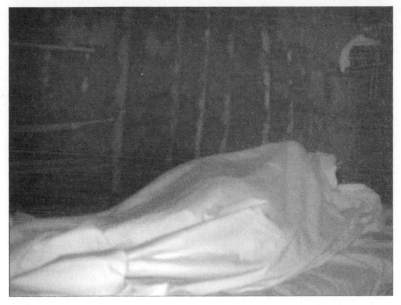

"This picture, as you see, seems to show a woman sleeping. But this woman has been raped and later brought to our women's center where we gave her some medicine. Here she is resting. We covered her face because we did not want to show her identity—and she could be any one of us."

—Evelyne M'Makalele, DRC

worst perpetrators of atrocities, but every armed group, even the UN peacekeeping force, was guilty of rape. Men singly or in gangs raped women and girls of all ages, as women had been telling me every day. They often tortured women *during* rape, as the Réseaux studies found in 71.7 percent of cases. Survivors and medical personnel told me of other things the rapists did as well. They cut off women's nipples or breasts; they mutilated or cut off the external genitalia. They eviscerated living pregnant women to remove and kill fetuses. After rape, men commonly inserted foreign objects into the vagina: sticks, sand, rocks, knives, rifle barrels, bottles, broken glass, pestles covered in pepper, burning wood or charcoal, or molten plastic made by melting shopping bags. They inserted a handgun or rifle in the vagina and fired it. They blinded women by gouging out their eyes or driving nails into them. They chopped off women's arms and/or legs and left the women to die in the forest. They abducted women, and especially girls as young as ten or eleven, as captive "wives." They kept women and girls chained to trees for months and gang-raped them day after day. They murdered some captive women and girls, often by slitting their throats, as disciplinary examples to the others. They abandoned in the forest captive women and girls who were no longer serviceable for sex.

It's true that long before the war, Congolese men treated women as lesser creatures, forbidden to plant money-making crops such as coffee, cotton, and bananas—forbidden even to eat nourishing foods such as eggs and chicken. It's true that Congolese men routinely used force if necessary to compel women's labor and sexual service. It's true that many Congolese men hold notions that promote rape: the belief that having sex makes men stronger, for example, or that having sex with a virgin immunizes against AIDS. And it's true that child rape is traditionally considered an offense only against the father whose property is spoiled, an offense resolved by compromise. But all these cultural factors taken together are insufficient to explain the frequency and unspeakable brutality of rape in the DRC in the last decade. When I looked at the war in the DRC from my outsider's perspective, it was hard to see it as anything but a war against women. In 2008, long after war officially ended, Major General Patrick Cammaert, former deputy UN force commander in the DRC, said, "It is more dangerous to be a woman than to be a soldier right now in Eastern DRC."

But the women of Kamanyola had made me understand that rape has another dimension as well. It's not enough, they said, to get women to the hospital and patch them back together. The whole of life was falling apart. It is rape that makes that happen. It's often said that raping women is intended to "humiliate" men. (One Congolese man on the GBV staff revealed the usual male evaluation of woman's worth when he compared raping a man's wife to using his table without his permission.) But shaming or provoking enemy men is merely the beginning of a process meant to destroy the life of a whole community and/or "cleanse" an area. In eastern Congo, the process goes like this: Husbands cast out raped wives to fend for themselves, with or without their children. Or raped wives with no visible injuries conceal the fact of rape from their husbands and try to carry on. In either case, women are afraid to venture out to gather firewood, or fetch water, or cultivate their fields. For a time women band together to work the fields, until soldiers abduct a group en masse. Terrified, women begin to neglect their crops, or soldiers steal the produce, and families suffer malnourishment and hunger. With no surplus produce to sell at market, women have no money. They can't pay school fees for their children. Girls are afraid to go to school; now boys drop out too. Some men leave the village, shamed by a wife's rape. Some men leave to join a militia, voluntarily or by force. Some men leave to look for work and money in cities far away. Many men never come back. Some outcast women leave too, for cities or truck stops where they take up "survival sex," selling the only asset they have left, their already dirtied bodies.

The localized famine spreads. People weaken and grow ill, but there is no money to pay for a visit to the hospital, and the trip may be too dangerous to undertake. (Women have been raped on the way home from hospitals where they were treated for rape.) People begin to die of commonplace complaints like diarrhea, pneumonia, or malaria that they would have survived in better days. A study conducted by the IRC concluded that between August 1998 and April 2007, 5.4 million "excess deaths" occurred in the DRC, most of them from easily preventable and treatable diseases. Significantly, 2.1 million of those deaths occurred after the war formally ended in 2003.

Cultural norms die too when women are raped in the presence of their families; when boys and men are forced to rape their own sisters, mothers, or daughters, or are murdered on the spot for refusing; when boy soldiers are compelled to rape babies or grandmothers. A hospital administrator told me the story of a woman taken as a captive wife and separated from her two young children. Later her captors told her the children had been boiled, and she had eaten them. She arrived at the hospital carrying their skulls.

So divisive is rape, and the shame and terror that attend it, that even in the best case a family may fall apart. The rare husband who stands by his raped wife finds that his brother's family no longer visits him, nor his uncle's either. The durability of extended family ties, the allegiance of kinfolk, the pleasant give-and-take of hospitality at the heart of Congolese life—all fade and fracture. Fragments of families pack up and move to places they believe to be more safe, leaving empty houses in the village, soon looted by soldiers. In this way the community falls apart. Those who leave are desperate, penniless, often ill with sexually transmitted infections. Those who stay are old, ill, infirm. Those who return find their property ransacked, their tools stolen, their crops and livestock plundered, and their friends and neighbors vanished. They move away again. In this way the people who have not already been removed to serve the soldiers are cleared off, leaving an open field for armies to go about the real business of war, which is, of course, business. In the Congo, that business is—as it has been since the first sales trip of Henry Morton Stanley—extracting natural resources and selling them. All of that is made possible by rape used as a tactic of war—millions dead and a way of life gone. And along the roads, begging and threatening, are gangs of boys: orphans of war and unwanted offspring of rape who aspire to be soldiers.

Meanwhile, people like Fatuma and her family try to carry on, only to find that even when war ends, sexual violence against women and girls continues. The habits of warfare carry over seamlessly into the peace. And because rape was not acknowledged as a tactic of war prior to the passage in 2008 of Security Council Resolution 1820, soldiers could (and still do) continue to rape civilians while complying with peace accords merely by not attacking each other. "Peace building" goes on, "power-sharing" governments are formed, amnesty for ex-combatants is declared, even as the leaders in these negotiations continue to wage their shadowy war on women, the wedge of war against communities and cultures. The durable peace the UN seeks sinks in a slough of hypocrisy because so many men of affairs find the interests of women and their families—or those we might call the common people—inconvenient to the arrangements they make for the world.

The number of men penalized for crimes against women in the DRC is almost nil. One reckoning found that in 14,200 reported rapes in 2005–2007 in South Kivu Province, only 2 percent of rapists were "held accountable," whatever that means. A few men arrested, a few prosecuted perhaps; but those sentenced can be counted on one hand, and few actually stay in jail. A bribe does the trick: a spontaneous jailbreak as guards look away.

The failure to punish anyone for rape or torture gives everyone permission. In *The Greatest Silence*, a film by Lisa Jackson documenting rape in the DRC, a soldier laughingly admits to having raped and instigated gang rape many times; he calls it "making love." He says that rape "just happens" in wartime, and that when the war is over he won't rape anymore. But why should he stop? The absence of punishment creates a "culture of impunity" in which those responsible for punishing crime become complicit with criminals. Many men speak of the "culture of impunity" not as a barbaric breakdown of justice but as today's way of life, a free pass that encourages civilians—teachers, pastors, fathers—to take up practices popularized by soldiers. And as combatants are demobilized and reintegrated into civilian life, raped women meet their rapists in the street. For them the terror continues. One in ten of the patients Dr. Mukwege treats for traumatic fistula returns to Panzi Hospital, having been raped again.

Fatuma's raped daughter, who later married and had a child, was raped again two years ago, this time by six soldiers who beat her husband and forced him to watch. His response was something new, something influenced by CFK: "I saw what happened to my wife. I will not forsake her." CFK. If you pronounce the acronym in Congolese French with a Swahili accent, it sounds like *say-ev-ko*—"Save Co." Saving is what CFK does. It begins by saving rape survivors, but in effect it saves families, a village, and the idea of civic life. CFK and MED of Mubumbano are only two of many strong women's groups organized in the DRC, only two examples of what women can do, with a little security and a little help from the international community, to counteract the centrifugal force of hundreds of thousands of "acts of sexual violence against civilians" and make way for that elusive durable peace.

"A woman is receiving counseling after she was raped. I want all women to take courage because our women's group can help them. And I want our local authorities to defend women and punish the authors of rape."

—Kusinza Praxede, DRC

But the women worry about the future. Not long after I left the DRC in 2008—after UN Security Council Resolution 1820 had demanded an immediate end to rape—fighting flashed through North Kivu again while 6,000 badly outnumbered UN peacekeepers charged with preventing armed conflict and protecting civilians stood by. The National Army was trying again to turn back the forces of renegade General Laurent Nkunda, who professed to be protecting Congolese Tutsis from Hutu *genocidaires* in a relentless reprise of the 1994 Rwandan genocide in which one million people died; in the DRC, almost five and a half million have died in the ceaseless sequel. During this round of fighting, the roads of North Kivu filled with a quarter million civilians in flight, with no place to go. Cholera broke out among thousands camped in the rain outside Goma. Reports told of the massacre of civilian men of fighting age—and once again the mass rape of women and girls.

In January 2009, Rwandan forces captured Laurent Nkunda, their onetime ally; and in April 2009, DRC President Joseph Kabila told the *New York Times* that he expected Nkunda to be returned to the DRC to "answer questions" about the bad things he had done in eastern Congo. He did not mention whether the "bad things" to be investigated might include bad things done to women and girls. He talked as if the war were over and said that he has moved on from such incidental issues of "security" to "the other issue . . . development." Indeed, he had already announced a deal with the Chinese Railroad Engineering Company (CREC): in exchange for building infrastructure projects—roads, railroads, hospitals—worth $6 billion, CREC got the rights to extract enough copper and cobalt to kick back a bonus to Kabila and walk away with an estimated $42 billion profit. The DRC's Minister of Mines announced, "For the first time the people of the Congo will see a benefit from their resources"—which, as it happens, is just what Henry Morton Stanley said in 1871.

Contemplating the rich promise of that "development," President Kabila assured the *Times* that: "The main problem of security—we've dealt with that." Maybe so, but nobody has been disarmed. Nobody has been punished in the convenient, flourishing culture of impunity. Why should the army or militias give up raping? And why, now that they've got the habit, should civilians? Reading Kabila's complacent comments, I recalled a community meeting in the North Kivu village of Rwanguba, a village Laurent Nkunda's forces had overrun. Members were compiling statistics on the incidence of violence against women in their community: women *kupigwa* (beaten) and *kubakwa* (raped). That week, in this small village with a tradition of silence, one small civic organization had learned of sixteen cases. A twenty-one-year-old woman beaten by a neighbor. A twenty-eight-year-old woman raped in her home by a civilian. A fifty-year-old woman raped by a stranger. A twenty-one-year-old beaten by a neighbor. A forty-year-old beaten by her husband. Another forty-year-old raped and beaten by her husband. An eighteen-year-old beaten by her husband. A thirty-year-old raped and beaten by her husband. A twenty-eight-year-old raped and put out of the house by her husband. A nineteen-year-old raped by a civilian on the road. A thirty-seven-year-old raped by a civilian near her home. The list went on—and there wasn't a single soldier on it.

# BURMESE REFUGEES IN THAILAND:
## SOMEPLACE ELSE

I stared at the map. In nine months with the IRC I had carried the Global Crescendo Project to four countries, all of them in Africa, three of them neighbors on the same West African block. The project had become an African Crescendo, though only a small part of the continent had been given a chance to speak up. At the time, IRC GBV teams were also at work in Burundi, Central African Republic, Chad, Ethiopia, Kenya, Sudan, and Tanzania. At the rate I was going, it would take me another fourteen months to carry the cameras to African women in only the most desperate of the continent's troubled countries. Africa offered a lifetime of work, but if the project was to have a global dimension, it was time for me to move on.

I looked at Southeast Asia and zeroed in on Burma. At that time, the IRC was not allowed to work in Burma, where outsiders are not welcome, but just across the border in Thailand it worked with Burmese citizens who aren't welcome in Burma either: members of the country's ethnic minorities. There are nine refugee camps there, strung like beads along the Thai-Burmese border. It's a region of steep mountains cloaked in dense tropical forest cut by streams and rivers that turn torrential in the season of rain. Here, in a landscape that looks like the homelands they left behind in eastern Burma, refugees build houses of woven grass matting and leaf thatch on wooden platforms raised high above the floodwaters sure to come. The houses look like those they once owned in Karen, Karenni, or Shan State on the other side of the border, but they are not the same. These houses that cling to steep slopes or crouch on a bit of flat land too near a stream are often flimsy or incomplete; and they are chockablock. Those houses across the border were fine, and they were home; these are just temporary, just a place to camp really, until the householders can go back to where they belong. Today at least 150,000 refugees wait in these houses, in these camps. Many of them have lived here for twenty years.

In the IRC office in Mae Hong Son, I told two of my new Thai colleagues that just hearing about people stuck in refugee camps for twenty years made me depressed. After all they must have suffered in Burma, seeing families and villages destroyed, to somehow survive and struggle to find a safe place to build a quick shelter, a place to wait just for the time being, and then to find the time stretching on and yourself stuck: it seemed the sport of malicious gods. They had escaped from war into a kind of prison. "There are many old people in the camps who will never see Burma again," P'Jit said. "There are also many young people," said P'Meow, "who have never seen Burma at all." Then, seeing that I was distressed, they invited me to join them for the evening at the Wat of the Reclining Buddha.

We sat cross-legged amid buckets of lotus flowers on the wooden floor of the temple. P'Meow showed me how to peel back one layer of the bud of a lotus flower, fold the edges inward, and press the geometrically crimped tissue back into place; then swivel the shaft of the flower a few degrees and begin again.

"This picture is a view of the crowded camp showing how very near the houses are to one another. It is dangerous for people to live so closely together. Diseases spread quickly from house to house, and when one house burns down the next easily catches fire."

—Daw Meh and Phar Mo, Thailand

Eventually the whole ball of the flower's base was inscribed with the simple, painstaking three-dimensional design. I worked slowly, intent upon doing the task mindfully and well, and when I had finished my lotus bloom, P'Meow gestured to another bucket not far away where I was to deposit the flower. Close to the bucket I noticed another group of women weaving the crimped lotus blooms together in some inexplicable way that produced a great, tall tree of fantastically elaborate flowers. For a moment I felt chagrined that the lotus bloom on which I had lavished so much care was merely a tiny piece of a grander design meant to honor the great Buddha reclining gracefully at the end of the room. The moment passed, to be replaced by gratitude for this glimpse of the picture into which even my small imperfect part could fit. I smiled at P'Meow, and she put another lotus into my hand. P'Jit came in with her mother, who was losing her eyesight, and we all crept close to the Buddha, so she could see.

I had arrived only a few days before in Mae Hong Son, a small town in northern Thailand, not far from the Burmese border, where the IRC had established a base. The GBV team had been working in the camps since 2004. That first day I'd met my new colleagues: Abby Erikson, the GBV program manager—an unusual American, a tall, willowy, calm yogini, proficient in Thai, and a gifted mentor beloved by all her Thai and Burmese staff; and the Thai staff themselves, including P'Meow, a Buddhist nun worldly enough to manage the IRC's finances and generous enough to invite a newly arrived, newly met colleague to the Wat to prepare for the next day's celebration of the Buddha's birthday. That night, standing beneath the moon in the garden of the hilltop temple, I lit a candle and watched the flame take hold, meditating on all that I was grateful for, until, quite transported, I noticed the gentle tug at my sleeve and turned to accompany P'Meow back down the hill. I walked on alone, around the lake in the heart of town where the lights of street vendors still played across the water, and down a darkened lane to the guesthouse where the IRC had rented a room for me. There it was: a bed, a small table, a straight-backed chair, a rod with three hangers for my clothing, and a bathroom—a kind of tiled closet with a toilet and a shower head on a flexible hose. In the middle of the floor, a drain. The room seemed to me all that anyone might ever need. And it had a window, too, that opened on to a world behind the house, a world of trees and vocal birds.

I was far from Africa, I could see. Far from the world of brave, loud, laughing women wrapped in flamboyant print fabrics in which photographic images of the famous often figure prominently in ingenious designs: Ellen Johnson Sirleaf's face splashed across a broad bosom, or Pope Benedict's grim visage splayed on some faithful lady's ample behind. Here the fashions were quieter—a dark sarong, a simple blouse—and the demeanor of all the people was gentler, more restrained, tuned to a lower decibel. Here, I thought, our photo project would be different: perhaps not quite as lively, or as loud. But there is quiet courage, too. In the morning, we would begin.

The drive from the IRC office in Mae Hong Son to the refugee camps high in the forested mountains is spectacular. On the main road, before we turn off to climb a vertical slope on a skinny red track leading deeper into the dripping jungle, a white van speeds past us, full of gaping tourists who've paid top dollar for the view, knowing nothing of the people trapped up there in the trees. All the camps are closed, which means that residents are not to go out and others are not to enter without permission. Rules so stringent must be bent. Some camp residents slip out to clear the steep hillsides nearby; they gather firewood and building materials, or plant vegetables to supplement the camp's slim ration of rice. Others who need medical care or consultation at the hospital in Mae Hong Son catch rides on IRC trucks that travel daily between the town and the camps. Some camp residents are members of the IRC staff who travel back and forth with official permits or informal connivance. But everyone returns to camp. Refugees are strangers in a strange land, with no place else to go. They can't return to their own country, and they can't enter this new one that happens to house the overcrowded camps in which they live. Many refugees are grateful that camps offer things their villages lacked—things like free schools and health clinics—but nobody longs to be here. Nobody will ever be homesick for a refugee camp. Except for children born in the camps, everyone comes from someplace else—someplace just as beautiful just over the border, someplace that once was home.

That day, when I first went to Camp One to meet members of the Karenni National Women's Organization (KNWO) who had volunteered for the photo project, I wanted them to tell me about home, and how they'd come from there to here. As the truck nosed upward through groves of misty bamboo, I talked about it with my young translator, Moe Moe Aung, whose family lives in the camp. She echoed the words of other colleagues who had warned me that Karenni women are extraordinarily shy and self-contained. Their cultural traditions and the mission Christianity they learned long ago promote women's obedience and silence; and long confinement in camp swaddles the human spirit in passivity, fatalism, apathy, and despair. "It is difficult for women to talk," Moe Moe Aung said. I said I thought it might be easier for them to talk about the past, however dark, than about the dull present. Moe Moe Aung offered a wan, doubtful smile. "Maybe you will be lucky," she said.

We handed over our documents at the security checkpoint and drove into the camp. We dropped some staff members at the IRC-sponsored health clinic and climbed a steep track to the Women's Center, built like the houses of bamboo poles and grass matting and set in a compound with other small buildings—an office, a kitchen, latrines—enclosed by a bamboo fence. The women waited by the gate to greet us. They were mostly young women who had dressed with care in slim sarongs and pretty blouses and neatly braided their long black hair—prepared to meet what the day might bring. We got ourselves organized in the big, airy meeting hall, though it proved hard to find a place on the dirt floor level enough to support a plastic chair without wobbling. With Moe Moe Aung's help, we made the formal introductions and I told the volunteers about the project. Their faces were bright and eager, but after some time, when I asked them how they came to be living in this place, they went blank; the women stared at me in dismay, then looked away. We sat together through the long silence, and at last one young woman stood up and began to speak. Her name was Lu Khu Paw. She spoke quietly but with evident determination to finish the story. No one interrupted her.

"My father was shot by the SPDC when I was three years old," she said, referring to the army of Burma's ruling military junta. "After two years my mother got married again. Her husband didn't love us. The SPDC soldiers already made us suffer a lot, and my stepfather always hit and tortured us. SPDC troops often came to our village, and we had to hide in the jungle. The soldiers burned down our village, and we lived in the jungle for many years. We had no time to farm because we always had to run and keep moving from place to place, ahead of the soldiers. We didn't have our rice stores because the soldiers had burned down all the houses and stolen all our property, including our food. So in the jungle we had only bamboo shoots and bananas to eat. We had no other food and no housing, so a lot of people started to get diseases very easily. In 1996 a lot of people got malaria. They died because we had no medicine and no medic to treat them. Many people died that year.

"For me, I was faced with lots of suffering because my two brothers and one sister and I had to live apart from our mother. We wanted to be with her, but we didn't want to stay with our stepfather. When we were living in the jungle, my mother gave birth to a new baby; and we learned that the SPDC was coming in just a few hours, so we had to move to another place. It was the rainy season, and my mother started to get sick after giving birth because there was no medicine for her. My stepfather didn't take care of her and the baby when she was sick, so we tried to take care of her even though we didn't live together. But after some days she became very weak and she died.

"At that time, I really wanted to go to school, but there was no school for us because we always had to move from place to place. I thought, 'My mother has died, so who will send me to school?' I heard that there is a school in the refugee camp and that people support the refugees who want to go to school. So I decided to make my way to the refugee camp for my education. When I arrived, I had to stay with the family of my auntie who was already living in the camp. I had to work very hard and do all the housework. After I had lived with them for a year, other people who knew about my situation brought me to the boardinghouse for orphans. I am happy now to live at the boardinghouse and go to school. I thank God that he sent me to school and a safe place."

Lu Khu Paw was just learning the dialect most commonly used in camp, and she spoke with a strange accent. At first it made the others laugh a little, but in the end some were weeping. Then one by one they stood up and spoke about themselves. Common scenes recurred. SPDC soldiers enter a village; they steal chickens, pigs, rice, all the food supplies; they demand porters to carry the loot; they shoot men who try to run away; they take women into houses and do things that make the women afraid. Then the village in flames. The smoke. And after that the quick flights, time and again, just ahead of advancing SPDC soldiers, and each time the shedding of a little more of what they had once possessed until they are left with little more than the clothes on their back. People, too, are lost along the way.

Rosy said, "The SPDC always ordered the villagers to be porters and demanded fees and taxes every month. They made the villagers work for them as forced labor. Most of the men in our village, and all my brothers, had to hide in the jungle because of that. If the military didn't get men as porters, they arrested women and forced them to be porters. I couldn't continue my studies because we always had to run from the SPDC soldiers and hide in the jungle. We always felt afraid, especially young girls like us. It was very dangerous to stay in the village when the soldiers came. If they caught women as porters, they molested them and sometimes raped them. They didn't treat women as human beings."

Thaw Mar told about a time in 1996 when the SPDC forced everyone in her village to move to a relocation site; they gave the villagers no time to collect their things. "When we got to the relocation site," she said, "there were no houses to stay in and no food, no clean water. The people were crying. Some people went back to the old village, intending to farm, but when the SPDC soldiers saw them come back, they shot them dead." Reh Meh said that her village too was forced to relocate in 1996. Her father had already disappeared, and her mother decided to flee with five children to the refugee camp. Reh Meh was the eldest, though just a child. Leading a younger sister and brother, she followed her mother, who walked "for a long, long time," carrying two children, to the camp. When they arrived, Reh Meh's mother built them a house, all by herself. Reh Meh said, "I think my mother is great person."

Common themes emerged. Hunger—and the taste of bamboo. Death—in childbirth or from malaria or at the hands of the SPDC or a resistance militia. Fractured families. Beronica came to the camp with her mother after the SPDC killed her husband and her father; she brought her daughter along, but left her two sons behind in the care of a priest because she wanted them to go to the mission school while she was away.

"The woman in this picture is living alone with her children. Here she is building her own house with her own hands. Even men find it very hard to carry the wood and bamboo and collect leaves for the roof. This woman can do this job as well as a man, but she has suffered a lot, working so hard for her family."
—Naw Ra Htoo, Thailand

That was ten years ago. Thaw Mar, as a teenager, left her parents and siblings behind to come to the refugee camp by herself; she said she couldn't live with fear and violence anymore. Naw Bu Meh was separated from her parents on the trek to a relocation site; following other adults, she arrived instead at the refugee camp and found herself alone. Naw Ra Htoo also came on her own when she was six years old, tagging after adults who were walking to the camp. The SPDC had shot her parents in front of her. She said, "I had to leave home because my older siblings were still too young to be able to take care of me." She added, "I live in the boardinghouse now, but when I see my friends with their parents and brothers and sisters, I feel very sad." Naw Paw

Lweh, who lost some of her family when their village was raided and burned and others when they were hiding in the forest, said simply: "Our families were broken up."

Even in the camps, families split apart. Kee Meh's mother brought her children to the camp after her husband died. There, unable to provide for them, she married a man who said he would; but instead he drank and abused the children and kept them from school. On her mother's advice, Kee Meh got married very young, to get away from her stepfather. "Now," she said, "I live in a difficult situation just like my mother's, but I am not with her." Nearly everyone wanted to go home again to Burma, though they had spent most of their lives in camp; but some hoped for resettlement in a peaceable country. Rosy and her husband had applied to the United States; if the offer came, they would have to leave behind her husband's parents, who were very old and ill. To turn it down was to condemn their three bright daughters to life in camp. "We must choose the future," she said, "but to be forced to make such a choice—it is very cruel."

When the women finished speaking, we all seemed to feel that something had shifted. We sat together in silence again for a while, out of respect for the life they had lived and the courage they had summoned to speak about it. Then I gave them some cameras and we went to work.

In 1989, the ruling military regime transformed Burma into the Union of Myanmar, a name used historically to refer not to the country but to its dominant ethnic group. I call the country "Burma" because that's what the refugees call it. They were driven from their homes and villages by the same military regime that renamed the country. To them, the homeland they fled is still Burma, and it's still theirs. More recently the regime restyled itself as the State Peace and Development Council (SPDC). Perhaps the regime picked up Newspeak from George Orwell, who as a young man served in the British Imperial Police in Burma, a job, it's been said, that taught him everything about totalitarianism. To his great books on the subject, *Animal Farm* and *1984*, should be added another volume, the first in the trilogy: the early novel *Burmese Days*.

The totalitarian regime of the SPDC is now one of the most ruthless on earth, yet it has largely escaped the world's notice. In September 2007, the world got a brief look at protest marches led by long files of yellow-clad monks during the brave, improbable "Saffron Revolution." TV watchers glimpsed the regime's armed crackdown on the pro-democracy followers of Nobel Peace Prize laureate Aung San Suu Kyi. We witnessed the sniper shooting of a Japanese photojournalist. We saw him die in the street. I remember thinking, "If they do that to a foreign journalist in the public street in view of cameras, what will they do to the monks?" Then the news blackout resumed until May 2008, when Cyclone Nargis ravaged the southern regions, killing two hundred thousand people in the Irrawaddy Delta and displacing an estimated million more. The SPDC denied entry to the UN and international aid organizations that wished to help its citizens, the IRC among them.

Because of Aung San Suu Kyi, we know something—however vague—of Burma's pro-democracy movement. But there is another, longer war in Burma of which the world hears nothing at all: the forcible, genocidal displacement of Burma's ethnic minorities. After Cyclone Nargis, while UN Secretary General Ban Ki-moon and other prominent diplomats worked to persuade the SPDC to accept international humanitarian aid for the people in the devastated south, the SPDC's army was busy in the east of the country doing the same things that in years past had caused our photographers to flee to the refugee camps: raping and murdering villagers, driving them from their settlements, and burning their homes. Survivors were trekking to Thailand, cast out by a political cyclone that has howled off and on, below the horizon of the world's consciousness, for sixty years. The conflict between Burma's ethnic minorities and the government of Myanmar is the world's longest civil war.

It began soon after Burma gained independence from Britain in 1948 after more than a century of colonial domination. Britain had begun its conquest of Burma in 1824, folded it into the British raj in 1886, and made it a separate, self-governing colony in 1937. Then came World War II and the Japanese conquest of British Burma. A group of young Burmese soldiers dedicated to independence fought against one side and then the other—first against the British, then the Japanese—led by Aung San, a founder of the Burmese Communist Party. After the British retook the colony, Aung San became a leading politician and negotiator for independence. He was effectively prime minister of the colony when he was assassinated—at age thirty-two—on July 19, 1947, only six months before Burma gained the independence he had orchestrated. He is still venerated as the father of his country, though less so by the Karen minority, whose loyalty to the British put them at times at odds with Aung San.

When independence was granted, several ethnic minorities cited history to support their claim that their lands were separate jurisdictions and should properly be autonomous, if not independent. In fact, Britain had implied that separate status by signing an agreement in 1875 with several Karenni substates; and during World War II, in recognition of Karenni loyalty, Britain promised to safeguard the independence of Karenni

State. But against their will, the Karenni and other minorities were swept up into Burma, and when government troops entered Karenni State in 1948, the Karenni regarded it as an invasion. They organized armed resistance, as did other ethnic minorities. That was the beginning of the civil war that has no end in sight.

The conflict intensified after 1962 when General Ne Win, the head of the armed forces, seized power in a military coup. Under his regime, Burma slid deeper into poverty. Many people attributed the country's decline to Ne Win's mismanagement, but he blamed instability caused by the rebellious ethnic minorities. In the 1970s he adopted a new counterinsurgency strategy called the Four Cuts, designed to sever resistance fighters from four critical things they needed to carry on fighting: recruits, food, intelligence, and money. The people had provided all of these things. To carry out the strategy of the Four Cuts, the army turned their guns on them. What had been a conflict between the government and armed minority militias became the war the military regime wages against minority civilians.

The government intensified the pressure in the 1980s, but so did the resistance and the pro-democracy movement. Eight is a significant number in Buddhism, so when dissidents fed up with the authoritarian regime called for a general strike on the eighth day of the eighth month of 1988, the people must have thought their time had come. (It was, by chance, the year Aung San's exiled daughter Suu Kyi returned to Burma.) Citizens took to the streets to protest political repression and economic mismanagement. The army opened fire. In four days they shot thousands of people throughout the country and displaced thousands more. Yet the 1988 demonstrations reshuffled the regime, bringing to power a new junta with another Orwellian name: the State Law and Order Restoration Council (SLORC). This bunch promised free and fair multiparty elections in 1990, but to be on the safe side, they placed Aung San Suu Kyi and other leaders of her party under house arrest so they could not campaign. But SLORC had badly misjudged public opinion; Aung San Suu Kyi's National League for Democracy won resoundingly, taking 392 parliamentary seats to the government party's ten. In response to the drubbing, SLORC nullified the election results and hung on to power. Pro-democracy forces went back underground. In 2009, Aung San Suu Kyi, who had spent fourteen years under house arrest, was tried once again on absurd charges and sentenced to another eighteen months, a term just long enough to prevent her participation in Burma's next "free and fair" elections.

All the while, government violence against the ethnic minorities continued, in pockets of armed conflict, and it continues to this day. More than half a million people have been displaced from the minority states of eastern Burma alone, and an estimated two million have fled into Thailand. There hundreds of thousands work as legal migrant laborers; but they are the lucky ones. Thousands of others have no legal standing and no means of support. During the nineties, the junta compelled groups of resistance fighters to sign cease-fire agreements, even as it continued to attack civilians. As the Global Crescendo photographers said, the SPDC forced whole villages to move to distant relocation sites, where the people found no water, no food, no shelter, and no way to obtain these things. People died in wholesale lots of exhaustion, starvation, and disease. In Karenni State alone, the smallest of the minority states, it's estimated that seventy-five thousand people were forcibly removed.

And why? With resistance fighters badly weakened and civilian populations no longer able to support them, what did the government stand to gain by the forcible relocation of broken villages? The answer is vacant land and the fruit of torrential rivers: electricity, to be harvested by Chinese-built hydroelectric dams. The potential displacement of indigenous people by dam construction often sparks popular opposition and bad publicity for the builders, but in Karenni State and Karen State, the people have already been displaced. From a public relations perspective, it is as if they never existed.

The women who volunteered for the Global Crescendo Project caught on to photography in no time. Many of them were young, between eighteen and twenty-five. They were smart and literate, and though most were already married with children, they seemed happy to have something new to do during the unrelenting succession of similar days; for unlike the African women I had worked with, subject mainly to the rule of their husbands, these were more obviously, more officially, prisoners. They sorted themselves into groups of three, choosing teammates who lived nearby so they could easily pass the camera around; and each team huddled over its shiny new machine, awaiting instructions. They soon mastered the basics and more; they were the first Global Crescendo photographers who could actually read the words—such as "change batteries" or "card full"—that sometimes appeared on the screen and had terrified the nonliterate African women. Then we set off up the hill to practice shooting. They led me along invisible paths between and behind houses that had looked to me to be joined at the seams. One path led downhill past pigpens almost too small to confine the porkers inside. Space was at a premium in the camp, and pigs were even more cramped than people. Another path took us to a flat plot of ground in front of the school where men were playing ferocious volleyball. Another carried us uphill again to a building where women were weaving bright sarongs. Before long we were back at the Karenni National Women's Organization center, having completed the circuit of this section. There was much more to the camp, up and over the hills, but it seemed an impossible effort to walk on. The road was steep and muddy, the heat intense, the sun blazing. The women walked slowly, shielded by umbrellas. Why would you walk on in camp when you had seen it all before? When you knew that all too soon you would reach the point where you could do nothing but turn back? Why would you walk any-where in this heat? What I came to recognize as the ennui of camp settled over us so naturally it was indistinguishable from the weather. I asked the women to take photos of things impor-tant to them, both positive and problematic, and told them I'd be back in a week to take a look.

During the week I visited the camp again to start a second photo group there, and I traveled to a second, smaller camp, a three-hour drive from Mae Hong Son to organize a third. Camp Two lay along a river, on the floor of a narrow valley between abrupt mountains. Driving in, we forded the meandering river six or seven times, and in the following weeks, as the rains began, the river grew deeper, mounting over the hubs and over the tires. I asked the driver, "What happens when the river is too deep to cross?" "You walk in," he said. "Over the mountain. Long walk. Long time." Because the camp was so far from Mae Hong Son, my translator, Hom, and I often stayed there overnight, sleeping, as everyone did, on a grass mat on the floor. We stayed in the house of one of the medics, Naw Bu Meh, who had been trained by the IRC for work in the camp's clinic. She loved her career, especially because the war had kept her from getting much education; she hadn't been able to start school until she was thirteen. Not long after that, the SPDC burned her village and relocated the people. Separated from her parents in the process, she and her sister made their way to the refugee camp. When she married and built a house in camp, she planted a palm tree in the yard to help her measure the time. Two years ago she buried the husband she met in camp; she cares for their four children alone, but they are nearly grown. The palm tree has also grown to tower over the house, even though the house stands tall on stilts. One day, at her request, I took a photo of Naw Bu Meh and her eldest daughter standing on opposite sides of the tree, stretching out their arms, unable to encircle it, unable to encompass the time passed in this place. In the evening, after sharing a meal of noodles or beans, we would sit together on the floor, not far from the tree, and Naw Bu Meh would tell small pieces of her story to Hom, who softly translated them to me. She was grieving for her husband. When it was completely, absolutely dark—dark as it is only in the absence of electricity—we would creep away to our mats to sleep.

As the rains continued, the low wooden pontoon bridges within the camp washed away, and pedestrians switched to perilous suspension bridges of bamboo poles and rope slung over the stream. There, where the foaming river plunged between vertical green mountains, slim, delicate women would float over the bridges, holding aloft their bright umbrellas. I took photos then, and the images seemed to be exquisite renderings of an idyllic locale, romantic and dreamy. The contrast between the look of the place and the lives lived there set me back. A photo is not always worth a thousand words. Sometimes you need the words to grasp the photo; without them, you would never know that the graceful lady with the rosy umbrella passing over the pretty river has no place to go.

When I went back to the camps to look at the photographers'

work, I wasn't surprised that it was slim. At first only twenty photos from Pu Meh, almost forty from Su Meh, who took the most, and only ten from Bu Meh. There was a sameness to things in the camp, much like the women's names, that concealed distinctive subjects. Then there was the apathy, the heat, in addition to the chores of daily life. But the number of photos they shot increased from week to week as the women began to see that a photograph could uncover a subject that had gone unnoticed right there in plain sight. A photo could pin down a fact so that people could see it. A photo could open your eyes.

The first slideshow of their own photos amazed and pleased them. It was certain proof that they had succeeded in using the cameras. These women were much more familiar than the African villagers with modern imagery; they decorated their houses with glossy photos of Thai and Indian pop stars. In their own work they recognized themselves, their families, their friends, and they thought everyone looked just fine. But when I asked them to talk about the photos—about why they had taken them and why they were important—silence filled the room. Talking about photos seemed much harder than taking them. They had never done it before, and I suspected they were still suffering the aftershocks of the stories they had so bravely told during our first meetings. So we started small. Each woman sat down with a partner and told her about a photo: what it depicted, why she had taken it, what it meant to her. It was the partner's job to listen and then ask questions to learn more. Then we switched partners, and in this way the women made their way around the room, talking. Moe Moe Aung, the translator who had warned me that Karenni women don't talk, smiled approvingly as hesitant whispers grew like a rain-swollen river to a rush of voices. We brought the voices to full volume by asking each woman to explain what she had learned about another woman's photograph, this time to a partner who was not seated next to her but across the room. It was an absurd situation—Karenni women never raise their voices—and it made them laugh. After that, when I asked if anyone wanted to tell the whole group about her own most important photo, hands went up all over the room. Moe Moe Aung said to me, "You really are very lucky." Lucky, and like these women, ready to work in earnest.

By the third week they could take turns leading the discussion themselves, although very few had ever done such a thing before. One was so nervous, standing in front of the group, that

"I took this picture of a sick woman at the clinic to show that although there is illness and disease in camp, there is also basic free health care. Women get nutrition and medicine for their health, especially pregnant women."

—Say Meh, Thailand

she couldn't stop giggling. Contagion set the others giggling too and punctuated the whole discussion. Nevertheless, they produced long lists of the positive and negative things they had snapped with their cameras, and they numbered them in order of priority. At the top of the positive list stood the camps' free schools for girls and boys alike, and free schoolbooks. The free health clinics were a close second. (Aung San Suu Kyi reported that in Burma in the nineties, the junta spent less than 5 percent of its budget on schools, less than 1 percent on health; for Karenni women, having access to any school or clinic, let alone free ones, was an astonishment.) Next came the Karenni National Women's Organization—many thought it should come first—and the opportunities it provided for women to learn such money-making skills as weaving and sewing. Fourth on the list were the camps' elected Section Leaders (all men), whose responsibility it is to help solve problems and settle disputes. All the items on the women's list are manifestations of peace and order and good governance that no longer exist in Burma; and the schools suggest a better future. Also on the list was the support of the IRC and other NGOs that made possible the schools, the clinics, the women's center, and the work of KNWO in the camps. One woman likened refugees to trees and NGOs to the sun that enables them to grow. "Without the sun," she said, "we could stand up, but we would be standing in the dark."

Hope rests on future prospects, but problems lodge in day-to-day life. The greatest of these, the photographers said, turning to their list of problems, is the danger posed by the SPDC army, camped just across the border, less than an hour's march through the forest. "We are not safe," one said, and the others agreed. It is impossible to banish the fear of sudden attack, for everyone still remembers that the army crossed the Thai border more than once in 1996 to assault the refugee camps. Here, closed in these camps, they were sitting ducks. That insecurity was not simply the first problem on their list; it was a dark cloud of anxiety that never lifted from their lives. Beneath that cloud, their list of problems was a catalog of things they lacked. They had no freedom of movement. No jobs. No livelihoods. No future. Refugees are said to be "provided for." All those positive things the women mentioned—schools, clinics, livelihood skills training, and governance, plus allotments of staple foods—are given to them. Paradoxically, the gifts seem to require gratitude that diminishes the value of the gratitude they genuinely feel. Somehow they can never be grateful enough for the gifts that ease their lives, though the gifts also abrade their self-respect. Self-sufficiency dims in memory, and the future folds into the endlessly repeating present where depression lies, attended by its classic medication, alcohol, that leads in turn to neglect, abuse, and violence.

Domestic violence was high on the list of problems. The women said it is widespread among the more than twenty thousand people crowded into Camp One. They wanted to document it in photographs, as so many African women had done. (I'd shown them photos taken in Côte d'Ivoire and Liberia of men beating women in the streets.) They wanted to show such photographs to the camp leaders so that men would have to acknowledge the violence women face every day. But here the violence takes place indoors, they said, and not in the streets. Here no one dares to interfere. People live on top of each other in the camp, separated from neighbors by walls of grass. "You know your neighbors can hear what's happening," one photographer said, "but if you cry out, no one comes."

I had to remind them that photographers must consider their own safety. They did, and none of them dared enter a neighbor's house to photograph—or help—a woman under attack. Instead they started to photograph women after the fact. They produced many portraits of women and children who, they said, were regularly beaten and abused and sexually violated by the man of the family. But I had to ask, "Can we show these photos without exposing the women to shame, or danger?" The photographers said no. Frustrated and angry, they had questions too. How would the men be punished? How would they be stopped?

The photographers told me that women endured violence because they saw no other choice. Many thought that complaining would end their hopes (and their children's prospects) of resettlement in another country and they believed that if they divorced their husbands they would be in greater danger. One divorced woman had been raped thirteen times by her ex-husband. Confined to camp, she had no escape. I asked the women why, when everyone had run away from violence in Burma, there was so much violence here. "Women run away from violence," one said. "Men carry it with them."

The GBV program had been working closely with the camp community, especially KNWO, to tackle the problem. The GBV program had started a men's violence prevention project called "Men Involved in Peace-building" (MIP); it tried to work with men to quell their smoldering violence. Older men especially, who had been robbed of their country, their land, their work, their status, and almost all the traditional roles that once defined their identity, had little left but their despair and rage; they took it out on the only people over whom they still seemed to be able to exercise some control, their wives and children. They showed little interest in building peace at home. To protect women and children in camp, the IRC built Women's Community Centers (WCCs) where they could find help and temporary shelter, while MIP turned its attention to youth groups—teenage boys and girls together—in an effort to stop the generational recycling of family violence. But the violence went on.

The photographers struggled with the problem of how to present the issue of violence in their photos, and every week they brought more somber portraits—that we couldn't show—of women and children they knew to be living with violent men. I pondered the obvious paradox: men and women alike worried incessantly about the slim possibility of an SPDC cross-border attack, while right there in camp countless women and children lived day after day under the repeated assaults of a single violent man.

At last the photographers came up with a solution to their quandary: since they didn't dare shoot violence in progress in another family's house, and they couldn't show photos of abused women without endangering them, they would photograph happy—nonviolent—families. These photos, they said, would give them a chance to talk about family happiness and its opposite: abuse, fear, violence, and disintegration. But photographing happiness wasn't easy either. Hla Won Nya showed us a portrait of another photographer, Martinar, with her husband and three little children. "This is a very happy family," she said, and because we all knew Martinar, we knew it to be true. "But I think it is a problem," Hla Won Nya said, "that they don't look happy." Faced with the task of posing for a formal portrait, Martinar, her husband, and the kids had put on somber faces fit for a funeral. The photo wouldn't work. But Beronica came up with a picture of a man squatting on the ground with his tools, making something out of wood, while his wife relaxed in a hammock close at hand. The woman had kicked off her sandals. Beronica said, "This is a happy family. This is how a family should be."

While the photographers snapped images to illustrate their

message of nonviolence, I thought about the questions they'd raised. How would abusive men be punished? How would they be stopped? GBV work almost always starts, anywhere, with prevention and protection. Here in the camps, the GBV program worked with women, men, and youth groups to raise awareness about violence. (That's prevention.) It built community centers where women and children could take shelter. (That's protection.) It formed special teams among health care workers—Response to Crisis Teams, or RCTs—and trained them to treat survivors of battery and rape. (That's also protection. That essential medical treatment, provided promptly, can protect a woman from unwanted pregnancy, and from HIV and other sexually transmitted infections as well.) Still, what about the perpetrators? What about justice?

In the refugee camps, justice lies with camp security officers who investigate and arrest, section leaders who mediate disputes, and judges who preside over camp justice courts. Almost all of these officials are men. The GBV team saw that abused women who brought complaints to them were more likely to be punished than helped; like many men everywhere, they were inclined to believe the old notion that women subjected to violence were asking for it. So the IRC came up with something new. In each camp, it established a Legal Assistance Center (LAC), a walk-in office staffed by lawyers ready to help complainants take their cases to camp justice or outside the camp to the Thai judicial system, as is their right. As far as I know, these are the first legal-aid centers to be established in refugee camps anywhere. The centers helped abused women seek justice, but it remained elusive. One frustrated Thai lawyer told me, "Camp authorities don't acknowledge women's rights. They're bound by the traditions of a culture that silences women, and those traditions are self-fulfilling: women don't get justice so they quit trying."

The LAC lawyers didn't give up. They realized that most cases adjudicated in camp came down to "she said, he said." She said he beat her or raped her; he said they had a family "discussion" or "made love." Such events don't always leave a woman with visible injuries, but often they do. The lawyers were sure that if authorities could see a woman's injuries, they would understand that real violence had occurred—and they would have to change their minds. What the lawyers needed to make a case was photographic evidence. With that in mind, nearly a year earlier, the LAC team had drawn up some guidelines, consistent with camp justice and Thai judicial requirements, and taught the Response to Crisis Teams how photographs could be used as evidence in legal cases. UNHCR provided funds for a couple of cameras, but there was no one to teach the women how to use them. Abby, the GBV manager, gave me the hint: "It would be great if the RCTs could learn to use those cameras they got from UNHCR." I offered to teach them, but I found that the cameras—still in their original packages—were outdated, inexpensive plastic film cameras, unsuited to the climate and the job. Thinking that the Global Crescendo Project would end in a few months, I e-mailed my boss in New York: "I think I've found a good home for a few of our loyal Global Crescendo cameras." She approved.

The GBV staff in Mae Hong Son quickly selected a team of forensic photographers for each camp, made up of first responders: medics from the Response to Crisis Teams, Women's Community Center staff, and key leaders of KNWO. We managed to include in each team one or two women who had already been shooting for a few weeks with the Global Crescendo Project.

The lawyers on the LAC staff updated the photodocumentation guidelines, and I led training sessions for the aspiring forensic photographers. The Global Crescendo Project donated five cameras—one for each place in Camp One and Camp Two where an assaulted woman was likely to turn for help.

Worried that the women couldn't master forensic photography in the short time we had to work together, I asked them to practice shooting fake victims. Within a few days they produced images—shot according to the legal protocol, in the right order from all the right angles—of several women terribly bruised, one with a broken arm, another with a massive head wound, another whose throat had been cut. All the wounds and injuries had been contrived with makeup, but they were

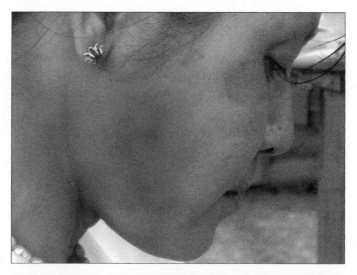

Global Crescendo photographer Naw Pa Lweh joined a forensic photodocumentation team and took this picture of a volunteer model with simulated bruises at a practice session. As a leader of the Karenni National Women's Organization in the camp, she was among the first responders to wife beating.

—Naw Pa Lweh, Thailand

modeled on real damage to real women that all these first responders had seen. Initially the photographers working in the Global Crescendo Project at Camp Two had told me that there was no domestic violence in their camp. None. It wasn't surprising that less violence occurred in Camp Two; it was much smaller and more spacious, its houses fewer and farther between and better built. Civic organizations and churches boosted community solidarity and raised spirits. But "none" seemed impossible to me. The medics from Camp Two provided evidence of the hidden problem when they applied makeup to their fake victims for photo practice. They duplicated case after case they had treated themselves but never spoken about, having been trained to abide by the medical code of confidentiality. They knew exactly what domestic violence was, and when it came to documenting abuse, they quickly learned how to do it.

Meanwhile, the forensic photographers at Camp One honed their skills, stuffing wads of toilet paper under a fake victim's hair to create a swelling on the back of her head. A medic trained her camera on the shredded white stuff peeking from the simulated head wound and said, "This contusion seems to be leaking brains."

Another medic on the team said, "That looks to me like a significant extrusion. Could be fatal."

The counselor from the Women's Community Center waved the printed guidelines. "Remember!" she said. "A life-threatening injury must be treated before you take the pictures."

Within two weeks, GBV's first-ever forensic photography teams documented two cases of wife beating for presentation to the authorities. A few months later, long after I had left Thailand, Abby sent me a newspaper article headlined "IRC-Trained Forensic Photographers Bring Justice to Refugees." The article quoted the woman who headed the legal assistance centers in the camps: "We have successfully used photographic evidence in a number of the cases." And it quoted Naw Paw, one of the first responders I'd trained at Camp One: "In the camp there was a lot of domestic abuse," she said, "but the community was not willing to do anything to help. I often hid beaten women in my house. With this job, I feel like I can make a difference. I talk to the women and help them get to the camp clinic for medical treatment. And now, with my camera, I can also help bring the perpetrators to justice." There it was—the answer to the "culture of impunity." But to get past impunity to accountability, women needed more than a camera. They needed a functioning system of justice already in place. In so many crippled countries in Africa and elsewhere, that was the catch. But here in these closed camps in Thailand it was the opportunity.

While the forensic photographers practiced, I worried about the photo exhibitions—the grand finale of the Global Crescendo Project. Most of the women had never spoken in public before they joined the project, during which they had spoken to groups consisting of only fourteen other women. I remembered my colleagues' early warnings that these women are too shy to speak; so although they had been speaking nonstop for weeks, I tried to give them the opportunity to practice. I suggested they invite only their family and friends to the photo show; and later, perhaps during the observance of International Woman's Day, the GBV staff could arrange another show for important community leaders.

The women stared at me as if I'd lost my mind. They huddled to make a list of people they wanted to invite. Then they handed over the names of every prominent official in camp. So much for practice. And as for refreshments: they wanted fried chicken and sticky rice for lunch. Fried chicken and sticky rice is by Thai standards a relatively expensive dish. It's not usually available in the camps. My translator Moe Moe Aung was laughing. "It's good," she said. "You'll like it." I wondered what had become of "shy."

I wish I could say that when the big day arrived all the leaders came and listened and changed their ways and put a stop to violence forever. That didn't happen. Many of the leaders didn't attend. Perhaps they were too busy, or perhaps they too were subject to the ennui of camp life or the heat. But some Camp One leaders did make the long uphill climb to the KNWO compound, enticed by the prospect of viewing the first-ever, never-before-seen-in-our-camp All-Women's Photographic Exhibition and Ceremony.

The photographers gathered early to blow up balloons and hang a handmade banner modestly announcing the "Karenni Women's Photography Show." They arranged the furniture and set out programs and cans of soda and water for the audience. Then they cracked betel nuts as they waited for their guests to arrive, and when it became clear that many of them would not come, they began the show. After welcoming speeches from KNWO and the IRC, I explained our project, with Moe Moe Aung's help. Then Lu Khu Paw, the brave young woman who had been the first to speak at our first meeting, stood before the audience and held up a photo of some men and women sitting on the deck of a house. The men in the photo look startled; although they are seated on the floor, they seem to be backing away.

"I took this photograph," Lu Khu Paw said. "It shows men getting ready to run away from the visit of some women from the camp's Gender-Based Violence working group. I want to talk about such men who turn away from the education and awareness-raising offered by the domestic violence team. Most of the men in camp don't want to listen and learn. But if they listen to people from the domestic violence team, they will learn how the problem starts and how they can solve it by themselves. They will even learn how they can help the community solve such problems. We know that most men don't like to listen; but we hope that at least men can see. We took these photographs of things going on in our community so that men can look and see and learn."

She stepped aside, and one by one the other photographers came forward to join her. They held up their pictures and spoke about life in the camp as they saw it. There were photos of polluted streams and piles of garbage standing nearby.

"In this picture you see many people bathing in a small outdoor enclosure. Men, women, and children are bathing at the same time in this crowded space. Women are very sensitive about it, but they have no choice. The bathing place is very near the road where lots of people are walking, so it is neither private nor safe for the women who are bathing."

—Pu Meh, Thailand

Photos of flimsy grass-walled houses crowded together. Photos of men, women, and children huddled around water spigots right next to the road, trying to bathe modestly with their clothes on. Photos of widows and old women doing hard labor: building their own houses, hauling firewood, cultivating near-vertical fields. A photo of students sharing a meager meal in the overcrowded Camp One boardinghouse for orphans. A photo of a longtime camp resident glassy-eyed with depression. There were photos of schoolchildren, carrying in their bookbags the hopes of two or three generations; and photos of women weaving and wearing the traditional garments that anchored their lives in a valuable past. There were photographs of refugees in the churches, heads bowed in prayer for the victims of Cyclone Nargis—prayers of the survivors of one disastrous storm for the victims of another, back home.

When the women finished, Moe Moe Aung and I presented their certificates, and then those few male dignitaries in attendance—section leaders and camp security committee members—rose to commend the women on their work. Each speaker groped for words to respond to what he'd seen and heard. One apologized for the absence of leaders who'd failed to come. One suggested the women should have a photo gallery so young people and civic leaders alike could see their work. Another suggested a book. A few days later, after the show at Camp Two, a camp security man said, "The pictures showed us many things like health care and education, and they showed us many difficulties women have faced because of the political crisis." (Political crisis is an Orwellian term for war; people learn to speak that way, coming up against the junta.) "The pictures showed us difficulties we might not have noticed or paid enough attention to. The women who attended this training must continue documenting things in camp. As your teacher said, 'You are a camera, even when you don't have a camera.' I would like to encourage you to continue working on these issues because you are making a very important contribution to the community."

Many staff members from the IRC office came with us to Camp One to see the first photo show, including Mubi, the young Karenni woman who was Abby's right hand in the GBV program, training to take over soon. I could see that Mubi was moved by all these young women speaking up, and afterward she rose to speak herself on behalf of the IRC. "Normally," she said, "Karenni women are quite shy and do not really express what they think or what they believe, but it doesn't mean that they are ignoring the problems. It means there is a gap between women and action." The gap was there, she said, because Karenni women had little education, little support, little to inspire their confidence or encourage them to step forward. "That is why women are limited at the community level, the national level, and the international level—reticent to give voice to improve the peaceful ways in their society. It is important to empower women," Mubi said, "because they can make change to improve conditions for the whole community. This project supports Karenni women," she said. "And it empowers them to use their eyes, to speak up, and to use their voices for voiceless people. Now the women are able to present their photos to the community leaders. The women are able to stand in front of the public and express what their photos reveal about our community, both positive and negative things. This exhibition made people aware that women must be part of the community to make change. It made the community leaders aware that women are important. Unless women take part in making change, there will still be a gap between the roles of female and male in the community, between the beliefs of women and the action of men; and problems in the home, in the community, and in the nation will never be solved."

There stood Mubi, making the case that women are essential to crafting durable peace just as it might have been presented to the UN Security Council contemplating passage of Resolution 1820. (Later she sent me a letter with a copy of her remarks, signed with a flourish: Mubi, A Karenni Woman.) Without the voices of women there can be no lasting peace anywhere in the world, yet men the world over have devised systems to silence them, and even to make their oppression appear picturesque. I had visited Mubi's mother and grandmother— her father and grandfather are dead—who reside in a refugee village purpose-built as a tourist attraction. Mubi's mother and grandmother were offered homes there because they still proudly wear the brass neck rings and ankle-to-knee leg bracelets that are the traditional earthly treasure of Karenni women.

Thai tour companies bring international vacationers to see an "authentic hill-country village" and buy authentic weavings from authentic Thai hill-country people, still enjoying the freedom to practice their own traditions. Except that they are not really authentic Thai people and not really free to remove their neck rings and leg bracelets, though each set weighs a good twenty-five pounds. And they are not free to come and go as they please because they are really Karenni refugees and the authentic Thai village is really a refugee camp—though tourists are spared that troubling information. One day we all had lunch in the kitchen at the back of Mubi's mother's house and talked politics, and then we moved to the breezier front deck that faced the main pathway through the village. A tour group passed on the trail below, gaping up at us. They pointed. They snapped pictures. As if they were visitors to a human zoo where on exhibit were colorful hill-country women—who may truly be an endangered species.

Yet, as Mubi said, our photography project did make some difference. A few months later, on the occasion of International Women's Human Rights Defenders Day, KNWO held a women's march and an assembly that included an encore presentation of the Karenni Women's Photography Show, this time before an audience that included almost all of the community leaders. And when Pu Meh presented her photo of men and women bathing together and argued that women should have separate places to bathe, the chairman of the Karenni National Refugee Committee came forward to support the idea as a matter of protection. UNHCR took the issue seriously, and the IRC, responsible for water and sanitation in the camps, soon began to change the bathing stations into separate facilities for women and men. It seems that officials had never thought of it before because no one in the Karenni community had mentioned that it might be a problem. It had been a problem only for women, but this time they spoke up, and they presented evidence. And things changed. Now life will be just a little easier, a little more comfortable, a little safer for women and girls in the camps. And next time, those shy Karenni women will speak up again. That's a victory. But the camps are still camps where a woman may marry and grow old and bury a husband. And they're still closed.

When I drove out of Camp Two the river had risen above the door sills, and the driver said, "Next time, you walk in." But there wasn't to be a next time. Abby had gone on leave, so I worked in the office alone for a few days, finishing up my work. I paid a last visit to the Wat, took leave of my colleagues, and left. I expected to go on to another assignment in Jordan or

Iraq, but the IRC was not yet fully established in the region and GBV would have to wait. In the meantime, I helped the IRC plan its big exhibition of the Global Crescendo photographs to take place at UN headquarters in New York when the General Assembly was in session. Then I waited for the GBV unit to set up shop in the Middle East; but I soon grew tired of waiting and took off by myself.

# 6

# IRAQI REFUGEES IN JORDAN, SYRIA, LEBANON: BLOWN APART

Now it was my turn to take photos. I squinted through the viewfinder of my 35mm digital camera and framed a shot: a stolid middle-aged woman standing in the living room of a small ground-floor apartment in Amman, Jordan, behind three of her daughters seated on chairs. The daughters might have been triplets, but in fact they were stairsteps, two years apart in age: Rania was thirty-one, Roula thirty-three, and Ruba thirty-five. They were very pretty, with the round, soft look of women who stay in the house and don't get much exercise. Patriarchal authority keeps many women at home, but Siham's daughters had been confined by illness and war.

Ruba's hands flew to her hair. "Oh," she cried. Her sisters laughed and clutched their heads. Ruba reached between the cushions of her chair and pulled out a long tube made of some stretchy knit fabric. She tugged it over her head to hide her hair. In the Alps it might have been a ski hood, but among Iraqi women it was a handy modern Islamic veil. Roula found hers on the coffee table, and Rania drew one from her pocket. I had already taken some shots, but the women made me promise never to show the photos in which they were not properly covered. They are respectable. They had forgotten their hijab only because we were all women together in their own living room on a sunny morning, and because they were so excited. They are refugees from Iraq who can't go home again, but they had been accepted for resettlement in Sweden. They expected to leave very soon.

"We have given so many things away," Ruba said. "That is why our rooms seem bare."

"They told us we would leave last month," Rania said, "so we even gave away our warm clothes."

"Yes," Roula said, laughing. "And now we are cold."

"What do you know about Sweden?" I asked.

The daughters laughed so uproariously that even their weary, serious mother joined in. "Nothing!" Ruba said. "Nothing at all."

"Have you been to Sweden?" the mother asked.

I admitted I had, and then there was no escaping their questions, the answers to which unavoidably included some mention of the beauty of snow. But when they realized the foolishness of discarding warm clothes in preparation for a move to Sweden, they laughed all the harder. "It is a good joke on us," Roula said, and they were off again.

I caught the eye of Fatima, the woman who had brought me here, and she cocked an eyebrow as if to say, "I told you so." What she had told me was that the spirit of Iraqi women is the gift of Allah. Fatima was an Iraqi refugee too, but she was a civil engineer who had come to Jordan with her college-student sons and her businessman husband, who had deposited $100,000 in a Jordanian bank and thus acquired for the family a limited but legal residency. The family had fled Baghdad because one of the sons had been kidnapped there and held for ransom. As violence increased in Iraq, many people fled for the same reason; but

The widow Siham (standing) with her daughters (*left to right*) Ruba, Roula, and Rania, in the apartment in Amman, where they waited to depart for Sweden.                                        —Ann Jones

Fatima and her family, having money, had landed on their feet in a comfortable apartment in a good neighborhood, though not quite good enough to safeguard the family cat from having its whiskers burned off by a Jordanian neighbor resentful of Iraqi "guests." Fatima consoled the cat and went to work to help other Iraqis. She took a job as a project director at a women's shelter run by a Jordanian women's organization and funded by UNHCR. That's where I met her and where she told me about the strength and resourcefulness of Iraqi women in the face of disaster. "I will show you," she said, "so you can see for yourself." That morning, at her insistence, I met her at a beauty parlor, where she had just had her long, lustrous black hair washed and beautifully styled. She donned her own Islamic ski tube, squashing her lovely hair, and took me to Siham's living room.

There's another layer to the story, for the way to the heart of the matter is a trail that leads from one person to the next. My odyssey had started at the UNHCR office in Amman. The IRC was still delicately negotiating to establish a presence on the unsteady ground of the Middle East, but UNHCR had been at work here for a very long time. In Jordan, in years past, UNHCR had assisted thousands of Palestinian refugees, and now it was working overtime to help Iraqis. I offered to contribute photographs and stories for its media campaigns to draw the world's attention to a humanitarian crisis already out of hand. The director passed me on to the protection officer, the person who could introduce me to refugees wanting to tell their stories; and she asked a colleague to take me to the shelter to meet Fatima, who later drove me to the small apartment where she sat on the couch drinking tea while I photographed Siham and her daughters and listened to their story.

Siham said she had been a widow for most of her life; her husband had died in 1977, when she was just twenty-five years old, leaving her with five small children. "My life since then," she said, "is my jihad, my struggle to preserve our lives."

I asked the obvious question: "How do you live?"

She touched her fingertips to her forehead and her lips. "God exists," she said.

But it was Siham who had done the work. She and her children lived in Tikrit, a small city famous as the birthplace of mighty militarists: Saladin and Saddam Hussein. There Siham had bought cheap produce and prepared meals to sell to fancy shops. She made clothing for her children and for sale. Even now she made beadwork jewelry for Jordanian boutiques. The family was very poor, but they survived; and the children went to school. Siham's oldest daughter married at nineteen, just before the start of the first Gulf war, and moved away.

Then in 1991, American forces bombed Tikrit. Even that, Siham and her children survived.

A few years later, when Ruba had become a secretary and Rania and Roula were still in school, the girls began to complain of pain in their muscles. They felt weak and unsteady. They were overcome by fatigue. They went to the hospital for help, but they found none. The bombing had destroyed diagnostic equipment and labs and pharmacies. These things could not be replaced because sanctions were in effect. Many physicians had already left the country, and the pace of departure quickened when war threatened to come again; soon there were few physicians left, all of them overworked. Gradually the girls lost control of their muscles, but it had become too difficult and dangerous to travel to the dysfunctional hospital. By the time the United States invaded the country a second time, Siham's daughters could barely stand. As the second war went on, they lost control of their bodily functions and their hands, and because the tongue is also a muscle, they lost the power to utter intelligible speech. Desperate, Siham somehow managed to get them to a doctor who thought he knew what was wrong with them. He thought it had something to do with the toxic effect of bombs and smoke and burning chemicals in Tikrit in 1991, and indeed their symptoms resembled those of many American veterans of the first Gulf war whose mysterious illnesses forced the Pentagon to acknowledge the reality of Gulf War Syndrome. But the Iraqi doctor who knew what he was looking at had no medicine to treat the condition. And so, one by one, Siham's daughters sat down and stopped speaking and folded their useless hands and consigned themselves to the care of their mother.

In 2007 Siham caught the attention of a small Iraqi charitable organization that arranged for her and her daughters to move to Amman where the daughters could receive physical therapy.

The treatments had no effect. In Amman Siham sought help from a European humanitarian organization that sent her daughters at last for proper diagnostic exams. All three were found to have an infection in what Siham calls "the base of the brain." Medication was prescribed, and the Red Cross agreed to provide it, though now Siham must make a long trip once a month and wait in line to collect it. Siham registered the family with UNHCR and received some financial support. CARE offered a monthly payment to help with rent. Fatima found her a sewing machine. After six months on the medication, the daughters showed improvement. The infection lessened; their mobility increased. When I met them that morning, they had been taking the medication for ten months. They could wiggle their fingers and clench their fists; they could speak again; and by holding on to the back of her chair, Ruba could stand up. They laughed as though life were a lark.

The doctors couldn't say whether Siham's daughters would ever be fully restored. But in Sweden their treatment would continue free of charge in the public health system. And Siham had been told that an aide would come to their home to help her care for her girls. She had asked her son to come to Jordan to help her, and he had tried; but Jordan doesn't admit single Iraqi men of fighting age. Having nothing left in Iraq, he went to Egypt to live with his eldest sister and her husband, who had fled the second American invasion. Siham said sadly, "Sweden is very far from Egypt, I think." But she went on, "In Sweden, a woman will come sometimes to help us." She smiled for the first time. "I hope I may take a rest. Just a small rest. You understand."

Later Fatima said to me, "That was a story of the Iraqi woman's spirit."

It was also a story about the long-term consequences of war. Made sick by one war and deprived of medical care by the punitive sanctions, Siham's daughters were made worse by a second war. They may be saved—and Siham may be saved from a life of caretaking—only if international humanitarians transport them far away from home and homeland to a snowy place that offers hope and care conducted in a language they do not know.

"Fatima," I said, "I know I should feel uplifted by Siham's spirit, and her daughters' too. But their lives are so difficult and so sad, I can't help feeling depressed."

"You should be depressed," she said. "Your country did this."


The flight from Iraq began long ago. Iraqis fled Saddam Hussein's regime (1979–2003) to escape political persecution or military service during the Iran-Iraq war (1980–1988). They fled the first Gulf war (1991). They fled the suffocating sanctions (1990–2003). Some of those refugees in exile nurtured sectarian agendas and, like Ahmad Chalabi, coached the Americans for the Shock and Awe invasion of 2003. In its aftermath, three hundred thousand exiles returned to Iraq, either voluntarily or because their legal standing as refugees from Saddam Hussein's persecution was revoked by host countries when the regime fell. But even as they returned, others left. Those with the most to lose led the way. Hundreds of academics, doctors, judges, and lawyers were murdered; thousands of their colleagues fled the country. Iraq's education and health care systems, once state-subsidized first-class services, were devastated—as were citizens, like Siham's daughters, who needed them. Justice, law, and order dissolved. Militias, religious fanatics, and criminal gangs ruled. UNHCR reported that they targeted all sorts of Iraqis, for many different reasons: "their public status, (perceived) political views, sectarian identity, engagement in 'Western' activities or other alleged 'un-Islamic' behaviour, and perceived wealth." As Iraq descended into chaos, life grew ever more difficult and dangerous. Analysts usually cite the bombing of the gold-domed Shiite shrine in Samarra in February 2006 as the event that turned random "sectarian violence" into "civil war." Perhaps more important, it turned widespread flight into mass exodus.

American officials in Washington and the Green Zone fortress in Baghdad routinely used those terms to blame Iraqis—for *their* sectarian violence, *their* civil war—and belatedly they groped for a plan to stop it. A year later, they embarked on "A New Way Forward," a strategy to restore order to Baghdad with a "surge" of 28,000 soldiers: one brigade in January 2007; another in February, when Operation Imposing Law was launched; and another in March. In April a fourth brigade was deployed to Diyala. A fifth and final brigade arrived in Baghdad in May. But by that time an estimated 4.7 million Iraqis—17 percent of the population—had been driven from their homes, and at least two million of them had fled the country.

Only a few months later, in September 2007, General David Petraeus, the acknowledged architect of the strategy, cautiously reported to Congress that as a result of the surge, violence in Baghdad had been reduced significantly and "fragile" and "reversible" improvements had been made. He told Congress that the surge produced "improvements" in Baghdad in part because it deployed forces to "protect Iraqi civilians." But Iraqis told a different story. Civilian casualties had increased—to more than 1,500 killed in July 2007—and so had the body count of unidentified Iraqi corpses found each day in Baghdad streets. In April 2007, the UN High Commissioner for Refugees reported that "one in eight Iraqis have been driven from their homes." In August the International Organization for Migration and the Red Crescent confirmed that the number of Iraqis fleeing their homes had "more than doubled" with the onset of the surge, and the tally of those fleeing the country had risen dramatically. At the same time, formerly mixed neighborhoods became distinctly homogeneous. It was hard to avoid the conclusion that the surge, which George W. Bush described in his 2007 State of the Union address as an effort to "help Iraqi forces to clear and secure neighborhoods," had organized the chaotic criminal violence so many refugees describe into efficient ethnic and sectarian cleansing. During the surge, Baghdad's Shiite citizens increased their relative numbers from 65 percent to 75 percent of the population, turning Baghdad into a Shiite city, much like Tehran, in which Sunnis could no longer hold their own.

During the course of the war, millions of Iraqis became part of what UNHCR describes as "the most significant displacement in the Middle East" since the movement of Palestinians following the creation of Israel in 1948. Thousands of Iraqis fled to Europe or beyond, but most refugees slipped into the neighboring countries—Syria, Jordan, Lebanon—where they rented apartments to wait for the war to end. For the most part, Iraqi refugees are urbanized, educated people who—before the war at least—had property, jobs, businesses, careers, and savings. They look like anybody else from the Middle East. They share a common language. To Western visitors, they are indistinguishable from local citizens; to the outside world they are invisible because they are not crowded together, confined behind bamboo walls or barbed wire, or massed in blue-tented camps visited by Angelina Jolie, snapped by news photographers and spread on TV. They are scattered. Except for the assistance some get from UNHCR, they are on their own.

As they were in their calamity. Listen to Iraqi refugees and "sectarian violence" and "civil war" become oversimplifications that don't cover what's gone on. Every refugee has a story of loss and terror, a personal disaster that inspired flight. Yet, as UNHCR reported, "the sheer number of actors actively engaged in violent activities in today's Iraq" has made it almost impossible for their victims to know who attacked them, or why. Many refugees scarcely know what hit them. They don't call it civil war. One explained: "Saddam used to be the bad boss. Now every gang in Iraq has a bad boss. Any Iraqi can be a little Saddam." Indeed, Saddam was notorious for wholesale extortion; he imprisoned citizens and solicited bribes for their release. In post-Saddam Iraq, kidnapping for ransom became everybody's game.

Othman, twenty-eight, came to the UNHCR office in Amman to talk with me. We sat together on the roof looking out over the sun-washed city as he told his story. He said that on February 10, 2006, as he was driving home from work with his father, he was stopped by men he took to be Iraqi police. They handcuffed him, hooded him, drove him to another location, and handed him over to men he couldn't see. Somebody lifted his hood and said, "That's the guy." Somebody knocked him out. He woke up hanging by his feet in an airless cell. He hung for three days; the pressure in his eyes blinded him. His captors—four or five unknown men—beat him with hoses, partially asphyxiated him by running a noxious generator just beneath his head, and jolted him with electrodes attached to his fingers and penis. They phoned his father so he could hear Othman screaming. His father handed over $20,000 and the kidnappers threw Othman out, half dead, in a vacant lot, where a neighbor found him and dragged him from a circle of salivating feral dogs. While Othman was held captive, a Shiite militia seized his father's store, along with all the Sunni stores on their street in Sadr City, and shot several tradesmen who resisted. Three days after Othman was released, the whole family left for Jordan. For months, Othman was unable to leave his apartment in Amman and unable to sleep. At times he was filled with rage and became "aggressive" toward his wife, but he said that she "behaved very well" and helped him through it. She looked after him. When I talked with him, he was still stunned by flashbacks, confused by memory lapses, and haunted by the uncertainty of who had snatched him and why. Were they Iraqi police, Shiite militiamen, a criminal gang? Was the family targeted for their money and property? Their Sunni faith? What? Mostly he worried about his little daughter. If he could not protect himself, if he could not regain his equilibrium and be once again a good father, what in the world would happen to her?

Sayed, twenty-seven, was kidnapped by the Mahdi Army in February 2006, held for a month, beaten, and tortured. They broke his nose, his teeth, the bones of his eye socket. When I talked with him at a rehabilitation center for torture victims in Beirut, he couldn't speak of the other things they did to him; but he said that because they were done in the name of Islam, they had caused him to hate his religion. He was hauled before a Shiite sheikh who sentenced him to death by beheading. His wife's family delivered $10,000 for his release, and the kidnappers let him go. His is one of many stories in which money trumps sectarian fervor. But before they turned him loose, Sayed's captors cut off two fingers and the thumb of his left hand, marking him for execution if they catch him again. He asked me to photograph what remained of his hand and laid it flat on the glass-topped table. I had to ask him to quiet his legs, visible beneath the glass; during the hours we had spent in conversation, his legs had never stopped shaking.

The violence done by ordinary men to other ordinary men like Othman and Sayed destroys the victims. Men told me of being kidnapped as teenagers, beaten, confined without food or water, and coerced to provide sexual gratification to their captors. They spoke without apparent feeling, having retreated behind some psychic barrier where safety lay. Although most men won't tell—"A raped man is not a man," one said—UNHCR in Amman had recorded nearly three hundred cases of sexual violence against men. Captivity and torture of men in Iraq always seemed to have about it this peculiar quality of homoerotic sadism, the effluence of a culture that adores men far more than women yet sets them officially out of reach.

Kifah was kidnapped in Baghdad at age nineteen and sexually coerced by his captors, who denied him food and water for days, then offered an exchange for "favors" that included hand jobs and blow jobs and more that Kifah said he couldn't speak about. Not long after his captors released him, he was slightly wounded by a bomb that killed his best friend—the only person he had been able to tell about what had happened to him. Kifah fled to Amman and then, after learning that his parents and younger brother were missing, he returned to Iraq to search for them. For two months he scoured his parents' old neighborhoods, including the hospitals and morgues, but found no trace. Then, fearing for his life, he returned to Amman, where he registered as a refugee with UNHCR and asked to be resettled far away. We sat together on a bench in a public park; and looking straight ahead at nothing he told me his story haltingly, in a quiet, level voice. Only at the end did he turn to look at me and say, "I can't shed tears. I can't feel anything anymore." When the Americans invaded, he was studying to become a dentist.

Iraqi men and boys had such awful stories to tell. Even those in Amman who made good money as male prostitutes and admitted to having fun—partying with Western military contractors and war correspondents and rich male sex tourists from the Gulf states—were deeply troubled about performing sexual acts forbidden by Islam. One boy of seventeen told me that he enjoyed dressing up (scantily) like a girl, along with several of his friends, to dance for a French journalist, a regular client, because "this is not forbidden in the Quran." But he was studying the Quran, to make sure.

In these Islamic countries I heard many stories of men because it was men who put themselves forward. At UNHCR registration centers, men overshadow the veiled furtive figures of women and girls. They fill out the forms. They do the talking. They are in charge of the families. They are used to speaking on behalf of women and children. It is their responsibility. They do business, manage money, hold property, conduct the affairs of public life. In modern cultures still dominated by men, like theirs and ours, this is still most often the way civil life is organized. But attached to almost every man are women and girls whose names appear on the UNHCR certificate that bears his photograph and is issued to him as the head of the family; and I also felt their shadowy presence—Kifah's lost mother, Othman's devoted wife and cherished daughter, the spectral women and girls of their households who must have wept for them.

Women without men—widows like Siham—have their own stories to tell, and there is no shortage of widows in Iraq. Haifa Zangana, exiled to London after being imprisoned and tortured as a communist by Saddam's regime, reported in *City of Widows* that by 2007 there were at least three hundred thousand widows in Baghdad. Today some estimates place the number of widows nationwide at close to a million, a figure almost impossible to believe, and yet like most statistical estimates of Iraqi suffering probably too low.

Most widows lost their husbands to war. Um Adel, who lived in Falluja, lost her husband and most of the men of her family. She had married as a young girl named Nadia, given birth to her first son in 1991, when she was eighteen, and become by customary practice Um Adel: mother of Adel. Two more sons followed. In 2004, when she was thirty-one, American soldiers shot her husband during the assault on Falluja and left her a widow with three children. Adel was thirteen; her youngest boy was six. She maintained her husband's hardware shop for almost a year before someone burned it down. After arsonists struck her home as well, she moved with her children to her parents' house. Al Qaida operatives tried to persuade her eldest brother to work with them; early in July 2005, when he refused, they cut his throat. Later that month, when her second brother opened the front door of their home to look around, an American soldier shot and killed him. In August, Shia militiamen dragged her father away, and he never returned. Um Adel fled with her boys to Damascus, but a few months later she learned that her mother was ill, and with her son Adel, she went back. Along the way, she ran into Al Qaida. They beat and tortured her, breaking her sternum. They hung the boy by his wrists, distorting his shoulders in ways that have left him permanently in pain. What they wanted to know was where her eldest brother was; after seventeen days, they finally checked her story—that her brother was dead—and let her go. She returned with Adel to Damascus without ever seeing her mother.

War creates new widows all the time. Like Swaad. Before the war, she said, she had lived "an almost perfect life," married to a generous husband with a successful electrical business, living in a comfortable house in a good neighborhood in Baghdad with a four-year-old son and a new baby girl. Before the American invasion, she came and went as she pleased by herself; she met her friends anywhere she liked in the city. She enjoyed life. After the invasion, Al Qaida took over the neighborhood and imposed their Wahhabi ideas. She couldn't leave the house anymore on her own, and even when she went out with her husband, she couldn't wear pants or makeup. They were Christians, but she began to wear a veil. Then an engineer with whom her husband sometimes worked asked him to help with a job in the Green Zone. He didn't like Americans, but they offered him $2,500 a month at a time when a family could live very well on only $300. He bought new furniture and a BMW. He worked for the Americans for almost a year and a half before he got a threatening phone call in 2005. He thought a friend was playing a joke, but when he drove to the Green Zone to pick up his pay, two cars blocked him, in front and behind, and gunmen opened fire. After the funeral, papers were delivered to the widow's house saying, "Become a Muslim or pay us $7,500." "Become a Muslim *and* pay us $7,500." "Pay us $7,500 or leave this house." She left.

When I met Swaad in a threadbare apartment in Damascus, she was upset and angry. She had just had another fight with the landlord. "They are all greedy," she said. They kept raising the rent and she kept shifting apartments, on the downward slide. She was angry, too, with her son Hassan. She said, "He is violent and vicious. He beats up his sister and his cousins. He is uncontrollable, and he is only seven years old." Often his aggression brought her to despair, and then she became angry and beat the boy until he howled. She said, "I am very nervous, and sometimes I lose myself." Swaad's daughter Rita, then four years old, never spoke except once when they registered as refugees at UNHCR and the girl spontaneously announced, "My father is dead. They shot him in the stomach and the face."

Swaad shared the apartment with her sister-in-law Rasha, the wife of her husband's brother. It was Rasha's small son and daughter—the cousins—that Swaad's boy thrashed. They clung to their mother's legs when Hassan prowled the room. Rasha had lived in Baghdad with her husband and children in a house located on the divide between two sectarian areas; the house was hit by fire from both sides. In 2007, Rasha's husband brought her and the children to the safety of Damascus and went back to his job as a cashier, working for the Americans at an airport café in Baghdad. He drove back to Damascus every few months to visit his family, but the fourth time he returned to Baghdad, in March 2008, he vanished. Rasha said, "I think he has been kidnapped by Al Qaida. I think if I could raise some

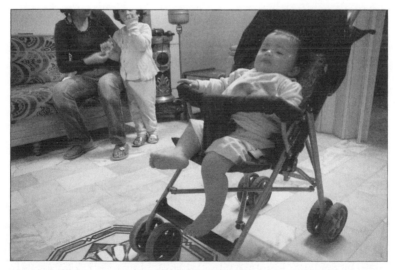

The young widow Swaad comforts her silent daughter Rita in their apartment in Damascus. In the stroller is the daughter of Swaad's sister-in-law Rasha, whose husband disappeared.                    —Ann Jones

money, I could get him back." She had no idea how to raise money, and depressed as she was—way beyond tears—she was too immobilized to try. "Al Qaida hasn't called me yet," she said. "But I know they will."

Swaad sat on the other side of the room with her silent daughter as her son paced up and down like some feral creature in search of prey. Her right arm was pinned to her side. She said she was receiving a course of injections to overcome what a Syrian doctor called "muscular stress." He gave her sleeping pills and tranquilizers as well. But her right arm had become a serious problem, contracting into paralysis. Lately she had been unable to move her right hand at all. It was the hand with which she had been beating her son.

There is more than one way to lose a husband. Illness, accident, assassination, murder, warfare. Rape is another. Many women lose their husbands to rape. How many thousands of Iraqi women and girls have been raped it is impossible to know; but rape is commonplace. Of 4,516 cases of sexual violence in Iraq reported to UNHCR in Jordan, women were the victims in 4,233 cases; and for each reported case, there are countless others. One UNHCR official told me that thousands of women and girls have been assaulted in their own homes or abducted and held captive—far more women than men, he said—and "99 percent were raped." Yet women seldom mention rape for many of the same reasons that Congolese women kept rape to themselves for so long. For Iraqi women rape is a terrible shame. In Kurdistan and some other parts of the country, rape may entitle a husband, father, or brother to murder the rape victim in defense of family honor; but honor killing is not the principal fear of most Iraqi women. Rape itself is enough. Women keep silent after the fact for fear of the social stigma that attends it. Many, having told their story once to a UNHCR protection worker, refuse to be referred to counseling for fear of having to tell the story again. One counselor said, "It is the legacy of Saddam Hussein: Iraqi people cannot trust each other." The refugees form no community organizations, no political action committees, no support groups. Each individual, or each family, seems to be alone and afraid. One counselor said of the raped women, "They have been well trained to keep silent."

I met many women full of sorrow because their once happy marriages did not survive the fact of rape. They're not widows really, but they might as well be, for rape destroys the relationship a woman had with her husband. No matter how sympathetic he may be, or how deep the love they share, the marriage as it was is over. Many women said they could not resume sexual relations with their husbands. A rape counselor said, "In a year or two, even the most devoted husband finds the end of his patience." But women can't forget. A common story tells of a gang of unknown men who forced their way into the house and remained for some time, terrorizing the family. I talked to women who were gang-raped—in some cases it went on for hours—and because their children were held hostage in the next room, they never made a sound.

Salma was abducted in Baghdad when she went to the market to shop for food. Until that moment, apart from the American occupation, she had felt happy with her husband and her little boy. She was twenty-five years old. Then a car stopped behind her, blocking the way, and two masked men in black held a gun to her head. "Please don't kill me," she said. "I have a son only nine months old." They forced her into their car and poured a liquid into her eyes and mouth. "It would have been better if they had killed me," she says. Then she was in a room.

A Sabaean Mandaean woman (in dark dress) sits with her three adult daughters in the living room of a Damascus apartment. They cover their faces for fear of reprisal and pray to be granted asylum in another country.
—Ann Jones

Her hands were tied over her head; she was suspended with her toes just touching the floor. "We know everything about you," one of her captors said. But they wanted to know exactly how much gold her husband had. Salma and her husband were Sabaean Mandaeans, neither Muslim nor Christian but followers of John the Baptist; working in gold was the traditional occupation of Sabaean Mandaean men. Salma told her captors that her husband was merely a worker; he owned no gold at all. Then, she said, the men gave her sleeping pills. Half conscious, she felt she was raped; she awoke in other clothes only to be drugged again. They taped her eyes shut, and then they raped her for days. At last her husband and his father delivered $5,000, and her captors threw her into the street. She had been abducted at the end of October 2007; by December her husband had divorced her. Their religion has strict rules; a husband can never again touch a wife who has been touched by another. Salma took her baby and fled to Damascus to join her parents who had left a year before. The boisterous baby proved too much for her sickly father. He found another room. Um Salma—mother of Salma—goes back and forth between two small, shabby flats, caring for her husband in one place, her daughter and grandchild in the other. Another daughter has gone to Australia, a son and his wife to the Netherlands, a brother to Sweden. Um Salma said exactly what I had heard from many others: "Our family has been blown apart." Every Sunday, Salma and Um Salma put on the white cotton garments of their faith and attend services at a nearby swimming pool where all the worshippers are baptized anew by immersion, and cleansed.

Mona was attacked in her Baghdad home by a gang of men in black who broke down the door at four o'clock in the morning. They dragged her about by her hair and slapped her around, demanding to know where her husband was. She told them the truth, that he had fled to Lebanon for fear of kidnapping. She said she had stayed behind so that her children could finish school. (Iraqis value education above all else.) They told her to write down the names of people in the neighborhood and whether they were Sunni or Shia. (She asked me, "How could I do that to my neighbors, knowing they'd be killed? They were already killing Sunni—twenty-two in our area since my husband left.") She refused. They broke her arm, they ripped off her nightclothes, they twisted her broken arm behind her back, and they raped her. She begged for mercy, saying, "I'm a Muslim, like you." One of them said, "You are a Sunni infidel. If you were a Muslim you would not let your daughter do gymnastics." It sounds absurd: to be raped and beaten because your teenage daughter takes a gym class at school, but this is the nature of "sectarian violence." Mona was one survivor who knew what happened to her and why. "They raped my sister, too," she said, gesturing toward the corner where a skeletal figure lay on the floor, staring at us with vacant eyes. "She was an invalid; she couldn't use her legs. The rape finished her. All those men. Now she just lies on her mat and pisses herself." That night, Mona feared for her children, but after the men left the house, the two little boys crept out of the cupboards, and she found her daughter on the roof, hiding in the water tank. She phoned her husband, and he blamed her. A year later, long after her brother had helped her move the family to Damascus, her husband came to join her. He raped her too, and she became pregnant, but before long he beat her so badly that she miscarried. He left again for Lebanon and sent notice of their divorce. Her daughter was not able to finish school.

Everyone has a story, and all the stories are about the past, about what happened. All the stories end in this exile, this uncertain time that can't last but seems to go on and on. For many in exile life slides downhill, especially when the money runs out, when the ends cannot be made to meet. For Um Adel it all happened fast. When she returned to Damascus after the doomed attempt to visit her mother in Falluja, she had just enough money left to pay one month's rent and feed her children for a week. She found a job in a clothing factory that hired illegal refugee workers at substandard wages. Earning twenty-one dollars a week, she couldn't make her monthly rent of one hundred and fifty dollars, so she took a second job in the evenings and on weekends in a hair salon. She left her son Adel, then fifteen, in charge of his younger brothers. The hair salon paid her a bit more than two dollars a day, but added to her factory wage that still left her short on the rent; and the family had to eat. At the hair salon, her customers told her about the clubs where they went to dance. They invited her to come along and meet the club owners. Soon she was pulling in close to $1,800 a month.

A lot of Iraqi women and girls dance in the nightclubs in Damascus and leave in cars with men who pay them for sex. To call it "prostitution" implies a greater degree of choice than they have. "Survival sex" is more accurate. In Jeremana, the seedy low-rent Damascus neighborhood where I lived among Iraqi refugees, I met sex workers in the clubs, at the beauty shops, and at the restaurants where they socialize with regular clients during the day. Many sex workers, like Um Adel, are single mothers, widowed or abandoned—some after having been raped—and desperately poor. They pay club owners for the privilege of sitting at a table night after night and buying bad food. They get up to dance woodenly to deafening music together with ten- and twelve-year-old girls whose sad-faced mothers sit on a bench near the toilets, watching and waiting for sex tourists from the Emirates or Saudi Arabia to buy their daughters' virginity. The going rate is $5,000, but there's a bargain price of $600 for penetration only of the anus, which can be sold any number of times.

Sex work is dangerous enough to be almost suicidal. Stopping at Um Adel's one evening, I met a young woman named Duaa whom she had taken in to share the apartment. Um Adel's earnings had fallen off sharply; there were fewer sex tourists coming from the Gulf and more girls competing for their attention. We talked in the bedroom while the two women tried on clothes, searching for just the right outfit for the night's work. Duaa told me that about a year earlier she had been beaten and gang-raped for two days, thrown from a car and left for dead by four men from the Gulf who were later sought by Syrian police for gang-raping a thirteen-year-old girl to death. The police brought photos of the men to the beauty salons frequented by sex workers, and Duaa recognized them. Later she learned that the same men had killed an eight-year-old Iraqi girl in the same way. Duaa hadn't gone to the police herself, and she didn't tell those who came around with the photographs what had happened to her. In Jordan, Syria, and Lebanon, any refugee caught working at any job is subject to detention and deportation, and prostitution is a crime. Instead, she had gone back to work. She needed the money. Duaa finished dressing—low slung leopard top, shiny tight green pants, strappy spiked sandals—and prepared a bottle for her new baby boy. (She never talked about the father, and I didn't ask.) She turned the child over to Adel who cares for him while the women are out. Cradling the baby, Adel lay down on his mother's bed amid a pile of her clothes.

Women sell their bodies. Men sell their daughters. Well, women also market their daughters, but men are more likely to sell them outright. Like the man who sold his fourteen-year-old daughter to a group of Syrian men who trained her in erotic dancing and sold her at a profit to a Saudi who runs a little "hospitality" business for visiting Saudi men. The Saudi ditched her when it became apparent that she was pregnant. Jordanian police picked her up and eventually turned her over to UNHCR. The traumatized girl did not want to have a child, but the high-minded morals and laws of Middle Eastern countries forbid abortion and recommend abstinence. The best UNHCR could do was get her quickly to another country in the West where she could safely have the baby and decide whether to keep it or not, as she tried to start a new life. That's a trafficking story that might still turn out with a halfway happy ending, but you can be sure that this girl's place in the Saudi stable was quickly filled and refilled many times over by now. Trafficking women and girls for prostitution is an old game in this part of the world. Lebanon has institutionalized a system of legal, licensed prostitution that imports women from the countries of the former Soviet Union, while captive women from many impoverished and troubled parts of the world are routinely shipped through Amman and Damascus on their way to brothels, or reshipment, in Saudi Arabia and the Gulf States. In Amman's women's shelters I met trafficked girls from Somalia, Nigeria, and Morocco who had escaped and were hoping to go back home. But now more and more trafficked women are kept in Amman and Damascus to meet the demand of new clubs and new massage parlors proliferating on the outskirts of war. The presence of so many desperate refugee women keeps the prices down, while profits are promised by hordes of men on the prowl: contractors, sex tourists, traveling businessmen, journalists, diplomats, aid workers, refugees. War, being a man's business, is good for other businesses controlled and patronized chiefly by men: the sex industry, narco-biz, arms trading, trafficking in child labor, trafficking in body parts. All these profitable private enterprises grow in the shadow of war, usually with the patronage and cooperation of local men whose inadequately paid job it is to fight crime.

Police often arrest sex workers and use the threat of deportation to extort money or sex; but generally they seem to go easier on "respectable" women who work illegally—or at least that's what people believe. So in a great many refugee households, it's the women who leave the house for paid work and necessary errands. They go out. The men stay at home, doing nothing, in small, bare apartments sometimes strikingly reminiscent of the rooms where they were held and tortured. Like Karenni men in the refugee camps of Thailand, Iraqi men in exile have lost house, land, livelihood, status—all that once identified them as men. But in Amman, Damascus, and Beirut, someone must make a living for the family. Someone must bring home some money. Women take on a double burden—their husband's role as well as their own.

As the family sinks deeper into poverty, and waiting becomes intolerable, men try to reclaim their sense of identity by reasserting control over their wives and children. Domestic violence sweeps through Iraqi refugee communities like cholera. A man afraid to go out to look for work sometimes keeps his wife at home too, as if forcing her to return to a woman's traditional role will restore the status and power he once enjoyed. Having a wife at home shows that a man can support his family. But he can't. Amal, who had been a professor in Iraq and the sole support of her husband and four children during three years of exile, finally "surrendered"—after a year of increasing violence—to her husband. When I went to see her, she had abandoned her job with an international NGO that helps refugee women. The bruises on her face from the last beating were fading to yellow. There was no food in the apartment. The children were at home too, withdrawn from school for lack of money. They looked thin and depressed. "They are malnourished," Amal said. Her oldest son had taken to beating his sister. "My daughter cries and cries," Amal said. "And me, I am now a 'good' wife. I am at home. I am dying here." She may die a martyr to her husband's ego. Many women willingly assume the burden of their husband's suffering. Ahmad's battered wife says, "I choose to share this life of misery with him." But others, like Amal, are forced.

———

No Iraqi family has been spared the collateral damage of this war. Every Iraqi can name at least one lost relative dead or disappeared. Most I spoke with had suffered multiple tragedies. Too poor or too damaged to leave after the first assault, they were struck again. Hassan, a Shiite, was a driver for an oil company and the head of a family consisting of a wife, Faiza, who is Sunni, and seven children. Everything changed in March 2006 when he was kidnapped. Suddenly the family was hers. Faiza had been a schoolteacher, and as a condition of her state employment, a Baath Party member; she had lost that job in 2003 when the Americans de-Baathified the country, and the family was struggling. Now, with her husband gone, how was she to care for seven children? In April, a month after her husband disappeared, seven armed men broke into the house. They threatened to rape her daughters, and when her eldest son intervened, they shot him and cut off his head. He was sixteen. The unknown men remained in the house for seven hours, during which they forced the next-oldest boys— fourteen-year-old twins—to hold their dead brother's body and his head. What the men did during seven hours to Faiza and her daughters, Faiza declines to say. Not long after that, she learned that her husband was alive. She gave the family savings to ransom him and, after forty-five days in captivity, he came home. But he had been tortured. He was partially paralyzed and unable to stand. A month later, another group of unknown men entered a nearby school and forced the students to watch as they gang-raped their teachers. Among the students was Faiza's second daughter, Zahra, then eight years old. The men abducted Zahra and seven other girls, ages seven and eight, held them in a windowless room, deprived them of food, and forced them to watch as they gang-raped captive women. After about a week, the men set fire to the girls' hair, slit their throats, and threw them onto a rubbish heap. Foreign soldiers spotted the girls' bodies and noticed that Zahra was still breathing. She was the sole survivor. Eight months later, in January 2007, unknown men for unknown reasons set a fire that consumed the family's house and belongings. Destitute and homeless, Faiza fled with her paralyzed husband and six surviving children to Damascus where they live in a one-room apartment. I occasionally visited them there, bringing fruit and cookies for the children. Hassan lies on a mat on the floor and smokes. The children are afraid to go to school. Faiza confesses in a whisper that she often thinks of suicide. "But," she says, raising her eyes to her daughters. She tells me that Zahra always wears a tight knit cap because her hair hurts.

The younger daughters of Hassan and Faiza enter the kitchen to help their mother. Zahra (*center*) wears the tight knit cap that eases the pain of her hair.

—Ann Jones

For Faiza and her family and for millions of Iraqis uprooted by war, the very idea of exile is a hardship. Some refugees, against their better judgment, have gone back to Iraq to collect the $800 payment the Iraqi government offers returnees. Some returnees have been killed. Many do not regard returning as an option. Aziz, who had been an English teacher, tried to help his neighbors in Baghdad by speaking to American soldiers on their behalf. Zealots wrongly accused him of working for the Americans. The accusations were false, but the charge stuck. I visited him and his wife, Nadima, and their four children in a tiny one-room apartment in suburban Damascus. Although they had no furniture, shawls were spread on the floor and their belongings were arranged along the walls with tidy precision. Nadima took me to see the quarters they'd occupied the year before, when she was pregnant, on the roof of a five-story building at the top of a steep hill. (Still fearing reprisals, Aziz stayed home; he never leaves the house.) She showed me the storage room where the family had slept. Corrugated plastic covered some sections of the roof, but it was full of holes. She told me that on very cold, wet days, a woman in an apartment below had taken her children inside. She was immensely grateful for that, and for their new ground-floor apartment that flooded only during heavy rains. She led me to a sink in the far corner of the roof. A nylon mesh body scrubber hung from a nail on the wall. It was pink. "This is where we bathed," she said. And then she began to weep.

It's the task of UNHCR to look after these refugees, especially those like Aziz and Nadima who can never go home again. UNHCR determines when it registers refugees whether to refer them to a third country for possible resettlement. Then it's up to that country to interview the referred refugees and decide whether to accept them. Many refugees have waited months or years for a host country to summon them to an interview, though of all Iraqi refugees in the Middle East, only about 1 percent are offered resettlement. Only the most "vulnerable" make the cut. Eleven categories of vulnerability include female-headed households, persecuted religious and political groups, and those who are on everybody's hit list because they aided Americans, whether from conviction or, more often, financial need. While refugees wait, UNHCR supports the neediest. In Damascus it provides a monthly cash payment for rent or an allotment of staple foods. Refugees can choose between shelter and food. The terrible irony of UNHCR's underfunded struggle to cope is that its inadequate response so often seems, even to grateful refugees, another almost unbearable trial.

The George W. Bush administration strictly limited resettlement of Iraqis in the United States. Families that had redeemed relatives from kidnappers were excluded on the grounds that paying ransom amounted to providing "material support" to terrorists, a practice forbidden by the Patriot Act. (That provision of the act was found unconstitutional in 2007, and this cruel policy challenged, but at this writing, it has not been reversed.) Another excluded category, sex workers, disqualifies many of the most vulnerable women and men. By the fourth anniversary of the invasion, early in 2007, the United States had admitted only 463 Iraqis. Even when the number of post-invasion refugees passed 1.5 million, the Bush administration argued that they would return home any minute and thus were not real refugees. The United Nations, which had strongly opposed the illegal American invasion, continued the task of mopping up after the increasingly costly American disaster. UNHCR issued an urgent appeal for $60 million to aid Iraqis, and the Bush administration, under intense international criticism, reluctantly announced that it would provide $18 million and process 7,000 Iraqis for resettlement in 2007. In 2008, the United States admitted 13,000 Iraqis and pledged to take 17,000 more in 2009. But those quotas didn't begin to cover even those Iraqis still in danger for having worked with Americans. For comparison's sake, consider that in one eight-month period in 1975 the United States took in 131,000 Vietnamese, persuaded by the moral argument of President Gerald Ford; and since the end of that war, the United States has accepted 900,000.

To resettle refugees in the United States, the State Department's Bureau of Population, Refugees and Migration (BPRM) contracts ten organizations—including the IRC, which works in twenty-two American cities. For each refugee, an organization receives $1,800 (until January 2010, the sum was $900), half of which must be spent directly on the resettling person. The BPRM sets forth strict requirements. The refugee must be met at the airport, offered a "culturally appropriate" warm meal, and settled in "permanent" housing that has been equipped with so many pots and pans, so many beds and chairs, and for which one month's rent has been paid in advance. After that the IRC at least undertakes to help enroll the refugee in Social Security and the children in school. It connects the family to Medicaid or whatever state and local health services are available. It helps the refugee find a job, often in minimum wage service occupations—hotels, fast-food restaurants—where English is not strictly necessary. By this time the BPRM's allotment is long gone, and the IRC is falling back on its donors because it is not in the habit of leaving people flat. Initially the IRC was able to make its slim budget stretch for a month or two until the Iraqi refugees found jobs. After that they were supposed to make it on their own. Sometimes there were problems when Iraqis quit jobs they considered beneath them—a surgeon, for example, might not want to subject his hands to dishwashing—but once they understood that scrambling for low-wage jobs is the opening act of the famous American dream, most of them tried again. Then came the crash. In Phoenix, where refugees once could expect to find minimum wage jobs in one or two months, in 2009 it was taking eight or nine. Landlords who might have cut a refugee some slack for a couple of months couldn't wait that long for the rent. For nonprofit NGOs like the IRC, this quickly became "a crisis situation." It was a crisis, too, for refugees who had missed the blessings of democracy that the United States promised to bring to Iraq, yet hoped to find them here.

I knew that because of the harsh terms of resettlement in the United States, staff members at UNHCR tended to refer the most vulnerable refugees to other, far more generous countries. (It wasn't a policy; just the instinctive practice of experienced humanitarians.) It's not by chance that Siham and her helpless daughters were referred to Sweden, with its public health system and social services among the best in the world, and not by accident that they were accepted. In the United States, even with the best efforts of organizations like the IRC, they would get less assistance than they were receiving in Amman. That assistance was funded largely by UNHCR and international donors, but little Jordan, Syria, and Lebanon shouldered enormous social and economic costs. Considering that Iraq's neighbors are not rich, and that none of them is obliged by international treaties to protect refugees (as the United States is), they have been remarkably hospitable. Jordan, with a population of six million, accommodates at least half a million Iraqi refugees— equal to 8.5 percent of its population—in addition to the 400,000 Palestinians it has harbored for decades. Tens of thousands of Iraqi children enroll in Jordanian schools. Syria, with eighteen million citizens, received an estimated 1.2 to 1.5 million refugees, mostly in the capital. That's the equivalent of the United States opening its arms to more than twenty million refugees, mostly in the neighborhood of the White House.

Given what I knew, I wasn't surprised when the Iraqi refugees who frequented the smoky Internet café in my Jeremana neighborhood started getting discouraging Skype calls from friends who had been resettled in the United States. The message coming back was: "Don't accept the United States." Most reported that rents were beyond their means and jobs almost impossible to find, even below minimum wage. No one could support a family on the wages from a single job. And all the things that sophisticated Iraqi urbanites were used to—from free higher education to public transportation to a neighborhood mosque—were missing in America. Most could not speak English and could not find an English course. Many met hostility from Americans who regarded Iraqis as terrorists; others said Americans expected them to be grateful for having been "set free." Well before the Skype calls started coming, many Iraqis had told me they would never agree to go to America. How could they possibly live in a country that had destroyed their own? But some desperate refugees had accepted—there is no second choice—and now, said their friends, they were being cruelly punished.

Soon I heard in Damascus a theory I'd already picked up in Amman. According to this supposition, spreading along the Skype lines, America's strategy for the destruction of Iraq consisted of three stages. Stage One was thirteen years of sanctions to weaken the country and the culture. Stage Two was the occupation, which set off violence like a bomb to blow apart all that remained. And Stage Three was resettlement, contrived to condemn masses of Iraqis who survived the war to slave labor in the United States. From here to eternity, Iraqis would do America's dishes. The coup de grâce is the requirement that Iraqi refugees repay the American government for their airfare to the United States. When I first heard of this last provision, I thought it was a joke, a bit of the dark humor that helps Iraqis through overwhelming adversity. But it's not. Every refugee must sign a promissory note—the average airfare runs about $1,500—and pay a monthly installment on time. Welcome to America.

In Beirut, nearing the end of my stay in the Middle East, I used to walk along the Corniche each afternoon as the light began to fail, relishing the salt air and the sound of the sea against the shingle. The sweep of open water drew me away from the testimonies and gave me space to think about war, and women, and photography. The singular image of this war had already been shot: the photo of the hooded figure with outstretched arms at Abu Ghraib. I thought about the women refugees I'd met and wondered what they would have photographed if I had been able to give them cameras.

In Beirut, I had sat with a group of battered women. Organized by a Lebanese women's center and called a support group, it was conducted by an Iraqi woman who lectured the women on how to conduct themselves to avoid being beaten: "Kiss his hand, kiss his feet, touch (you know), massage, compliment, praise, get naked, listen, hug (if he likes that), ask him for sex, give him what he wants, be a mother to him." The battered women stared at her blankly. One said, "It's not like that at all." I had visited a shelter in the hills to talk with a woman whose husband had tried to kill her because she did not always promptly obey him. (He stuck a carving knife in her belly to teach her to move faster.) There I had also talked with two teenagers, a reserved brother and his vigorous younger sister, whose father had sold them into hard labor, splitting rocks. The sister had planned and led their escape. But most of the Iraqi women I had talked to were individuals, isolated in their separate houses with men who kept them at home. These women might have photographed the four walls, the empty cupboards, the tattered sleeping mats. The children—always the children—and their school notebooks and pens. The plastic bags of medicine—every refugee had a lot of medicine for ill-defined anxieties and pains. Maybe the markets that held all the things they could not buy. Or the UNHCR office in Damascus, or the reception center at Douma where hundreds of refugees stood in line. I thought of photos Iraqis had asked me to take. A hand deprived of its fingers. Purplish toes that bore deep pitted scars where toenails had once grown. The thin white scar on the neck of the child Zahra. And I thought I knew what the women—and men, too—would have said, if they had been asked to speak up, to join a global crescendo, about what it is they want. You'll have to take my word for it because Iraqi refugees are in no position to speak for themselves. They want peace. They want security. They want a future—meaning a peaceful future complete with jobs and schools and health care and some self-determination for their children. They want their children to be educated. They want their families to be reunited, but they know it isn't going to happen; so they want their children to have a chance at such families, the kind of families Iraqis used to have. The women want all those things and something more. They want respect and support. They want to dress as they choose, go where they choose, do what they choose. They want their husbands to stop trying to keep them at home. They want their husbands to stop beating them.

They want to work, for their families and for themselves. They want their husbands to realize that in this war, and in this life, women are not the enemy.

After some months spent listening to Iraqis and photographing them in Amman and Damascus and Beirut, I began to edit my pictures for UNHCR. I had tried, at the subjects' request, to take photos that did not reveal their identity. Their safety might depend upon that privacy. At first I had photographed my subjects from behind or at odd angles that concealed faces. Then, in Damascus, I began to photograph my subjects from the neck down. I beheaded them. They became in my photographs decapitated bodies reminiscent of the hooded torture victims in the snapshots from Abu Ghraib. It was my intention to protect them, but in discarding their faces, severing their heads, I obliterated their identity as individual human beings.

In Beirut I photographed Ahmad, the man I spoke of in the introduction to this book as the only Iraqi I met who actually was liberated by the American invasion. He was still suffering from the consequences of torture he had endured during eighteen years in Saddam Hussein's prison and more recently fifteen days in the hands of the Mahdi Army. I photographed him with Azhar, the woman he had married shortly after he escaped from prison. He loved her desperately, yet at times he couldn't stop himself from beating her. When he told me about this, in her presence, he wept. I took a photograph of the couple, holding cherished photos of their own. Azhar clutches their formal wedding portrait, and Ahmad holds a picture of the two of them with their little boy, taken when they were alive, and joyful, and full of hope; but there they stand in my photograph in their grim apartment, headless as corpses. It wasn't what I

In their one-room apartment in Beirut, Ahmad and Azhar display family photographs taken in Baghdad, where they once had a home.

—Ann Jones

meant, but there was the fact in shot after shot: war makes even living people dead.

What emerged from all my fractured photographs were glimpses of a civilization, among the oldest in the world, blown apart. Fatima said, "I want to go back, but to what? Our world is gone." Families are decimated or dispersed. Fatima has seven brothers and sisters, all highly educated, multilingual professionals—professors, judges, scientists; they are needed in Iraq, but they live and work in Australia, Canada, Egypt, Germany, Switzerland, England, Oman. Iraq becomes another Afghanistan: the citizens capable of reconstructing the country scattered like shrapnel by the explosion of their culture, the destruction of their cities, the devastation of their land. I heard that story over and over again from Iraqis of every description, as I had heard it in years past from Afghans. It was enough to make me want to sit down in a chair, like Siham's daughters, Ruba and Rania and Roula, and fold my hands, and stop speaking. What saved me was remembering the real Ruba and Rania and Roula. They were laughing. In Sweden, in the snow, they would be laughing still. I like to think of them, though I cannot see it in my photographs, standing up.

# AFTERWORD:
## IT'S NOT OVER

Early in the photography project, with the amazing accomplishments of the women in Côte d'Ivoire fresh in my mind, I went to see Rachel Mayanja, a Ugandan who serves as special adviser on gender issues to UN secretary-general Ban Ki-moon. My purpose was simply to let her know what we were doing at the IRC, but right away she saw the great promise of the project, and she proposed an exhibition of the photographs at UN headquarters when the General Assembly was in session. She wanted delegates from all over the world to see the women's work. I carried the idea back to the IRC and they ran with it. So at the end of my Global Crescendo travel, I helped a designer choose and arrange the images for the exhibition; I pored over my notebooks and tapes to find the remarks each photographer had made about her pictures at her town's First-Ever All-Women's Photography Exhibition. The designer had the images printed on eight enormous canvas banners together with the photographers' statements. In October 2008, the banners were hung in the gallery of UN headquarters in New York.

The opening was a grand success, my colleagues in New York

reported. Then, for a few weeks, delegates to the United Nations had to pass through the gallery and walk among the eye-catching banners to enter the assembly chamber. At the time, I was in Damascus and sorry to miss this last grand exhibition. But soon my colleagues sent word that it was causing a stir. Some African delegates—men—grumbled that the show made them look bad because so many of the global voices came from Africa. They complained that Africa had been unfairly singled out when everyone knows that men fight wars and mistreat women all over the world. That is certainly true, though it misses the point the women were trying to make about the ways that war and violence tear families and communities apart, and it is blind to their ardent images of peace: happy families, girls at school, a woman on a motorcycle making sure the roads are safe. But what can you say to a man who thinks a community's photographs are all about him?

I only wish that all the delegates had acknowledged the truth of the grumblers' defense: that women suffer the consequences of war all over the world. What if they all confessed to the facts and pledged to work together—the delegates from Europe, Asia, Australia, Africa, and the Americas—to overcome once and for all this ancient injustice? They might have turned the Global Crescendo volume way, way up.

To be fair, that's what the UN Security Council has been trying to do in passing the resolutions mentioned in the introduction to this book: SCR 1325, adopted in 2000, calling for women's full participation in peacemaking, and SCR 1820, passed eight years later, demanding an immediate end to violence against women and girls in war. Both resolutions were celebrated—and then universally ignored.

In 2009, the Security Council tried again. It passed Resolution 1888, asking the secretary-general to appoint a special representative to oversee a long list of UN mechanisms aimed at protecting women and children from sexual violence during armed conflict. Chairing the meeting, U.S. Secretary of State Hillary Clinton said, "We are here to address an issue that has received too little attention, not only in the Council but also by all Governments around the world." Since the passage of the earlier resolutions, she noted, violence against women and girls in war had not diminished, but increased in some places—such as Bosnia, Burma, Sri Lanka, the DRC, and "elsewhere." The secretary-general expressed regret that nothing much had come of those resolutions, once hailed as landmarks. "Parties to armed conflict continue to use sexual violence with efficient brutality," he said. "The perpetrators generally operate with impunity."

The Security Council noted that "despite its repeated condemnation" of such violence, these "acts continue to occur, and in some situations have become systematic or widespread." What could be done? Resolution 1888 reiterated the demand "for the complete cessation by all parties to armed conflict of all acts of sexual violence with immediate effect." But nowhere did the violence cease.

One week later, the Council passed another resolution urging all nations and international organizations "to take further measures to improve women's participation during all stages of peace processes, particularly in conflict resolution, post-conflict planning and peacebuilding . . . by [among many other things] promoting women's leadership, . . . supporting women's organizations, and countering negative societal attitudes about women's capacity to participate equally." Just as Resolution 1888 repeated the demands of SCR 1820, Resolution 1889 repeated SCR 1325—only louder. That may count as a global crescendo of sorts. Yet exclusion and oppression continue unabated.

During the session, many male delegates spoke fervently about the need of women and girls for "protection." All civilians—men, women, and children—need protection in wartime. Yet protection is by definition either a racket or a courtesy extended by the strong to the weak. The Global Crescendo photographers showed us that while women need protection as much as other people, they also urgently need a voice, a seat at the table, within earshot, where they might actually be heard to pronounce demands and plans of their own. In the Security Council discussion it was left to Vitaly Churkin, the delegate from the Russian Federation, to suggest that there is more at stake than women's bodies. He said that though sexual violence is "an appalling crime," it is one among many other offenses, such as excluding women from peacemaking and post-conflict planning, that block the path to human equality. To be excluded from decision-making processes that determine your country's future and your own is a less brutal but no less effective kind of evisceration.

As the Security Council resolutions say, women should be involved every step of the way in peace negotiations and reconstruction, but not simply because of that longed-for yet conveniently distant abstraction called equality; women should be heard because their concerns so perfectly coincide with the interests of civil life that they know best what real peace might look like and how it might be achieved. As I write, aid organizations distributing food to earthquake survivors in Haiti have begun to hand the packages directly to women because women will feed the children and share what is left, while young men have been pushing women, children, and old men aside to snatch all the food for themselves. It is a fact that women, who even in the midst of cataclysm have the sense to share food, are far better equipped to plan equitable and durable peace than are those men who for too long have squatted on the seats at negotiating tables: the commanders, diplomats, and private financiers whose interests run to military, political, and economic supremacy.

Yet what happens when an opportunity is at hand for world leaders to enlist the full participation of women? Consider, for example, the chance to hear the voices of Afghan women presented when representatives of more than sixty nations and organizations—"the international community"—met in London in January 2010 to discuss the future of Afghanistan. It was the women of Afghanistan, after all, who under the Taliban regime were the world's most oppressed—confined, deprived, denied, and stoned to death in public stadiums. Yet curiously enough, not the United States nor the UN nor any of the other interested nations convened in London thought to extend an invitation to a single Afghan woman. Not even to the Afghan Minister for Women's Affairs.

All the while, in other countries officially at peace, ex-combatants in West Africa still jockey for power, the junta in Burma still drives minorities from their land, and militias in the DRC still rape and kill. Yet ordinary "unqualified" women given cameras choose to document polluted water supplies, shattered houses, broken bridges, ruined fields, gutted schools, drunken policemen, corrupt judges, pregnant schoolgirls, and raped women. They also organize to help each other. They speak of what needs to be done to save their families and their towns. Even as I write, hundreds of women, Muslim and Christian together, march in northern Nigeria, demanding an end to sectarian and ethnic slaughter. The solutions the women suggest—the better world they envision—has to do with social justice, or what many call simply "being fair." We carried out the photo project to see what ordinary women think about in the aftermath of war, and we found blueprints for peace.

While the world turns a deaf ear, women keep trying to effect change themselves. With money raised abroad and technical help from the IRC, Fatuma Kayangele and the women's organization she started to counteract the plague of rape in the Congo—the Collectif des Femmes de Kamanyola—has put up a building to double as a community hall and a warehouse to store the maize they grow. This will make it possible for them to play the market, selling their maize only when the price is high. The profits will sustain their work on behalf of women survivors and their families and communities. Considering that these women must be ranked among the most violated, oppressed, and ignored people on earth, their accomplishments are stunning.

But the bravery of these remarkable ordinary women would go much further if it were matched by the courage of enlightened men. This was brought home to me when I returned recently to Afghanistan, where a colleague working to rebuild her country spoke of her sorrow that there a woman can do nothing without a man's permission. "If I did not have the full support every day of my husband and my father," she said, "I could not come to work. Those of us who have that support are still few. We are doing all we can, and we are growing stronger. But in all honesty, I think that we cannot do this alone." Husband, father, leader. The United States emerged from the London Conference muttering of plans to negotiate peace with the Taliban. If successful, such bargaining will permit the United States to declare the war in Afghanistan "over" even as the war of Afghan fundamentalists—the mujahideen and the Taliban— against Afghan women goes on.

Clearly, we need more leaders with the simple clarity and courage of the chief of Zatta—men who will raise their arms for all the world to see, and say: "This violence must stop." Not violence against women and children only, but the violence of war. For any man, taking a stand against violence shouldn't be such an extraordinary event. The chief of Zatta came to it on his own, with a little push from the women photographers of Zatta, who still sit on his advisory council to this day. And he encouraged the women when they came up with a plan to start their own radio station in nearby Yamassoukro, the nation's capital. Not a radio program, a station. They have plenty to say, but they might not have been able to realize their radio dream without the backing of the chief and the IRC, which offered some technical equipment and advice. That's what women need. Not protection, but a little help from their friends and support from men who also imagine and yearn to inhabit a just and peaceful world. Soon their voices will be on the air.

# NOTES

## INTRODUCTION: WAR IS NOT HEALTHY

1    *As a young man, Ahmad*: Interview with Ahmad (pseudonym) and his wife Azhar (pseudonym), Beirut, Lebanon, November 10, 2008.

5    *For many years I studied violence in the family and wrote about it*: *Women Who Kill* (New York: Holt, Rinehart and Winston, 1980; New York: Feminist Press, 2009); *Everyday Death* (New York: Holt, Rinehart and Winston, 1985); *When Love Goes Wrong*, with Susan Schechter (New York: HarperCollins, 1992); *Next Time She'll Be Dead* (Boston: Beacon, 1994, 2000).

7    *it is civilians who die in far greater numbers*: For current statistics on U.S. military deaths, see http://www.icasualties.org. For documented Iraqi civilian deaths by violence, see http://www.iraqbodycount.org. The highest and most controversial estimate of civilian casualties, a study by the Johns Hopkins Bloomberg School of Public Health, placed Iraqi civilian excess deaths by the end of June 2006 between 426,369 and 654,965. See *The Lancet*, vol. 369, no. 9556, January 13, 2007, pp. 102–3, or www.thelancet.com, and "Updated Iraq Survey Affirms Earlier Mortality Estimates," at Johns Hopkins School of Public Health, www.jhsph.edu/publichealthnews/press_releases/2006/burnham_iraq_2006.html. See also Lawrence K. Altman and Richard A. Oppel, Jr., "W.H.O. Says Iraq Civilian Death Toll Higher Than Cited," *New York Times*, January 10, 2008.

7   *in an earlier book: Kabul in Winter: Life Without Peace in Afghanistan* (New York: Metropolitan Books, 2006).

8   *the International Rescue Committee*: The organization was founded in 1933 at the suggestion of Albert Einstein. See the website http://www.theirc.org.

9   *the Security Council passed Resolution 1325*: See the full text at http://www.un.org/events/res_1325e.pdf.

9   *SCR 1820*: See the full text at http://www.stoprapenow.org/pdf/Security%20Council%20Resolution%201820.pdf.

11  *Susan Sontag*: Susan Sontag, *On Photography* (New York: Farrar, Straus and Giroux, 1977), p. 4.

12  *A Congolese nurse in North Kivu*: Interview with Fred Kahunde at Heal Africa Hospital, Goma, Democratic Republic of Congo, April 12, 2008.

12  *The architects of disastrous U.S. ventures*: See Yuki Tanaka and Marilyn B. Young, eds., *Bombing Civilians: A Twentieth-Century History* (New York: New Press, 2009).

### CHAPTER 1: CÔTE D'IVOIRE: "GRÂCE À L'APPAREIL"

16  *From Aka's campground on the Gulf of Guinea*: On the history of Côte d'Ivoire and Houphouët-Boigny, see http://country-studies.com/ivory-coast/history.html; Pierre Nandjui, *Houphouët-Boigny: L'homme de la France en Afrique* (Paris: L'Harmattan, 1995); Amadou Kone, *Houphouët-Boigny et la crise ivoirienne* (Paris: Karthala, 2003).

16  *the World Bank . . . and the International Monetary Fund*: On the operation of the World Bank and the IMF, see Joseph E. Stiglitz, *Globalization and Its Discontents* (New York: Norton, 2003). On operations in Côte d'Ivoire, see Shantayanan Devarajan, David Dollar, and Torgny Holmgren, *Aid and Reform in Africa: Lessons from Ten Case Studies* (New York: World Bank, 2001), pp. 374–78.

17  *"exploited ethnic divisions"*: " 'My Heart Is Cut': Sexual Violence by Rebels and Pro-Government Forces in Côte d'Ivoire," Human Rights Watch, vol. 19, no. 11(A), August 2007, p. 15, at http://www.org/en/reports/2007/08/01/my-heart-cut. On the conflict and peacekeeping operations, see pp. 16–18.

19  *"The scale of rape and sexual violence"*: "Côte d'Ivoire: Targeting Women: The Forgotten Victims of the Conflict," Amnesty Inter-

national, March 15, 2007, p. 1, at http://www.amnesty.org/en/library/info/AFR31/001/2007/en.

19   *"cases of sexual abuse are significantly underreported"*: "'My Heart Is Cut,'" p. 4 et passim. See also "Côte d'Ivoire: Targeting Women," p. 2 et passim.

20   *"The brutality of rape"*: "Côte d'Ivoire: Targeting Women," p. 29. On the absence of health care, see pp. 33–35.

20   *commonly referred to as Dioula*: "Côte d'Ivoire: Targeting Women," pp. 6–8; "'My Heart Is Cut,'" pp. 67–73. The term "Dioula" is used to refer to those people residing in northern Côte d'Ivoire whose origins lie in other countries in the region, such as Burkina Faso, Mali, and Guinea, and to those with Muslim family names.

22   *The IRC started working in Côte d'Ivoire*: Interview with IRC country director Maurizio Crivellaro, Abidjan, Côte d'Ivoire, September 11, 2007.

## CHAPTER 2: LIBERIA: "LIFE CAN CHANGE . . ."

57   *Liberia had been awash in waves of war*: Ellen Johnson Sirleaf, *This Child Will Be Great: Memoir of a Remarkable Life by Africa's First Woman President* (New York: Harper, 2009); Gabriel I. H. Williams, *Liberia: The Heart of Darkness* (Bloomington, Ind.: Trafford, 2007).

57   *By the time the fighting ended in 2003*: "United Nations Development Assistance Framework for Liberia 2008–2012: Consolidating Peace and National Recovery for Sustainable Development" (Monrovia: UN in Liberia, May 2007), p. 7.

58   *women were targets*: "Majority of Liberian Women Suffered Sexual Violence During War, Says New Study: UNFPA/CDC Survey Indicates Steep Reproductive Health Challenges in Lofa County," UNFPA, November 6, 2007, at http://www.unfpa.org/news/news.cfm?ID=1060.

58   *A World Health Organization study in 2005*: Marie-Claire O. Omanyondo, "Sexual Gender-Based Violence and Health Facility Needs Assessment: Lofa, Nimba, Grand Gedeh and Grand Bassa Counties" (World Health Organization, September 2005).

58   *A study by the IRC and Columbia University's School of Public Health in October 2007*: The observation and statistics are drawn from an IRC internal report.

58   *An earlier IRC study (2003)*: The statistics are drawn from an IRC internal report.

59   *Some people call Liberia America's stepchild*: On the history of Libe-
     ria, see Ryszard Kapuscinski, *The Shadow of the Sun* (New York:
     Random House, 2001), pp. 233–60; Tom W. Schick, *Behold the
     Promised Land: A History of Afro-American Settlers in Nineteenth-
     Century Liberia* (Baltimore: Johns Hopkins University Press,
     1980); and Williams, *Liberia*.

62   *"the emergence of a class of marginal young people"*: Paul Richards
     et al., "Community Cohesion in Liberia: A Post-War Rapid
     Social Assessment," Social Development Papers: Conflict Pre-
     vention & Reconstruction, paper no. 21 (World Bank, January
     2005), p. 1 et passim.

65   *When the IRC surveyed Liberian women in 2006*: The statistics are
     drawn from an IRC internal report.

69   *a Médecins Sans Frontières study*: "Shattered Lives: Liberia: Ensur-
     ing Care for Rape Survivors in Health Facilities," Médecins Sans
     Frontières, March 4, 2009, at http://doctorswithoutborders.org/
     publications/article.cfm?id=3463&cat=special-report.

73   *evangelist Pat Robertson*: On Robertson's secret involvement with
     Charles Taylor, see Colbert I. King, "Pat Robertson's Gold,"
     *Washington Post*, September 22, 2001, p. A29.

### CHAPTER 3: SIERRA LEONE: ABOUT GIRLS

93   *Foday Sankoh*: Derek Brown, "Who is Foday Sankoh?" *Guardian*,
     May 17, 2000; Lansana Gberie, *A Dirty War in West Africa: The
     RUF and the Destruction of Sierra Leone* (Bloomington: Indiana
     University Press, 2005); Stephen Ellis, *The Mask of Anarchy: The
     Destruction of Liberia and the Religious Dimension of an African
     Civil War* (New York: New York University Press, 2006).

94   *Like the SOA*: The curriculum of the SOA was revealed when its
     secret training manuals came to light in 1996. See Dana Priest,
     "U.S. Instructed Latins on Executions, Torture," *Washington Post*,
     September 21, 1996.

95   *Charles Taylor from Liberia*: On Charles Taylor, Prince Johnson,
     and the war in Liberia, see Gabriel I. H. Williams, *Liberia: The
     Heart of Darkness* (Bloomington, Ind.: Trafford, 2007).

95   *Sankoh's band of guerrillas*: On Foday Sankoh, the RUF, and the
     conduct of the war, see "'We'll Kill You If You Cry': Sexual
     Violence in the Sierra Leone Conflict," Human Rights Watch,
     January 2003, pp. 9–15, at http://www.hrw.org/reports/2003/

sierraleone/sierleon0103.pdf; Gberie, *A Dirty War in West Africa*; and Ellis, *The Mask of Anarchy.*

96  *Human Rights Watch reports*: "'We'll Kill You If You Cry,'" p. 26.

97  *forcibly conscripted children*: On child soldiers, see Ishmael Beah, *A Long Way Gone: Memoirs of a Boy Soldier* (New York: Farrar, Straus and Giroux, 2008).

100  *During the war about fifty thousand people*: No reliable statistics are available on the number of people killed, mutilated, and displaced, and estimates vary widely. See, for example, Twentieth Century Atlas—Death Tolls, at http://users.erols.com/mwhite28/warstatz.htm#s. See also "Sierra Leone: Getting Away with Murder, Mutilation, Rape," Human Rights Watch, July 1999, at http://www.hrw.org/legacy/reports/1999/sierra/.

100  *poorest country . . . highest rates of maternal and infant deaths*: "War-Related Sexual Violence in Sierra Leone: A Population-Based Assessment," Physicians for Human Rights, 2002, p. 31, at http://physiciansforhumanrights.org/library/documents/reports/sexual-violence-sierra-leone.pdf. Since the end of the war in 2002, Sierra Leone has advanced slightly, and at this writing it is ranked as the tenth poorest country with one of the highest rates of maternal mortality. See "Out of Reach: The Cost of Maternal Health Care in Sierra Leone," Amnesty International, 2009, at http://www.amnesty.org/en/library/asset/AFR51/005/2009/en/9ed4ed6f-557f-4256-989f-485733f9addf/afr510052009eng.pdf.

100  *its trademark atrocity: amputation*: "Special Report: Sierra Leone: 'A suffering that knows no end,'" BBC News, July 8, 1999, at http://news.bbc.co.uk/2/hi/special_report/1999/01/99/sierra_leone/251286.stm.

101  *the number of women and girls sexually assaulted*: Physicians for Human Rights estimated that some 257,000 internally displaced women and girls "may have been affected by sexual violence": "War-Related Sexual Violence in Sierra Leone," pp. 3–4. Human Rights Watch, citing that estimate, notes that it is probably too low and documents countless atrocities based on its own interviews: "'We'll Kill You If You Cry,'" pp. 25–50.

101  *Rainbo Centres*: Amie-Tejan Kellah, "Establishing Services in Post-Conflict Sierra Leone," Forced Migration Review, no. 27, January 25, 2007, at http://www.reliefweb.int/rwarchive/rwb.nsf/db900sid/YAOI-6XT8YW?OpenDocument.

102 *But women and girls were still being raped every day*: Statistics provided by the IRC Rainbo Centres.

## CHAPTER 4: THE DEMOCRATIC REPUBLIC OF CONGO: RAPE

131 *Leopold laid claim to the Congo*: Adam Hochschild, *King Leopold's Ghost* (Boston: Houghton Mifflin, 1999).

133 *Patrice Lumumba . . . Joseph Desiré Mobutu*: See Hochschild, pp. 301–4.

134 *And the Interahamwe continued their war on Tutsis*: On the Congo wars and Laurent and Joseph Kabila, see Johann Hari, "Congo's Tragedy: The War the World Forgot," *The Independent*, London, May 5, 2006. On the historical roots of the conflict in Rwanda, see Ryszard Kapuscinski, *The Shadow of the Sun* (New York: Random House, 2001), pp. 165–82.

150 *the report of the two Réseaux said 95.1 percent*: "Women's Bodies as a Battleground: Sexual Violence Against Women and Girls During the War in the Democratic Republic of Congo, South Kivu (1996–2003)," *Réseau des Femmes pour un Développement Associatif* and *Réseau des Femmes pour la Défense des Droits et la Paix*, Bukavu, 2005, p. 39.

151 *Dr. Denis Mukwege*: Interview, Panzi Hospital, Bukavu, DRC, April 15, 2008.

159 *They often tortured women during rape*: "Women's Bodies as a Battleground," p. 34.

160 *Major General Patrick Cammaert*: Testimony before an international conference entitled "Women Targeted or Affected by Armed Conflict: What Role for Military Peacekeepers?" Wilton Park, Sussex, UK, May 27–29, 2008.

162 *A study conducted by the IRC*: "Mortality in the Democratic Republic of Congo: An Ongoing Crisis," International Rescue Committee, 2008, p. ii, at http://www.humansecuritygateway.com/documents/IRC_MortalityInTheDRC_OngoingCrisis.pdf.

163 *One reckoning found that in 14,200 reported rapes*: Interview with anonymous court official, Bukavu, DRC, April 7, 2008.

164 *One in ten of the patients Dr. Mukwege treats*: Interview with Dr. Denis Mukwege, Panzi Hospital, Bukavu, DRC, April 15, 2008.

166 *In January 2009, Rwandan forces captured Laurent Nkunda*: Jeffrey Gettleman, "A Congolese Rebel Leader Who Once Seemed Untouchable Is Caught," *New York Times*, January 24, 2009.

166 *and in April 2009, DRC President Joseph Kabila told*: Jeffrey Gettle-

man, "An Interview with Joseph Kabila," *New York Times*, April 4, 2009.

166    *Indeed, he had already announced a deal*: John Vandaele, "Development: China Outdoes Europeans in Congo," IPS News, February 8, 2009, at http://ipsnews.net/print.asp?idnews-41125.

## CHAPTER 5: BURMESE REFUGEES IN THAILAND: SOMEPLACE ELSE

169    *Today at least 150,000 refugees*: Interview with Abigail Erikson, GBV Program Manager, International Rescue Committee, Mae Hong Son, Thailand, May 17, 2008.

178    *In 1989, the ruling military regime transformed Burma*: Michael W. Charney, *A History of Modern Burma* (Cambridge: Cambridge University Press, 2009).

179    *George Orwell*: See George Orwell, *Burmese Days* (New York: Harper, 1934). See also Emma Larkin, *Finding George Orwell in Burma* (London: Penguin, 2005).

179    *Burma's pro-democracy movement*: Aung San Suu Kyi, *Letters from Burma* (London: Penguin, 1997).

179    *the forcible, genocidal displacement of Burma's ethnic minorities*: See *Living Ghosts: The Spiraling Repression of the Karenni Population Under the Burmese Military Junta* (Bangkok: Burma Issues, March 2008). See also Pascal Khoo Thwe, *From the Land of Green Ghosts* (New York: Harper, 2003).

182    *Aung San Suu Kyi . . . was tried once again*: Seth Mydans, "Burmese Activist Receives New Term of House Arrest," *New York Times*, August 12, 2009.

182    *More than half a million people have been displaced from the minority states*: Inge Brees, "Forced Displacement of Burmese People," *Forced Migration Review*, Bangkok, April 2008, pp. 4–5.

183    *Chinese-built hydroelectric dams*: *Dammed by Burma's Generals: The Karenni Experience with Hydropower Development from Lawpita to the Salween*, Karenni Development Research Group, 2006.

## CHAPTER 6: IRAQI REFUGEES IN JORDAN, SYRIA, LEBANON: BLOWN APART

N.B. All the stories of Iraqi refugees related in this chapter are based on interviews conducted in Jordan, Syria, and Lebanon during September, October, and November 2008. The names and other identifying characteristics of all the Iraqis have been changed for their protection.

210    *In its aftermath, three hundred thousand exiles returned*: "UNHCR's Eligibility Guidelines for Assessing the International Protection Needs of Iraqi Asylum-Seekers" (Geneva: United Nations High Commissioner for Refugees, August 2007), p. 21.

210    *"their public status, (perceived) political views"*: "UNHCR's Eligibility Guidelines for Assessing the International Protection Needs of Iraqi Asylum-Seekers," p. 13.

211    *they embarked on "A New Way Forward"*: "Fact Sheet: The New Way Forward in Iraq: An Update," Office of the Press Secretary, The White House, George W. Bush, June 28, 2007.

211    *General David Petraeus . . . reported to Congress*: "Transcript: Gen. Petraeus Testifies Before Congress on the Status of Iraq," *Washington Post*, September 10, 2007.

211    *the UN High Commissioner for Refugees reported*: Antonio Guterres, UN High Commissioner for Refugees, April 17, 2007, in "UNHCR's Eligibility Guidelines for Assessing the International Protection Needs of Iraqi Asylum-Seekers," p. 21.

211    *the International Organization for Migration and the Red Crescent*: Ian Black, "Displaced Iraqis Double Despite US Military Surge," *Guardian*, August 27, 2007.

212    *During the surge, Baghdad's Shiite citizens increased*: Juan Cole, "A Social History of the Surge," July 24, 2008, at http://www.juan cole.com/2008_07_01_juancole_archive.html.

212    *"the most significant displacement in the Middle East"*: Antonio Guterres, UN High Commissioner for Refugees, April 17, 2007, in "UNHCR's Eligibility Guidelines for Assessing the International Protection Needs of Iraqi Asylum-Seekers," p. 21.

212    *most refugees slipped into the neighboring countries*: On refugees in Jordan, Syria, and Lebanon, see Stephen Glain, "Exodus," *The Nation*, June 11, 2007.

216    *no shortage of widows in Iraq*: Haifa Zangana, *City of Widows* (New York: Seven Stories Press, 2009).

217    *the number of widows nationwide*: Timothy Williams, "Iraq's War Widows Face Dire Need With Little Aid," *New York Times*, February 22, 2009.

220    *4,516 cases of sexual violence in Iraq*: Statistics provided by UNHCR.

232    *Bush administration strictly limited resettlement*: On the admission of Iraqi refugees to the United States, see "UN Welcomes US Iraq Refugee Plan," BBC News, February 15, 2007, at http://news.bbc

.co.uk/go/pr/fr/-/2/hi/middle_east/6362289.stm; Matthew Harwood, "A Lifeline for Iraq's Refugees," Guardian.co.uk, July 30, 2008, at http://www.guardian.co.uk/commentisfree/2008/jul/30/iraq.immigrationpolicy; "How to Confront the Iraqi Refugee Crisis: A Blueprint for the New Administration" (New York: Human Rights First, December 2008) pp. 1–4. Reported statistics vary wildly because many commitments were not met.

233 *To resettle refugees in the United States*: Interviews with Robert Carey, IRC vice president for resettlement and migration policy and chair of Refugee Council USA, January and May 2009.

234 *of the harsh terms of resettlement in the United States*: Tom A. Peter, "Struggling in the US, Some Iraqi Refugees Now Want to Go Back," *Christian Science Monitor*, January 10, 2008; "For Iraqi Refugees, Life in America Has Left Them with Few Options," MCT (McClatchy–Chicago Tribune) Information Services, October 28, 2009; and interviews with Robert Carey and IRC resettlement officers Robin Dunn Marcos, May 20, 2009, and Ellen Beattie, May 28, 2009.

## AFTERWORD: IT'S NOT OVER

242 *It passed Resolution 1888*: For a summary of the Security Council meeting and text of the Resolution, see "Security Council Adopts Text Mandating Peacekeeping Missions to Protect Women, Girls from Sexual Violence in Armed Conflict," Security Council: SC/9753, September 30, 2009, at http://www.un.org/News/Press/docs/2009/sc9753.doc.htm.

243 *One week later, the Council passed*: For a summary of the Security Council meeting and text of the Resolution, see "Security Council Urges Renewed Measures to Improve Women's Participation in Peace Processes, Reaffirming Key Role Women Can Play in Rebuilding War-Torn Societies," Security Council: SC/9759, October 5, 2009, at http://www.un.org/News/Press/docs/2009/sc9759.doc.htm.

# ACKNOWLEDGMENTS

All credit for the project at the heart of this book goes to the dedicated professionals of the International Rescue Committee who took a chance on this volunteer, especially Edward Bligh, John Keys, Sue Dwyer, Carrie Welch, Robert Carey, and most of all, the GBV technical unit, especially Heidi Lehmann, Karin Wachter, Kristin Kim Bart, Carmen Leah Ascensio, and Betsy Pollard. GBV launched the project on faith and a shoestring, and we were all grateful when the NoVo Foundation stepped in with generous support. I'm also indebted to Rachel Mayanja and Natalia Zakharova at the UN, who welcomed the photography exhibition to the UN gallery. In the field, it was a privilege to work with great IRC colleagues: in Cote d'Ivoire, Tanou Virginie, Monika Topolska Bakayako, Gbozie Marie Chantal, Karamoko Aminata, Bedi Bienvenue, Tia Gbogen, Bomisso Dramana, Ehouman Emmanuel, and Gergey Pasztor; in Liberia, Navanita Bhattacharya, Gertrude Garway, Musu Oberly, Esther Karnley, Marian Rogers, Hannah Sammie, Joseph Ballah, Edwin Morlu, the late Bockarie Gamoh, and Annette Runge; in Sierra Leone, Amie Kandeh, Natsnet Gebrebrhan, Christiana

Massaquoi, Christiana Gbondo, Rosa Vandi, Hawa Demson, Baimba Syllah, Aminata Kaikai, Mary Sheku, Lilian Karimu, Christopher Briama, and Shiv Nair; in the Democratic Republic of Congo, Francine Nsinda, Marlene Musimwa Bahizire, Oswald Chishugi, Edmond Suluku, and Erika Beckman (of PMU); in Thailand, Abigail Erikson, Annabelle Mubi, Moe Moe Aung, Hom Pamelar, The Ka Oo, Jennate Eoomkham, Inbal Sasani, Nyein Chann, Sai On, and Wisitpong Yangyuentawee. To Dr. Jeff Kambale Mathe: thanks again, Jeff, for saving my life.

I'm indebted to the Nation Institute Fund for Investigative Journalism, which supported my work on Iraqi refugees. It was my good fortune to be able to conduct that work with the generous cooperation of UNHCR staff in the Middle East. Thanks to Arafat Jamal, Rana Ksaifi, Hanin Shukri Hamzeh, and Dana Bajjali in Amman, and Stéphane Jaquemet, Carol El Sayed, and Laure Chedrawi in Beirut. I appreciated their graciousness and herculean hard work in the face of a monumental refugee crisis. My thanks also to Alaa Hasan and Fanella Ferrato, and to Faiza Al Araji for all she taught me.

I'm exceedingly lucky to have a wonderful agent in Ellen Geiger and great editors. My thanks to Betsy Reed, who helped me refine my thoughts in articles for *The Nation*, where two pieces of this book first appeared in different form. And thanks to Tom Engelhardt, who was an enthusiastic supporter of the project from the first appearance of some early blogs from West Africa, and who edited an account for the indispensable www.tomdispatch.com. Thanks also to my friend, writer Deborah Campbell, and Ruth Baldwin of Nation Books, who nudged me toward this little volume in thoughtful conversations. I couldn't have put it all together without the artful, incisive editing of Riva Hocherman at Metropolitan Books, and the encouragement of publisher Sara Bershtel; every writer should be so blessed.

Thanks, too, to my friend Irene Young, who edited the photographs, and to Grigory Tovbis, Rita Quintas, Kelly Too, Rebecca Seltzer, and all the Metropolitan team. This book is certainly the better for all their help; its failings are my own.

Living out of a duffel bag as I do, I'm especially grateful to friends in the United States, the UK, and elsewhere who take me in from time to time, support my work in countless ways, and look after my four-footed family in my long absences. Thanks to the late Marilyn French for unfailing encouragement, and to Valerie Martin and John Cullen, Maxine and Victor Kumin, Suzy Colt, Shari Diamond, Mary O'Neil, Patricia Lewis, Marion Miller, Alison Baker, Catherine Ruocco, Katha Pollitt, Diane Ebzery and Peter Lobel, Donna Ferrato, Rachel Wareham, Gurcharan Virdee, Mary Clemmey, Nigora Igamberdiyeva and Manav Sachdeva, Revan Schendler, Barbara Hadden, Virginia Bell, Nina Weisenhorn, Tess and Cahal Creamer. Their generosity makes my obsession possible. And very special thanks to my beloved friend Eleanor Torrey West, patron of prickly artists and pigs, who welcomed me once again to Ossabaw Island, where most of this book was written, and inspired me as always with her irreverent and irrepressible high spirits.

My greatest debt, of course, is to the women and girls who bravely volunteered for the improbable photography project and to the Iraqi refugees who confided to me their appalling stories. Their voices are a humbling gift and an obligation.

# INDEX

Page numbers in *italics* refer to photographs and captions.

# ABOUT THE AUTHOR

ANN JONES, writer and photographer, is the author of seven previous books, including *Kabul in Winter,* *Women Who Kill,* and *Next Time She'll Be Dead.* Since 9/11, Jones has worked with women in conflict and post-conflict zones, principally Afghanistan, and reported on their concerns. An authority on violence against women, she has served as a gender adviser to the United Nations. Her work has appeared in numerous publications, including *The New York Times* and *The Nation.*